FIVE MINUTES TO MIDNIGHT

Other books by Richard Lapchick

The Politics of Race and International Sport: The Case of
  South Africa
Oppression and Resistance: The Saga of Women in
  Southern Africa
Broken Promises: Racism in American Sports
Fractured Focus: Sport as a Reflection of Society
On the Mark: Putting the Student Back in the Student-
  Athlete
Rules of the Game: Ethics in College Sport

FIVE MINUTES TO MIDNIGHT

Race and Sport in the 1990s

Richard E. Lapchick

MADISON BOOKS
Lanham • New York • London

Published by Madison Books
4720 Boston Way
Lanham, Maryland 20706

3 Henrietta Street
London WC2E 8LU England

Distributed by National Book Network

The paper used in this publication meets the minimum
requirements of American National Standard for
Information Sciences—Permanence of Paper for
Printed Library Materials, ANSI Z39.48–1984. ♾™
Manufactured in the United States of America.

Library of Congress Cataloging-in-Publication Data

Lapchick, Richard Edward.
Five minutes to midnight : race and sport in the 1990s /
Richard E. Lapchick.
p.   cm.
Based on an earlier work by the author entitled: Broken
promises: racism in American sports, 1984.
1. Discrimination in sports—United States—History.
2. United States—Race relations.   3. Lapchick, Richard
Edward.   I. Lapchick, Richard Edward. Broken promises.
II. Title.   III. Title: 5 minutes to midnight.
GV706.32.L36   1991
305.8'96073—dc20   90–29903 CIP

ISBN 0–8191–8066–1 (cloth : alk. paper)
ISBN 0–8191–8166–8 (paper : alk. paper)

British Cataloging in Publication Information Available

For Ann

who has taught me how to love again
and who has shown me that life can be better
if we slow down and stop
to smell the roses

Contents

Acknowledgments

It is with a profound sense of appreciation that I acknowledge the encouragement of Jean Mahoney, director of the Reebok Foundation, and Ken Lightcap, vice president–corporate communications for Reebok, to go ahead with this project. Jed Lyons of Madison Books must be singled out for his can-do approach to the entire project.

Several people at Northeastern University's Center for the Study of Sport in Society were most helpful, including Aaron Thomas, who helped with some research, and Keith Lee, who was a sounding board for my thoughts.

My wife, Ann, was my best critic, and my oldest daughter, Chamy, typed the first draft.

Finally I want to thank Bill White, Lou Carnesecca, Joe Paterno, Bill Bradley, Rafer Johnson, and Benjamin Hooks for their support for the project.

Introduction

When I finished *Broken Promises: Racism in American Sports* in 1983, it had been more than thirty-five years since Jackie Robinson broke the color barrier in professional baseball. Americans were witnessing numerous black athletes being paid more than $100,000 per year to play baseball, basketball, and football. Most thoughtful, intelligent Americans believed that this was a sign of society's progress. Many young men and women, black and white alike, believed that sport was a great racial equalizer.

A virtually unknown man named Al Campanis changed all that in April 1987 with his words on Ted Koppel's *Nightline* that blacks might not have "the necessities" to be head coaches or general managers. The sports press, which until then had rarely surfaced stories on racial problems in sport, was finally forced to take a penetrating look at how far we had to go.

Now that same American public watches even more black athletes earn not $100,000 but literally millions of dollars each year. But we cannot shake the image of Campanis or subsequent stories like the Shoal Creek controversy in 1990 in which golf, one of America's most popular sports, was shown to be played in almost 100 percent segregated circumstances. By the 1990s we finally developed more of a sense of how far we have to go to keep the promises we made to those who came to our country. While having that sense surely does not mean that the promises will be kept, we have at least emerged from our state of denial.

Born into a great sports family just before the Jackie Robinson era, I too was in denial and a believer for most of my youth. Being part of a white middle-class family with a sports celebrity for a father made my early life both easy and happy. I wanted nothing more than to emulate my father's path to athletic glory.

That desire made me oblivious to reality, even to the reality of my own father who was himself a quiet pioneer in bringing about racial change in American basketball. As the country's star pro center in the 1920s and 1930s, his Original Celtics team was among the first to play against the Rens, the nation's first great black team. While becoming one of America's most successful coaches during a thirty-year career, he brought Nat "Sweetwater" Clifton to the Knicks in 1950 to help break the color barrier in the NBA.

By doing so, he became a "nigger–lover" to many. Four decades after Clifton came to the Knicks, not only have I been branded a "nigger–lover" for my own efforts to end racism in sport, but my own son Joe has been called a "nigger–lover" because of those he has chosen to call his friends.

This book is, in part, the story of how I became involved in the struggle for racial equality and why I remain involved despite several life-threatening situations. It took me more than three years to be able to write about those events, which took place mainly in 1978. The trauma of those times made it difficult to share these experiences with others. This book is also the story of what it was like to grow up with a famous father who cared about more than just a game.

The first eleven chapters were taken from *Broken Promises* and I retell my story, a story which remains relevant in these times of turbulent and traumatic racial relations. The final six chapters are all new, beginning with the three that look at the early days of black versus white in sport as traced through the rivalry between the Celtics and the Rens. Recognizing the power of that rivalry reinforced the positive potential for playing with and against players from different racial groups. Writing those three chapters also reinforced my own limited experiences and made me believe that sport could really be a model for better human relations.

Broken Promises was also the story of how little had changed since Jackie Robinson took that courageous first step. *Five Minutes to Midnight* is much more optimistic. Perhaps my views are being colored by the lessons of the Celtics and the Rens or the perspective that comes from the faithful and fearless smile of Emily, our baby girl who has only learned about love. *Five Minutes to Midnight* brings some hope that in the ensuing years since *Broken Promises* was published, we are on the right path in sport. Sport may yet show us a better way.

But America has made many unkept promises to its people. The promise of racial equality is one that has been broken time and time again. A decade ago, some commentators were saying that time was running out, that it was five minutes to midnight. Events in places like Bensonhurst and Howard Beach make it seem like we may now be closer to Spike Lee's vision in *Do The Right Thing* and the racial clock may be about to strike midnight.

I saw the other side of midnight in 1978. It is an ugly place that I hope my children never see. Racial violence was supposed to be a thing of the past when I was attacked. Now we read about such attacks almost every day. I originally wrote *Broken Promises* to attempt to ensure that my children would never have to live in fear. Now the entire nation seems to sit at home, fearing those who live in other neighborhoods. Promises have been made again. This time we cannot afford not to keep them; this just may be our last chance.

Part One
The Attack in Virginia

Chapter 1

No Defense

" 'Nigger,' they carved 'nigger' on his stomach!" As I heard one of my students say this to his friends while pointing to me, I realized with horror that my life might never be the same again. Still dazed, I tried to reconstruct the night. Within a week I would have to try to reconstruct my life.

It was Valentine's Day, 1978. Early that day, I told my wife Sandy (we were divorced several years later) that I couldn't go out to dinner since I had to work late in my college office to prepare for the next day. There had been little time for dinners in recent years; the pace of our lives had accelerated too fast. My belief that I "had to work" usually prevailed.

We had both reached a stage where we felt comfortable with our individual lives. Sandy, who had retreated from a career as a commercial artist after achieving early success, was now re-emerging into the art world. I had somehow learned to balance my life as an academic teaching political science at Virginia Wesleyan College in Norfolk, Virginia, as an activist on civil rights and anti-apartheid issues, and as a father. Being a husband was getting less attention. So on this particular Valentine's Day, neither of us worried about missing time together.

Several of my students tried to persuade me to go to the basketball game at the college that night. It was hard to say no to them. This was partially because I would do almost anything to enrich the relationships I had with my students. However, on this night I especially wanted to prove to that small part of the world that cared about these things that I was not anti-sport. I was a critic of racism in sport, both in South Africa and in America, and I had heard myself accused of being anti-sport more frequently during the preceding weekend than ever before. How could I be anti-sport? How could the son of Joe Lapchick, a legendary figure in basketball, be anti-sport? When my father criticized basketball for not being integrated, did his contemporaries think he was anti-sport? That was a question I would reflect on frequently after this night.

But now it was my time to be judged. As National Chairperson of ACCESS (American Coordinating Committee for Equality in Sport and Society), I had been campaigning to end all sports contacts between the United States and teams from South Africa as long as sport and society there were segregated. I had spent two years writing a book on the subject, *The Politics of Race and International Sport: The Case of South Africa,* which was published in 1975, and had already been involved with the issue for eight years. However, at this time, there was a new intensity over this issue in the United States.

The tone of South Africa's press coverage in America and Europe had significantly changed. Images of the slaughter of children in Soweto in June 1976 were still fresh. The South African police were trying to explain how Steve Biko, the founder of the Black Consciousness Movement and one of the most important contemporary black men in the country, had died in their custody as a result of a crushed skull in September 1977. The Western press could hardly ignore the October 1977 bannings of most of the other important voices of dissent in that country. News items were beginning to appear about the scandal in the Ministry of Information—a scandal that would eventually bring down Minister of Information Connie Mulder and Prime Minister Vorster with him when it was revealed that huge sums of money were spent to buy favorable foreign opinion.

With its image tarnished, South Africa felt it was even more crucial to successfully stage its Davis Cup tennis match with the United States. Having an integrated team play the matches at

Vanderbilt University in Nashville, Tennessee, before thousands of spectators and possibly millions of television viewers might do for South Africa what a ping-pong match did for U.S.–China relations in 1972. If investment dollars, bank loans, and trade, which had been reduced due to anti-apartheid criticism, were to resume on a grand scale, the South African government knew it would have to win this battle in its propaganda war.

Therefore, my visit to Nashville from the tenth through the thirteenth of February was not warmly welcomed by either South Africa or its supporters in the United States. The earlier announcement that the National Association for the Advancement of Colored People (NAACP) would make the Davis Cup a focus of its efforts guaranteed the high level of attention we wanted on what apartheid meant for black South Africans. My visit generated a great deal of attention in Nashville as to why we wanted the matches canceled.

The Nashville sports media wanted to raise the accusation that I was anti-sport. However, the news media and the people of Nashville concentrated on what apartheid was about and the oppression it created in South Africa. By the time I spoke at Vanderbilt on October 13, I could feel the momentum shifting. This was confirmed when the news came, during my speech, that the financial backers of the tournament had pulled out. When I flew home to Norfolk that night, I sensed that, possibly for the first time in all my years as an activist in the 1960s and 1970s, I had made a real contribution. Although I was tempted to go to the basketball game that night, I told my students that I needed to work and couldn't go out.

My office was situated on a balcony that circled the main reading room of Wesleyan's library. At about 9:30 P.M. there was a commotion in the library, which had begun to temporarily fill up with students after the game. When I looked out I saw Lambuth Clarke, the president of the college. I liked Lambuth and had always gone out of my way to greet him. However, I gave him a special greeting that night because I wanted him to know I was working late in my office. Although I had no classes to teach on Friday and Monday, I felt slightly guilty that I had been in Nashville and not on campus. We exchanged pleasantries and I went back to my office to work.

At approximately 10:25 P.M. I went to the water fountain for a drink. The two librarians still there were about to leave. I told them I would be working late and said good night. I returned to my office and began typing a quiz that I would give to my urban studies class the next day.

There was a knock at my door at 10:45 P.M. I assumed it was campus security police routinely checking the library.

Although I could not clearly see who or what stood outside when I opened the door, my life began to change with one rough shove across the room. My shoulder was slightly cut as I landed on one of the railroad spikes that comprised a steel sculpture. As I stared up at the two men attacking me I realized that they were both wearing stocking masks.

I was terrified and confused all at once. Was this a robbery? If so, why would they choose a college professor in his office? Were these Cuban exiles coming after me because of favorable remarks my students and I had made after returning from two weeks in Cuba in January? I knew that the Cuban exile community of Norfolk was extremely upset, but could they be doing this to me now?

My confusion grew along with my fear as they tied me up in my chair and stuffed one of my thick winter gloves into my mouth. I felt like I was gagging and losing my breath. The first man, speaking without an accent, said, "Will you continue doing what you have been doing now?" Had my trip to Nashville provoked this?

The second man, also speaking without an accent, said, "Nigger–lover, Nigger–lover." The first man then said, "You know you have no business in South Africa." The confusion about why they were there was over.

All the time the attackers were saying these things, they used the top two drawers of my file cabinet as battering rams on my chest and face. I did not believe they were trying to kill me; they could have been hitting me with much greater force. Also, they were turning my head from side to side so the blows never hit me squarely and were cushioned by the glove in my mouth. No, it was to frighten me. And they succeeded.

They untied me and one held me up with a hammerlock so I could not move. The hooded hunters were both behind me as I faced the file cabinet. Unable to see them, I listened carefully to their voices. Were they Klansmen? South Africans? All they said were the three phrases, repeated as if they had been rehearsed. They were definitely American although I could not tell where they came from in the United States. Of course, I later realized that if South Africa was behind the attack, the last thing they would do was send nationals with South African accents.

After the file cabinet beating was finished, I could examine at least the one man who was not holding me. Beyond the impenetrable stocking, I could tell he was white, about six feet tall, and well built. He reached for the steel sculpture.

The spikes were set in a four-by-four-inch wooden base. The attacker wielded it like a bludgeon, working his way up the backs of my legs to my back and my arms while the man holding me asked, "Will you continue doing what you have been doing now?" His friend said, "Nigger–lover, nigger–lover," and then he repeated, "You know you have no business in South Africa." It seemed so orchestrated, so set, but their fury was genuine. He pummeled my stomach; the ferocity of the bludgeoning made me wonder if they were still only trying to scare me. I passed out as the pain and horror became too much.

When I came to, both men were kneeling over me. My shirt had been ripped open and one of the men was using what appeared to be my office scissors on my stomach. I was scared, not knowing what they were going to do. The pain was intense; my terror grew.

I thought I heard a noise from the library. The men pulled me up as if they had also heard something. The one who had been holding me said, "Let's get out of here." That was the only deviation from their script. He was slightly taller with broader shoulders than his partner. He was also white. He opened my door and was gone. The other pushed me to the floor and, as a farewell gesture, knocked a bookcase on top of me. It hit me in the head and I passed out again.

When I regained consciousness I was in great pain and my head was ringing. The office was dark and quiet. The door was closed. I had only one thought—to get out of there. I could not stand and had to use whatever I could to prop myself up. I half-staggered, half-crawled along the balcony of the library to the stairs, where I began to make my way down until I lost control and rolled down the last eight or ten steps.

Finally I made it to the library desk, where I reached for the phone. I noticed the clock on the wall—it was 11:40 P.M. What seemed like an eternity of torture had begun and ended within an hour. I dialed campus security but, amazingly, there was no answer. I called Sandy.

I told her what had happened but that I was not badly hurt, and asked her to call the police and rescue squad. It was obvious that she was worried, but at the same time she was remarkably calm. When we were finished I called campus security again—this time they responded and said they would be right there.

I fell back and rested on the stacks of newspapers that lined the inside of the library desk. It seemed forever before anyone came. At first I was afraid that the attackers were still somewhere in the building. Worse yet, I worried that they or their associates might go to my home. Our house was always open to students and people from the community, even at late hours. It was too vulnerable.

I thought of my mother, who was living in an apartment that adjoined the house. She had been through this before with my father, who had paid an emotional price for his commitment to racial equality in sport, and with my sister Barbara's second husband, who had been a political prisoner in Uganda.

At that point two members of the campus security force entered the library. I did not have the strength to yell to them and they seemed to walk around endlessly. Finally, the older man found me. He ordered his assistant, a young black man, to go up to check the balcony. I don't remember him saying anything to me as he scurried around the library desk. I guess he wanted to make sure that no one was around; maybe he was embarrassed that this could have happened while he was on duty.

"It's a wreck up here," the black guard shouted, but the older man seemed to ignore him. The library suddenly came alive with men from the rescue squad and with students. As I was being examined by the rescue squad, Mike Mizell, a student whom I did not know well at that time, took a long look at my abdomen, which had been exposed during the examination. Although I was quite dazed, I will always remember the expression on his face, which changed from simple concern to horror. He got up, walked over to his friends, and said, " 'Nigger,' they carved 'nigger' on his stomach!'' I had forgotten about the scissors but suddenly realized that this was what the attackers must have done with them.

"Nigger–lover, nigger–lover" began to ring through my head. Images of my children flashed in my mind. Chamy, a soft three-year-old with a golden Afro, would be sound asleep and was surely too young to be affected. Joey, an intense, high-energy five-year-old, might not be able to escape being traumatized by the repercussions of the attack. Only one week before, he had come to me in my study and asked, "Daddy, are you a 'nigger–lover'?" I was stunned until I recalled my own experience when I was his age.

My father, as coach of the New York Knickerbockers, had just integrated the team by signing Nat "Sweetwater" Clifton, who had been playing for the Harlem Globetrotters. We lived in Yonkers in an old three-story house. Like other children, I loved to answer the phone. I had picked up the phone upstairs when my father picked it up on the first floor; it was one of a number of "nigger–lover, nigger–lover" calls. At five, I didn't know what a "nigger" was, but it certainly sounded wrong to love one. The callers obviously hated my father. I could not understand this because to me he was such a sweet, gentle man—the center of my universe. Why did he love a "nigger" if it was such a bad thing to do? It hurt to hold it in, but it was half a lifetime before I had the courage to ask him.

I had asked Joey, "What do you think a 'nigger–lover' is?" He replied, "I don't know. But some mean man on the phone just told me that you were one." I was enraged that people would still play on the minds of children to get to their parents. I didn't want Joey to carry images of doubt about his father around with him as I had done, so I tried to explain to him what I was doing that would provoke racists to call me "nigger–lover." Why did a five-year-old have to understand such ugly things? He would have to know soon enough.

I was brought to Bayside Hospital in Virginia Beach and underwent a number of tests. The doctor in the emergency room was Dr. Martin Lorenz. He was very sympathetic to my injuries and became even more so after he heard about the attack.

Sandy arrived and I regained a sense of reality when she said, "Did you know that they carved 'nigger' in your stomach?" When I said I did, she responded, "Did you know they misspelled it: *n-i-g-e-r*?" We both laughed. The injuries didn't seem so bad now and I hoped I could go home. I wanted to teach a class the next day. After the tests were over, Lambuth Clarke, the president, Bill Wilson, the dean, and Alan Stowers, the college information officer, came into the emergency room. Lambuth said, "They misspelled 'nigger.' At least we know it wasn't one of our students." I told him it was obvious he hadn't read any student papers recently.

Sandy told me that Dennis Brutus, one of the founders of the movement to end racism in sports in South Africa in the 1950s and still one of the leading voices in exile, had been trying to reach me. Two police detectives entered the emergency room and began questioning me. Sandy excused herself to call Dennis and tell him what had happened. I knew he would empathize; he had been banned, imprisoned, and shot in the stomach by police for his work in South Africa. I thought that at least here the police would be on my side and would try to help.

They were pleasant enough and my trusting nature did not lead me to read anything into their questions at the time. I recounted what had happened. They told me they knew nothing of my "political" background and asked a great many questions about it, about my trip to Nashville, about my local involvement with race relations and migrant workers, and about my recent trip to Cuba. At the time, all their questions seemed directed at finding out who might have attacked me. Later, I began to wonder.

Dr. Lorenz returned to tell me that there was evidence of kidney damage since they had found blood in my urine. I also had a concussion and was forced to stay in the hospital for other tests. I began to realize there may have been more damage than I had thought.

One of the detectives stepped out at this point while the other remained to ask me to write out a description of the attack. The one who left approached Sandy and said, "When we heard who he was, we expected to find a screaming, shouting radical. We were surprised to see that your husband is so soft-spoken and gentle." She laughed and took it as a compliment, but it clearly indicated the attitude of the police toward political activists.

The officer returned to the emergency room as I was finishing my written account of the attack. I could not understand why they wanted a written statement from me since I was exhausted at that point and had already given a detailed oral account.

I was told, "We don't want this to get into the newspapers. Do not talk to the press under any circumstances." I was surprised at this request. I said, "It's hard for me to imagine how you could keep this quiet even if you wanted to. And why would you want to keep it out of the papers?" I was informed that "We don't want to spoil our chances of catching these men." "If they know what we are doing it would be more difficult," one of the policemen explained. I said I would try to go along with their wishes but considering the national and international implications of the attack, it would be almost impossible.

I was then told, "Okay, if the story does break don't, under any circumstances, say they used scissors, or refer to the statue or the misspelled 'nigger.' We must keep these clues to ourselves." This made some sense and I agreed.

"I just called Dennis Brutus and told him all of those details," Sandy interrupted. She was asked by the detectives to call him back and tell him not to say anything.

It was now 4:00 A.M. Just as the police were about to leave, a hospital orderly came in and asked Sandy to take my clothes home. "Don't you want the clothes for evidence?" Sandy asked the police. Much to our astonishment, they did not.

When Sandy finally reached Dennis at 6:00 A.M. he had already informed the protest organizers in Nashville. Sandy immediately called Yolanda Huet-Vaughn, a local organizer in Nashville, only to be told that they had already issued a statement to the *Nashville Banner* condemning the attack. Sandy asked her to call the paper and ask that they not mention that "nigger" was misspelled. Yolanda said she would try. Like so many other seemingly small details, this turned out to be important in the weeks to come.

For now I only wondered if the police would catch the attackers. I was still in a state of shock and could not think about the meaning of their behavior: the lengthy questions about my involvements, their surprise at my demeanor, the request for a written account of the attack at such a late hour, the plea to keep the story out of the press, the lack of interest in the clothes I was wearing. I didn't add these things up at the time. All I could think about was getting my attackers off the streets so I could be safe, so my family could be safe.

By the time I was left alone it was about 5:00 A.M. Exhausted, I finally dozed off. An efficient nurse woke me with the stark reality of an enema slightly after 6:00 A.M.

I called Sandy to tell her I was tired but okay and to find out what had happened when she called Dennis. Joey and Chamy were still asleep and unaware of what had gone on that night. The same was true of my mother.

The phone rang soon after I hung up. It was a Nashville radio station. I was amazed that the hospital switchboard had let the call through at that hour.

"Dr. Lapchick, all of Nashville is appalled to learn of this attack on you," the interviewer said. "You are being called a hero by your admirers here." I told her I was no hero and that I had merely followed my conscience. The Paul Robesons, the Malcolm Xs, and the Martin Luther Kings were heroes. They had been long-distance runners whose steel wills and compassionate hearts had been constantly tested by society.

This led to the inevitable question: "Will you continue your work now that this happened to you?" Although it was the obvious question, it stunned me. While she meant it sympathetically, it brought to mind the vision of the hooded hunters eight hours before. I lost control and began to cry. I was not sure whether the interviewer heard me. "How does your family feel about this?" she asked. "Do they want you to continue?"

I remembered my terror as a child when I would fantasize that those anonymous callers would hurt my father. I wanted to protect him. Now my own son would not only fantasize such fears but would have to cope with the reality of the attack.

What did it all mean? Was it worth it? Had the integration in American sports that took place in the 1950s, 1960s, and 1970s really made life any better for all but the minute fraction of blacks who had made it to the professional ranks? If my work, along with that of others in the movement, did result in the integration of all sports in South Africa, would it really change the lives of people there? Would it lead to the eradication of the heinous apartheid system? Do sports serve as a vanguard for change in our culture? Would I continue now? Who should be asking me this? Certainly not the attackers or the press. I was quite shaken now—more so than at any time since the knock on my door.

I replied, "Of course I'll continue. This has only strengthened my resolve to remain in the struggle. It proves that our efforts have been successful enough to provoke an attempt to destroy us. I'll go back to Nashville next week as planned." While I knew I would do all of this, I also knew I would have to ask myself all the hard questions I had thought about that morning. I knew I would have to confront my values. I would have to come face to face with all the assumptions I had made while growing up, with all that my father had taught me, and finally with what I had learned the night before.

Chapter 2

Offensive Attack

The scabs from the carving of *"n-i-g-e-r"* on my abdomen began to come off within a few days after the attack. But the physical scars were there, as were the mental ones that kept me awake at night. Calls of "nigger–lover, nigger–lover" played over and over in my dreams and wrenched me out of bed. First, my father with the Knicks; now me with South Africa. I knew I had to go back to Nashville to continue the fight over the Davis Cup. It was as reassuring to receive support from people all around the world as it was to hear from friends around the country. I was told that the attack had resulted in growing support for canceling the matches. That helped ease the pain. The strategy of the attackers was backfiring.

Trying to educate the American people about the reality of apartheid in South Africa had increasingly become my life's work and I was sure that our successes had led to the attack. Sport had become the vehicle for the message. But it is a reasonable question to ask why, with all the racism rampant in America and even in sport in America, I chose to work on the South African sports issue.

Part of the answer is fate. My meeting with Dennis Brutus while writing my doctoral dissertation on the subject and the publication of my book led me to confront the enormity of the oppression in South Africa and the role played by the United States in propping up the apartheid regime.

Part of the answer is analytical. I realized that many of the same institutional forces perpetuating racism in America were operating in South Africa. The same corporations that grow rich from the pool of cheap, unskilled, largely black labor in the United States, grow even richer from their operations in South Africa. American corporate exploitation of South African laborers, who work for extremely low wages, makes the position of black American laborers even more tenuous as they become increasingly expendable.

In the process, American dollars, through investments and loans, have helped South Africa remain "stable." "Stable" in South Africa means two things. First, that economic dislocations do not become too severe. Second, that part of the nation's wealth can be diverted to build its aggressive military machine, which in turn attacks its black neighbors to destabilize them.

With only 13 percent of its population white, and being surrounded by independent black African countries free from minority rule, the future of South Africa is clear. The forces of history dictate that it is not a question of whether black South Africans will be free. The question is when and how.

The situation inside South Africa had come under intense scrutiny by the American press after more than six hundred people were killed by the police in Soweto in June 1976. Most of those killed were schoolchildren. The murder of Black Consciousness leader Steve Biko in September 1977, followed by a series of bannings of remaining opposition figures in October, left South Africa's image badly tarnished as the scheduled Davis Cup tennis matches approached. Even the spending of $72 million for propaganda in the previous four years could not overcome the negative publicity. The Davis Cup was a potential propaganda coup desperately needed by the apartheid regime.

But the time was not right for South Africa. Nashville, Tennessee, the scheduled site of the Davis Cup, had many college campuses. And the campuses nationwide seemed to be coming alive on the anti-apartheid issue. The media was predicting— inaccurately as it turned out—that the protest against apartheid would rival that against American involvement in Vietnam. It was in this context that I had gone to Nashville on February 10.

The Davis Cup matches, in particular, and tennis in general, were the only areas left where South Africans were partially welcome. Successfully staged, the Davis Cup could reopen the flow of investments and loans. Better still, it could soften the image of apartheid and put a damper on the growing anti-apartheid movement in America. There was a great deal at stake for the Pretoria regime.

However, anti-apartheid groups in the United States were well aware of this and prepared a counteroffensive. Franklin Williams, who was president of the Phelps-Stokes Fund and the former U.S. ambassador to Ghana, took the lead with the civil rights groups. He organized the Coalition for Human Rights in South Africa, which included the NAACP and the Urban League. Franklin and I had spoken several times shortly after South Africa had defeated Colombia in Johannesburg in December 1977, "earning" itself a trip to Nashville. We exchanged ideas and materials and Franklin agreed to have the Coalition join ACCESS, the group of which I was chair, to plan the strategy to protest the matches. We both felt that the participation of the NAACP would assure a large demonstration in Nashville.

The creation of the Coalition was a major development. The traditional civil rights groups had historically been less involved in the anti-apartheid movement than predominantly white groups. Their priorities were, justifiably, at home where racism was on the rise. But Soweto, Biko's death, and the bannings helped make the connections. Black unemployment in the United States was steadily increasing as corporate dollars went to places like South Africa to exploit black labor there. The same banks that were "redlining" predominantly black and minority neighborhoods by denying them loans were making loans to South Africa. The same conservative politicians that opposed busing and the extension of the Voting Rights Act were supporting legislation that favored white minority regimes in Rhodesia (now Zimbabwe) and South Africa. The same men who fought as mercenaries were Klansmen with expert paramilitary training.

ACCESS had the information on the issue and kept it before

the public whenever sports contacts with South Africa came up. We were a coalition of thirty national civil rights, religious, political, and sports groups formed in 1976 to oppose sports contacts with South Africa until apartheid was eliminated.

Our main focus had been on tennis since it was the only remaining team sport in which South Africa competed for the world championship. The U.S. Tennis Association (USTA) had long been a supporter of South Africa's membership in the International Lawn Tennis Federation (ILTF), the tennis world's governing body. But South Africa was becoming more and more of a problem. Many countries refused to compete with them in the Davis Cup (men's) and Federation Cup (women's) championships. South Africa had won the Davis Cup in 1974 when India had refused to play against them in the championship round. As European, especially Eastern European, countries withdrew, the event became more of a farce.

For this reason South Africa was moved from the European to the North American Zone to compete. Most teams in this zone also withdrew except Colombia and the United States. The government of Colombia refused to allow the opening round with South Africa to be played in Bogota so it was moved to Johannesburg.

Thus, the confrontation was set up. We all felt that Vanderbilt University, under the leadership of its chancellor, Alexander Heard, would be the most likely to agree to cancel the matches. We were unfamiliar with the NLT Corporation, which agreed to back the event financially. We had been meeting with the USTA for two years. It had already announced it would press for South Africa's expulsion in 1979, but our concern was 1978. Therefore, ACCESS joined local Nashville groups in putting maximum pressure on Chancellor Heard. He agreed to meet me at the university.

I began the trip that would turn my life inside out on Friday, February 10, arriving in Nashville in the morning. The issue was catching fire and the exposure I received that weekend was amazing. I spoke on four university campuses, including Fisk and Tennessee State, the two major black schools. I appeared on two television shows, and did lengthy interviews with the *Nashville*

Banner and the *Tennessean*. We held press conferences on Friday, Saturday, and Monday. All three received top news coverage. I spoke at a black church on Sunday morning. We met with local organizers to plan strategy several times.

The only disappointment of the weekend was the meeting with Chancellor Heard and Vanderbilt President Emmett Fields. It was obvious that they were not going to change their decision to allow the matches to take place. On the one hand they said sports and politics don't mix; on the other they said that this was an "open forum" or free speech issue. I had been told by Vanderbilt's black students that the university's liberal reputation was a false one. My meeting with Heard and Fields accomplished nothing.

Other than this, everything else felt positive during these four days. You could feel the momentum of the city shifting toward cancellation of the matches. Local organizers had set up an excellent itinerary to maximize the impact of my stay.

On arriving Friday, I perceived the nature of the debate. Opponents of the matches felt that "South Africa is an evil country and we shouldn't play tennis with them," without having a deep knowledge of what apartheid meant on a daily basis for black South Africans. Proponents felt that "Tennis is a wonderful sport so let's see good competition and keep politics out of it." This was an issue I knew very well. The combination of being able to bring the information to Nashville, coming from a famous and respected sports background, and having the academic credentials enabled me to effectively deliver my message that weekend.

South Africa saw the momentum shifting and tried to change it by naming Peter Lamb to its Davis Cup team. Lamb was a "colored" (mixed ancestry) South African who was a student at Vanderbilt. He was a good player, but at eighteen was hardly of Davis Cup caliber. Announced on Sunday, February 12, the decision backfired immediately as the press perceived it as tokenism on South Africa's part. I knew that Lamb would soon find himself in an agonizing position—reviled by black Americans and by black South Africans for being unwittingly used by South Africa.

The element that I didn't recognize at the time was how much white South Africans resented my whiteness. I was later told that it was one thing to have a Franklin Williams or Benjamin Hooks do anti-apartheid work. It was, after all, blacks who bore the brunt of the oppression. More hated and less understood were whites like George Houser, then the executive director of the American Committee on Africa, or me. The same was true for white racists in America. It was "nigger–lover" time all over again.

By Monday afternoon, as I was about to address students at Vanderbilt, I knew that a great deal had been accomplished. There was an air of excitement, of anticipation. All three local television stations were there. One technician had a remote system back to the studio. Just as I was about to begin my speech, he told me that the NLT Corporation had announced that it had withdrawn its financial support for the Davis Cup.

I relayed the decision. The hundreds of students and faculty in the audience burst into a sustained applause. They were on their feet cheering several minutes. I told them, "The victory is yours. It is only the first." We were on our way to cancellation.

As I began the speech, the NLT decision made even the "Your father is a nigger–lover" call to Joey the week before seem slightly less painful. I told the audience about the incident. Usually a self-assured speaker, my eyes welled up with tears. I had to pause and drink some water. I had never said anything so deeply personal in a speech before. I caught my breath and went on with the speech. It was more passionate, more alive than the others that weekend.

I was feeling euphoric as I was rushed to the airport. We had the South Africans on the run. A Piedmont Airlines attendant at the gate said, "Well, Doctor, I guess there won't be tennis in March."

Sleep did not come easily that night after I got home.

I left at 7:45 A.M. for my 8:30 class on Tuesday. I had three one-and-a-half-hour classes on Tuesdays and Thursdays and usually was fatigued by the end of the day. But on this day I was flying, for it was the day after the NLT Corporation pulled out.

The only damper on the day was the word that Norfolk's

Cuban exile community was extremely upset about my "biased" reporting of what I had seen with my students in January. Peter Galuszka, a reporter from Norfolk's *Virginian Pilot*, was writing both sides of the story and called me for information. We went out for an hour or so to have a sandwich before I returned to my office to continue catching up on class work. I respected Peter as a journalist and watched how he tried to study the Cuban issue from all sides. Moreover, I liked him as a person and felt a friendship developing.

I opened up to him that night and told him about the call to Joey and about a series of calls I had received late in 1977. They began after a feature story on my anti-apartheid work appeared in a regional magazine.

I was called three times by the same person. At first I was told I had three weeks to live, followed by the tapping of a metal object—presumably a gun—on the phone. Exactly one week later the caller said I had two weeks to live. He again tapped the object. Another week had passed when the message that I had only a week left came through. The tapping was harder and louder. I slammed down the receiver, realizing that this could be serious.

I told Peter that I had gone to Bernard Barrow, a neighbor and friend. Barrow was a member of the Virginia House of Delegates. I had totally trusted his judgment when he told me to hold off calling the police until I returned from a one-week lecture trip. When I told Peter that the series of calls had stopped, I could see relief in his face. Yes, we could easily be good friends. As I ate the sandwich I could never have imagined the emotional wringer that Peter and I were about to be thrown into together.

Three hours after I left him, the attack began, lasting less than one hour. As it turned out, it only set the stage for the ensuing nightmare.

Part Two
The Aftermath of the Attack

Chapter 3

Riding Momentum

There was a sense of total unreality for a minute or two after I was awakened by the nurse. I could see I was in the hospital room. There was a nurse and a bed; I was in an antiseptic, nondescript room. Yes, it was a hospital.

Slightly dazed, I assumed I must be a visitor. After all, I had not been hospitalized in the twenty-five years since my brief bout with polio. There were remnants of my jock mentality left. A jock is invulnerable. My body was now a highly developed, muscular one hundred seventy pounds after years of consistent workouts three days a week at a gym.

My mind swirled. I thought of my three most recent visits to the hospital. I had come to watch and assist in the births of Joey and Chamy. I had come moments after the death of my father. The nurse did, at least, shake me back to reality. It was I who was in the hospital.

I thought of both ends of my family's life-cycle—Joey and Chamy, and my mother. I thought of last night—of masked men and of the police.

My body literally shook as "nigger–lover" rang through my head. But the image was of Joey asking me if I was a "nigger–lover" and not of the hooded hunters of the previous night. Were they the ones who had called Joey? Who had called me?

I called home. Everyone else at home was asleep. Sandy and I talked briefly about last night, about Dennis Brutus, and about the Nashville press release condemning the attack. Since a press release would obviously bring out the story, I asked her to call friends to tell them I was fine. Included in the long list was Peter Galuszka, the reporter from the *Virginian Pilot* whom I had been with shortly before the attack.

A few minutes later that Nashville radio station phoned and the circus began. Peter Loomis of the *Ledger Star,* Norfolk's afternoon newspaper, called to request an interview. He came by and I went over some details of the attack, deleting the parts the police asked me to leave out. Then I told him and he wrote that I was "beaten with a blunt instrument until he [I] lost consciousness." He reported that "nigger" (not "*n-i-g-e-r*") had been carved into my stomach "with a sharp instrument" and not with my scissors. He also wrote that I had cuts on my face, chest, and stomach. All he saw, of course, was my face. I wondered if deliberately withholding such details could really help the police to apprehend the men who had beat me. I wondered if the detectives were on the case. I realized they were probably asleep after their own long night.

Loomis was followed by Peter Galuszka. His was a welcome face, a face that told of his concern for me. We joked for a while, and then he told me he had been assigned to write the story for the *Pilot*. We talked about the details. He was puzzled when I repeated blunt object, sharp instrument, and "nigger." Peter assured me that the specific details were in the wire services stories already. He knew it was a steel sculpture, scissors, and "*n-i-g-e-r*." I abruptly realized that the Nashville people must have been unable to change their press release.

So I told him the whole story of the attack. By the end of the day I had told and retold the story more than a dozen times. The three local television stations sent crews. The networks, both television and radio, did phone interviews as did the wire services and the Nashville papers. Over and over I said I would go back to Nashville, that "As long as I'm able to get out of bed, I'm going to intensify my activities. This has strengthened my resolve." However, seeing the fear in my mother's face that afternoon when she came to visit made me question my bravado, sincere though it was.

I decided not to tell the children what had happened. When Joey called, I told him I was sick. He said that he had heard that "Bank robbers got you and cut out your heart and put it in your stomach." I was very upset, more so because I had no time to think. When I wasn't being interviewed I was being examined. Could I really go back to Nashville? Should I take the same risks? Time, I needed time to think.

A Sri Lankan physician, Dr. D. C. Amarasinghe, entered my room and announced that he would be in charge of my case. He gave me a thorough exam and ordered a battery of tests and X-rays. When he began to examine me for a hernia I protested, saying that I was sure there wasn't one since no one had hit me in that area.

Dr. Amarasinghe patiently explained that such a beating on the abdominal wall could easily cause one. Sure enough, when he said "cough" the bulge popped out. I was impressed by his competence and professionalism but distressed when I learned that I would eventually need surgery. The next day he told me that a liver scan showed that there were indications of minor damage to that organ. Dr. Lorenz had told me of blood in the urine indicating kidney damage the night before.

Wednesday afternoon was filled with friends. My adrenalin was pumping. Homicide Sergeant William Hayden, who was heading up the investigation, came by to talk. I could tell he was frustrated by having so many people going in and out of the room. When Hayden asked if he could come to my house when I got home to talk without interruptions, I agreed.

Then he asked if he could send the police doctor to examine me "to make sure you are okay." He had been talking about the massive press coverage the case was receiving and I assumed that he simply wanted another doctor to examine me to be sure I wasn't more seriously injured. I even thought that it was possible that he was concerned that Dr. Amarasinghe was not white and, therefore, somehow less qualified to provide adequate care. I had no objection to being examined again and agreed. I was, however, surprised that Hayden had not talked to either Dr. Lorenz or Dr.

Amarasinghe. I had no idea how significant all of this would become in the next few days.

Howard Cosell sent a film crew from New York to do a segment for ABC's *Good Morning America*. They arrived late in the afternoon. Much to my amazement, the hospital arranged at that moment for a series of lab tests that lasted an hour. It seemed to create a certain amount of tension among the crew. (I wondered if the black skin of some crew members and the fast pace of the "Yankees" prompted the hospital to insist on the tests at that moment.)

The interviewer was much more intense and insistent than the seemingly more sensitive local reporters. He said he wanted to film the scars on my stomach. I thought he was kidding but he was very serious. I told him I thought this might upset the police so I called Hayden, but he was out. The reporter assured me he would talk to the police before using it. I became really uncomfortable when they filmed the scars of "*n-i-g-e-r*"—it seemed too private.

It turned out that Bob Lipsyte, then a columnist for the *New York Post,* had called Cosell about doing the interview. Bob and I had a long conversation earlier in the day. I had respected him as a writer ever since he wrote the "Sports of the Times" column for *The New York Times.* One of the nicest things that happened to me was that I had become close friends with Bob. He was the most honest and forthright person I knew. His sense of humor was devastating. He began the call with "You'll do anything to publicize the cause." Bob and I both assume phone tapping is a widespread practice; we later wondered if his joke had given the police an idea.

One who had many insights was Mike Heaney. Mike was a graduate of Virginia Wesleyan who had joined the Norfolk police and was quickly moving up in the ranks. He came to visit me that evening because, he said, he was upset about the attack. But he was even more upset about the attitude of some of the local police. I had gathered from my conversation with Sergeant Hayden that the police were bothered by the media coverage. I asked Mike if that was it. No, what disturbed him was that some police were saying "he got what he deserved." I was so stunned that I asked him to repeat it. He did, adding that many policemen generally believed that anyone working for black rights deserved to be beaten up.

I remembered the first time I met Mike. He enrolled in the first class I taught on Black Politics in the spring of 1971. By then I had the reputation of being an activist in race relations. Students in the class I taught suggested to me that Mike was a racist. He seemed very uneasy in the class and the few times we met outside it. My first impression was that he was trying to be defiant, to show me I was wrong. I soon learned one of my first lessons as a professor. Mike had joined the class because he really wanted to shed the stereotypes that are the result of being raised in a racist society. Like others, he only needed to be exposed to the roots and consequences of racism to begin to change.

Mike mostly listened that semester, but you could see confusion, uncertainly, and anxiety melt away. The integrity and the sincerity were always there. In my eight years at Wesleyan, Mike probably grew more than any other student I taught. I don't mean he became radicalized. He became open. He came to look at all situations with an unbiased mind.

Mike was apprehensive one afternoon when he dropped by my office during his last semester. I sensed that something was wrong. Suddenly he blurted out, "Rich, I'm going to join the Norfolk Police." I said, "That's great, Mike." His jaw, rigid with tension, noticeably relaxed. "Great?" he asked, "I thought you would be angry." He knew I was critical of the police in many areas. But I was genuinely pleased to think of Mike—honest, caring, intelligent Mike—on the police force.

It hurt me to see Mike so tormented by the hatred of his colleagues for me. But I was also grateful that he was there. He gave me a feel for what was going on.

I had had dozens of moving, memorable moments at Wesleyan. That night I remembered what was probably the most memorable. In spring 1976 I taught a senior-level seminar on international race relations that compared racial questions in different areas of the world. The seminar gathered the best students I ever had together in one class.

One was Charlie Hatcher. A charismatic man, Charlie had

been among those who had integrated Norfolk's public schools, and in the process became an all-star basketball player. Although he had a satchel full of scholarship offers, Charlie entered the army. He was too burned out by the integration experience to do anything else.

Four years later he enrolled at Wesleyan as a twenty-three-year-old man. He quickly became the star of the basketball team. The other students, black and white, admired and respected him. If there was a cohesive force on campus, it was Charlie Hatcher. With two children to support, he eventually had to quit basketball and took a job working with juvenile offenders. I knew he would be late on this particular afternoon because he was to be a character witness in court for two black youths.

Leading the class that day was Leon Donald. Leon was from Milwaukee. Tall and thin, he was another ballplayer. But Leon was more into the black movement than basketball. He had shared with me some touching poetry that he had written about George Jackson, Malcolm X, Franz Fanon, and other important black American and Third World leaders. Intellectually, he was the brightest student in the class. That day he was giving a presentation on Jamaica's Rastafarians.

Listening and absorbing, as always, was Jack Schull. Jack was frail and almost never talked in class. But I knew he was sharp and quick from his writings and from discussions outside class. His shyness prevented others from seeing that he was sensitive and intelligent.

Charlie arrived an hour into Leon's presentation and, uncharacteristically, said nothing for the next thirty minutes.

During the break we took a walk. I was certain that something was wrong. Suddenly he stopped and turned to me. I could see that his eyes were filling with tears. His voice was cracking. This was a different Charlie Hatcher, a man losing control of his emotions. "Damn it," he said, "the judge gave both kids the maximum. Seven years for Bobby and six for Johnny. They're only teenagers. I was sure they would be put on probation. That judge was just another racist seeing two black objects in his court. And I was beginning to believe. It's all the same." He put his arms around me and I held him in turn. His feelings were so intense, so powerful, I could practically feel them through his body.

Charlie insisted on going back to the seminar. He sat quietly, listening to what was a good, academic analysis. Suddenly Charlie stood up. "I can't listen to this anymore. I have to go now. I appreciate that we can all talk so logically and even care about such problems. But the whites in this room, no matter how much they care, can never know what it is like to be black. Never!"

No one else knew what had happened in court. The class was stunned. No one moved. No one spoke. As Charlie moved toward the door, Jack Schull shouted, "Hold it, Charlie!" Like everybody else, I was amazed.

Jack said, "I appreciate what you said. I even agree with it. I only wish I could know so I could understand better. But you, Charlie, you will never know what it's like to know that my grandfather would have been likely to shoot you dead for being bold. My grandfather. A sweet old man who hated blacks. I have to live with that. I have to overcome that. You can never know what that is like."

The other thirteen students were frozen like statues. Charlie stared at Jack, then glanced toward me. Jack was shaking, tears in his eyes. Charlie went over to him, gave him his hand, and nearly crushed his slight frame with a hug.

Almost everyone was in tears. It was the most electrifying moment of my teaching life. We had always talked about understanding and about trying to understand. But at that moment Jack and Charlie understood, perhaps for the first time.

I thought about this moment early that evening. The beating I had absorbed and the misspelled "*n-i-g-e-r*" on my stomach had given me something that I thought no one else could ever fully understand. Yet I hoped that my going through it would serve to reiterate that some white people do care about blacks and vice versa. Then this otherwise senseless beating would have been given some meaning.

My thoughts were broken by Leon Donald, calling from Milwaukee. He had just heard about the attack on the CBS Evening News. I hadn't heard from Leon since 1977. When the phone rang again, it was Charlie Hatcher, calling from Chicago. He was flying in to see me the next morning. Ten minutes later Jack Schull phoned to ask if he could visit the following day. It had been a night of remarkable coincidences—proof of the sympathy that like souls have for each other.

I fell into an exhausted sleep at about 10:30 P.M. My last thoughts were of Mike, and the cops saying "he got what he deserved"; about Charlie's agonized "it's all the same," about Charlie embracing Jack.

I woke up early the next morning and began reading the morning paper. I read Peter's story titled "Masked Men Beat Rights Chief." When he came to visit I teased him about two errors, never thinking them to be important. The first was that I had gone to Nashville "as part of ACCESS's opposition against the inclusion of Peter Lamb . . . on South Africa's Davis Cup team." I told him we were simply against the team playing in the United States, no matter who was on it.

The second error was his reporting of the sequence of events in my office "according to Lapchick and Homicide Sergeant William Hayden." He wrote that the attackers first beat me with the steel sculpture and then beat me with the drawers from the file cabinet, at which point I passed out. Neither of us thought anything of this at the time.

Of all my visitors, the one that came as the biggest surprise was my brother, Joe. We had never quite seen eye to eye on politics, but this time he was on my side. That night he addressed a gathering of some two hundred fifty Wesleyan students. He began by saying, "The only one who can beat up my kid brother is me." My big brother. I felt secure with him around. We never had to say much to communicate. The Lapchick family bond was still a unifying force.

Ibrahim Noor, a Somali who was the assistant secretary of the United Nations Special Committee Against Apartheid, called to tell me that the U.N. would be issuing a statement condemning the attack. I was still in awe of the U.N. so this meant a great deal to me. I knew it would also help in Nashville. I received a call from Saundra Ivey (who was covering the story for the *Tennessean*) shortly after talking to Mr. Noor. She reported that the paper was moving toward calling for the cancellation of the matches. An editorial that day (February 16) had come close:

> There can be no doubt that this community would have been better off had it never heard of the Davis Cup matches. Dr. Lapchick's painful experiences should serve as a stark reminder that the mere debate of racism still has the potential for violence. At this point, that must be the real concern of every sane person in Nashville.

Saundra told me that one of the Nashville student leaders had received harassing phone calls, including a "warning call" on the night of the beating. This student was the same person who had taken me around Nashville for the weekend.

I tried to get permission to make a surprise appearance at the service held for me at Wesleyan although I knew what the answer would be. Instead, Dennis Govoni, the first faculty member to visit, arrived. His stay was interrupted by Faruk Presswalla, who identified himself as the doctor sent by the police. My initial theory that he might have been sent because my doctor was not white was instantly disproved. Dr. Presswalla was Indian.

When Dennis asked if he could stay, I eagerly agreed. It was nearly a month later that Dennis reminded me of it. How fortunate for me that he was there!

The other part of my theory about why the police would send their own doctor also evaporated during the course of Dr. Presswalla's visit. The examination he gave me lasted no more than a few minutes and was extremely superficial. He obviously wasn't there to make sure I was in good health.

However, I didn't make much of this at the time because we had a good one-hour discussion about politics. He told me of his involvement in a group called Indians for Democracy. I discussed my anti-apartheid work. Then I went over the details of the attack. Dennis listened with interest. I was surprised that Dr. Presswalla didn't take any notes, but not as surprised as I was about how cursory the examination was.

When he asked if I had ever thought that the attackers would kill me, I pointed out that they did not use much force with the file cabinet drawers and that they kept turning my head so I was never hit squarely in the face. I suggested that when they beat me in the abdomen prior to my passing out they might have gotten carried away.

After he left, I thought that, while I liked Presswalla, I wouldn't want to have him as my personal physician. I slept well that night with the good news that I was going home in the morning.

Chapter 4

Hidden Ball

I was feeling great on Friday morning—I was going home. Life would be normal again. When I arrived home, I felt compelled to prove to myself how well I was. But after taking a few steps in the front yard, I began to ache.

The day was again a full one with friends, students, and neighbors coming to visit. Sergeant Hayden dropped by in the midst of it all to try to talk. Frustrated but apparently understanding, Hayden asked me if I could come to the police station Saturday afternoon to "quietly discuss" where the case was going.

The best part of the day was being with my family. Although my brother Joe had left, my sister Barbara and her daughter Tayu had arrived from New York. But the stars of the day were Joey and Chamy. Their presence made life good again.

I called Lambuth Clarke, Wesleyan's president, and asked him if I could meet with the whole student body on Monday rather than trying to explain how I was to everyone individually. He agreed that this was a good idea and we set it up for 11:15 A.M., which wouldn't conflict with classes.

Father Joe, the priest from the church I attended, called to say that he was offering masses for me. He said he was proud that I went to his parish as I was an example of what he preached regarding social commitments. I told him I attended his church because he was so human and so inspirational. Not many priests had inspired me before and I rarely went to church in Virginia prior to discovering him.

On Saturday, however, my wounds began to ache and my adrenalin decreased. I called Hayden to tell him I had to take a nap and he said I could come down about 6:00 P.M.

When I awoke, the house was filled. Barbara had gone to the bus terminal to pick up a package from Nashville. I had a fleeting thought it might be a letter bomb, but it turned out to be news clippings sent from Nashville. Barbara read them and brought me one from the *Nashville Banner*. She was very disturbed.

It was the first article written on the attack and appeared on February 15. Although we had not yet met, Sergeant Hayden was quoted extensively.

The story began: "Authorities said Dr. Richard E. Lapchick . . . was beaten with a wooden statue and the letters N-I-G-E-R were scratched on his stomach with a pair of scissors." I found this quite perplexing since the only "authorities" I met in the hospital had emphatically asked me not to reveal any details. As I've said, I took this request so seriously that I was initially withholding such information.

The *Banner* explained that point awkwardly: "Huet-Vaughn's wife, during a telephone call this morning to the *Nashville Banner,* requested an editor change the letters scratched on Lapchick's abdomen to read N-I-G-G-E-R, instead of N-I-G-E-R, which actually was carved on the victim's abdomen." The article made no mention of why the request was made or that it was the police who had asked that the request be made.

As disconcerting as these inaccuracies were, they were nothing compared to the quotes attributed to Sergeant Hayden. First some misinformation—perhaps innocent: "Hayden said Lapchick apparently was assaulted as he walked back toward his office located in the same building as the Virginia school's library. He had gone outside his office to get a drink of water at a fountain and as he returned, he said he was accosted by two men wearing stocking masks." The attack, of course, took place entirely inside my office.

Then the article directly attributed the hold-at-all-cost details to Hayden. "The detective said Lapchick, thirty-two, suffered cuts and bruises when struck about the head and body with the wooden statue and cut on the abdomen with the scissors."

It proved to be only the beginning. "Most of his injuries were not tremendously serious at all," said Sergeant Hayden. But the two detectives had known of the kidney damage and concussion before Hayden said this. What is more, Hayden had not talked to Dr. Lorenz, the only one who had examined me, prior to talking to the *Banner*. When confronted with this later, Hayden responded, "The quote is true. Most of your injuries were not serious. I didn't say all weren't serious."

Then came the clincher. "Hayden . . . said he 'finds it rather interesting' that Lapchick's associates released a press statement before police had an opportunity to hardly start an investigation into the case." The Norfolk police knew exactly how the Nashville people learned of the attack.

I was outraged when I read the story. Nancy Lowe, a neighbor, said that her husband Fred, an attorney, would go with me to the police station to lodge a formal complaint.

We arrived and showed Hayden the article. He excused himself to "make a copy." Since he didn't return for twenty minutes, we assumed he was asking his superiors for advice.

When Hayden returned he apologized and said he could understand why we were concerned. I chose that moment to tell him that I had been told by a reliable source that one of the two detectives on the case was considered to be a racist. We were assured that he was no longer assigned to the case.

Then Hayden asked me to come with him to discuss the details of the attack, telling Fred to stay behind. I went through everything. At the end I pointed out that Peter Galuszka's article had reversed the order of the events, attributing his account to me and to Hayden. I said that considering what he had told the *Banner*, I assumed that he was the source of the confusion. However, I still saw no significance in this.

Sergeant Hayden had been very attentive. When I was finished he simply said, "You know, Richard, we have no suspects and leads in this case. I have faith in you, but you should know that it has been raised as a possibility that you staged the attack."

I might have been calm on the outside, but inside I was stunned and seething. "I want to prove this to be untrue so we can get on with the investigation," he went on. "I want to offer you the opportunity to take a polygraph. It just so happens that our polygraph expert is here tonight and has agreed to administer the test if you accept."

It was an interesting choice of words. He was "offering" me an "opportunity" to prove myself innocent of a crime that had been committed against me! I had a sudden flash of insight into how thousands of American women feel who had been subjected to a lie-detector test to prove they had been raped. For the victim to have to prove she was victimized in such a dehumanizing way is wrong.

If Hayden had looked into my background he could have easily surmised that I would refuse. I quickly realized that this would be an easy way for him to dismiss the case or to discredit me. I told him I would think about it but was almost totally sure that I would not subject myself to such a test. I suggested it was time for Fred to join us. When he did, I asked Hayden who it was that was raising the possibility of a staging. His response was unambiguous. "The local press."

"You mean Peter Galuszka and Peter Loomis?" I asked. Hayden said that he could not name individuals.

Fred asked what would happen now. Sergeant Hayden replied no one would know of the "offer" until I responded. If the press asked, he would then have to tell them if I said no. He requested me to sign over the hospital records to the police, and I complied.

We left the police station shaken and disturbed. I told Fred that I was likely to refuse the test because I was the victim and the police were making me the suspect. He said he agreed but warned me that many people would interpret any refusal as a sign of guilt. I kept thinking of all those rape victims.

Fred and I arrived home late. There were friends over for dinner, but I was not very good company. I felt I was being set up. But for what?

My physical strength was being eroded. Lack of sleep wasn't helping. My weight at the time of the attack was one hundred seventy. On Saturday I weighed one hundred sixty. Within a week it would be one hundred fifty.

I called trusted friends on Sunday morning. Franklin Williams promised to call other civil rights leaders. Bob Lipsyte said to refuse the request. Without exception, everyone agreed. Franklin called back and reminded me of the attacks on King and Malcolm X followed by police allegations of "staging." Franklin said, "We need to keep you alive."

I also called Peter Galuszka. I didn't believe Hayden when he said the press had raised the doubts. Peter said he had heard nothing like this. I was glad it wasn't Peter. However, he called back later to say that police had been leaking it everywhere that I had been asked to take a polygraph. They would have to write the story, he said, and suggested he call me later for a statement.

Fred and I got together to prepare it. I called Hayden. He denied that he was leaking the story and said he would try to stop the leaks. I believed him, just as I believed him when he said I wasn't being "set up."

The front-page story of Monday's *Virginian Pilot* was headlined, "Prof Suspected in His Attack." "Sources" claimed I may have staged the attack, but Hayden wouldn't say I was a suspect. He said I was being very cooperative with the police investigators.

The paper printed only two paragraphs of my statement. Curiously, the story did not say the police had requested the polygraph. Here is my statement in full:

> My initial reaction upon being asked to do this was one of shock, dismay, and anger. I asked myself, "Why aren't they out looking for the men who made the brutal attack on me instead of questioning the victim's truthfulness?"
>
> Since Sergeant Hayden has been most cooperative with me on a personal basis, I can only feel that this request made of me arises out of the traditional trend displayed by law-enforcement authorities in doubting those who are willing to take a stand on civil rights issues. More than a few people have suggested to me that the TV broadcast of the life of Dr. King last week may have created a climate for the police to attempt to discredit me as they had done to Dr. King prior to and after his assassination.

It is my firm belief that police procedures should not include placing the victim of a crime, regardless of its nature, in the position of having to submit to this type of humiliation. To do so only weakens the entire system of justice and threatens the ability of all people to feel secure with the protection that the police in our society should offer. We are paying the police to catch people who commit crimes.

After consulting all day yesterday with friends, family, and national civil rights leaders, I have decided not to succumb to the police request for a polygraph. There are several reasons for this: First, police have uncontroverted evidence of the seriousness of the injuries. Second, the two examining doctors have stated that due to internal bleeding, kidney damage, and a hernia, it is virtually impossible for the wounds to be self-inflicted. Third, there was absolutely no evidence to contradict my statements. But most important, to succumb would be to perpetuate the police use of this type of negative approach in the cases of civil rights assaults and other assaults such as rape.

As long as people agree to have their veracity challenged in this way, this process and practice will continue. I have decided that in this case it will stop.

As noted, the story quoted only two of the paragraphs. But it did cite Dr. Amarasinghe's doubts that the wound could have been self-inflicted and quoted Dr. Lorenz as saying that "the only wounds that could have been self-inflicted were the scratches on his stomach."

The *Nashville Banner* story was even more heinous. It quoted at length a "Virginia Beach detective official who asked not to be identified" as saying, "This whole thing just did not ring completely true." He added that my refusal to take the polygraph made me the focus of the investigation to see if I "was in on it."

The *Banner* quoted part of my response, then went for the jugular. "Lapchick, who recently returned from a trip to Cuba and has also visited Russia and Red China. . . ." No matter that I had never been to Russia. The truth was receding rapidly into police leaks.

Enter Sergeant Hayden again. "Dr. Lapchick and I had a conversation the other day and that conversation and what took place during our conversation are really between Dr. Lapchick and I," he told the *Banner*. "If Dr. Lapchick wishes to make comments with regard to our conversation, that's his prerogative. I'm not making any comments." The implication was that it was up to me to announce that I wouldn't take the polygraph test.

Both articles mentioned that I had been seen by the state medical examiner. Reading this was the first time I had thought of Dr. Presswalla since Thursday. Dr. Lorenz was again quoted as to how "the wounds on the professor's stomach could have been self-inflicted."

I was slightly confused by his comments. Saundra Ivey of the *Tennessean* probed him more deeply. "It amazes me that reporters are making so much out of this statement," Lorenz told her. "Obviously, you could inflict almost any wounds, so one could say of almost any assault that the wounds could be self-inflicted. I didn't feel, taking everything into consideration, that the wounds in this case were self-inflicted."

Again, Hayden declined to comment. "The comments you are seeing in the newspaper are not from me, because what I say, I put my name on," he told the *Tennessean*.

All of this had happened by 10:00 A.M. Monday. By the time I got in the car to head toward Wesleyan, I realized that I would have to address the polygraph issue with the students when I met them at 11:15 A.M. I decided to repeat my statement of the previous night.

My mind was filled with images. Security was tight at the entrance. This hadn't been the case last week. Driving into the parking lot reminded me of being put in the ambulance there, of the students swarming around me late at night, of Mike Mizell discovering the word "*n–i–g–e–r*" on my stomach.

The students were gathering outside Pruden Lounge where I was to meet them. Some greeted us in the parking lot, telling us that the lounge was packed with students and press. I wanted the meeting to be for my students alone, but knew it would become a press conference.

I was weak-kneed and couldn't catch my breath. Like a child wanting to please his parents, I wanted to please my students. I had always tried to get them to believe in themselves, to take responsibility for their actions, to stand on their principles, to be proud. They were also my family: Wesleyan had become an extension of my home.

So I worried about how the students would react to the morning headlines. Could I convince them that I was standing on principle by refusing the polygraph? Or that I was using good judgment in taking such responsibility for my actions rather than submitting to the police requests? Could I be proud at that moment? Did I really believe in myself?

I grew weaker and less determined as I wound my way up the stairs. I heard one student shout "Here he comes!" and the building filled with cheers. The students were on their feet, shouting, applauding. The television and newspaper people were everywhere, but all I could see were my students, my friends. I was home.

I began with words suggested to me the night before by Bob Lipsyte. "If you think you might be a murder victim," I told the group, "be sure you cross the city line so the Virginia Beach police don't claim you committed suicide!" The students roared. The ice was broken. I then read my statement. "For the first time, I clearly understood what a woman who has been raped must feel like when asked to take a polygraph." I concluded, "As long as people agree to have their veracity challenged in this way, this process and practice will continue. I have decided that in this case it will stop." The audience rose to its feet and applauded for several minutes.

I felt very good about both what I had chosen to say and the response I had gotten. The press began to ask questions, but I could sense they were not hostile. One reporter, whom I did not know, said, "The police told me this morning that the fact you have not received any threatening phone calls since the attack is very unusual. What's your response?"

More leaks from the police. I told the reporter that the attack was not likely the work of neighborhood kids who then make prank calls, that the business of sports relations with South Africa was a serious one. I didn't expect such calls. I added that I could not tell whether the Virginia Beach police were trying to discredit me or to close a difficult case in which they had no leads.

It clicked in my mind at that moment that there was no way I could get help from the Virginia Beach police. They had refused to give me around-the-clock protection as I had requested, choosing instead to beef up patrols near the house. We had noticed that even the patrols seemed to stop Sunday night, when the polygraph story was breaking.

I decided I had better consult with some legal experts and that I would follow the advice of the civil rights people and seek the help of the Justice Department.

After a friendly meeting with President Clarke, at which I told him I would ask the FBI to intervene, I taught my Urban Studies class and went home.

Andrew Fine, a lawyer who was an old friend from the Beach, had offered to help in any way he could. I called Andrew and he immediately arranged for a meeting the next day with the U.S. Attorney-General in Norfolk.

The local media was giving the statement I made at the college considerable coverage, although the *Pilot* put it on page B-3 after running the "suspect" story on page 1. The national press began to phone me at home. I was too exhausted to speak to many people.

I did speak to Bill Nack of *Newsday*. I felt he and his editor, Sandy Padwe, were two of the best and most serious analysts of the reality of sport as a reflection of society in America. Indeed, he wrote a scathing column on the actions of the police.

Franklin Williams issued a statement on behalf of the Phelps-Stokes Fund, the NAACP, and the Urban League, "deploring the libelous actions of the Virginia Beach police" against me. "Against reason, evidence, or acceptable standards of decency and honor, these authorities have cast doubts on Dr. Lapchick's veracity in the matter of his own brutal attack by racist terrorists. The suggestion that this man of integrity be subjected to a polygraph test says more about the method and morals of the police than it does about Dr. Lapchick, a fact that all who know the man are quick to grasp."

I was receiving calls and telegrams of support for my stand against the polygraph from all over the country. Several were from local women who still carried the scars of mistreatment by police after they had been raped and then forced to take a polygraph.

Andrew Fine and I met with the Norfolk U.S. Attorney-General on Tuesday at 11:30. I told him that I had lost faith in the police and that I felt that my civil rights were being violated. An interview with the FBI was arranged for that afternoon. I told Peter Galuszka about the morning meeting. He was anxious to write the story if the FBI agreed to take the case.

I had some misgivings while we waited for the FBI to arrive. As a child of the civil rights and antiwar movements, my image of the FBI was not of Ephraim Zimbalist, Jr., but of J. Edgar Hoover. The same Hoover who went after Dick Gregory, who tried to get Martin Luther King, who harassed innumerable dissenters and protesters, all the while breaking the laws he was supposed to protect.

I thought, "Times have changed," but then realized I was living proof that one still could not freely speak out without the potential of serious reprisal. I thought of the hate calls to my father and of how he internalized it all. I thought of the modern-day sports critics—Dave Meggyesy, Jack Scott, Tommy Smith, and Phil Shinnick. All were such threats to our society that in this February of 1978 they were all virtually unemployable. Harry Edwards was fighting to keep his job at Berkeley.

So I had no illusions as I saw FBI-Norfolk bureau chief James Healy and his partner drive up to the house. But I had heard good things about Drew Days, the head of the Civil Rights Division of the Justice Department, and knew that whatever help I got from the FBI would be better than what I was getting from the Virginia Beach police.

We talked for an hour. I was pleased by their reactions and they said there appeared to be grounds for the Justice Department to take jurisdiction in the case. As they left I asked how I should handle press inquiries. Healy said I could tell them that "the FBI had begun an inquiry."

I smiled as the agents drove away. It would be the last smile for a long, long time.

Chapter 5

Injury Time-out

The phone rang immediately. It was Peter Galuszka. "I guess you called about the FBI," I said. For the first time, Peter was abrupt.

"No. The state medical examiner has just announced that your wounds were self-inflicted. What is your response?"

I had no response. I just sat there, unable to speak. "Richard, Richard?" Peter kept repeating. Finally, I said, "Peter, I am absolutely astonished. How can he refute the doctors who treated me? Dr. Presswalla's exam was superficial. We spent most of the time discussing politics." Naively I asked, "Are you going to print this story?"

Peter advised me to call Presswalla, saying he had just spoken to him. He gave me his home number. He agreed not to write anything until I had prepared a response.

I just sat there a few minutes in a state of shock. Then I called Presswalla. His wife answered, pausing when I said who was calling. After a few seconds she said he was not there and that she didn't know where he was. I didn't believe her, and practically begged her to put me in touch with him. She could tell from my voice that it was imperative for me to reach me. She said she would try.

I collapsed on the bed, literally speechless. I just couldn't believe that this was happening to me.

I was being accused of a sick act of self-mutilation. What could I say? "I didn't do it." There would always be people now who doubted me no matter how much evidence I put on the table.

I knew I couldn't go ahead with plans to go to Nashville the next day. When I called to cancel, my friends encouraged me to come, but were understanding. Bob Lipsyte called. As usual, Bob was tonic for me. On this night I needed more than tonic, but still he helped.

"Who is this Presswalla? Was he paid off?" Bob asked. "You can't look back. If you don't go to Nashville, then they will have accomplished their aims. You have to go."

I said I didn't see how I could, but that I would reconsider it.

Then that unwanted call from Peter Galuszka came. I told him Presswalla hadn't returned the call and he said he was on a deadline. He was writing the story with Steve Goldberg, who had also coauthored the "Suspect" article.

Peter gave me the details. Dr. Presswalla based his conclusions on the markings on my stomach. He said they showed hesitation, that is, the person inflicting the wound was cautious not to cut too deeply. An attacker would not do that, but a person would do it to himself. In forensic medicine, such cuts are called "hesitation marks."

Presswalla told Peter that his decision to make his opinion public was based partially on the fact that the FBI had entered the case.

After our conversation ended, Peter called back. He said his editor realized I hadn't said whether or not I had self-inflicted the wounds. I said that the answer was obvious. Peter said "Then say it." "I didn't do it," I told him. It was hard to utter those words to Peter.

I was talking to Saundra Ivey at about 11:15 when the operator broke in with an emergency call from Presswalla. The timing was not insignificant; the deadline of the *Virginian Pilot* had long since passed.

My heart began to pound uncontrollably. I asked, "What are you trying to do to me? Do you really believe what you told the press?"

Dr. Presswalla responded that he was sympathetic to me, that as a political activist he knew the importance of publicity for the cause. He added, "What you did is not uncommon in India."

I said that Drs. Amarasinghe and Lorenz had contradicted him, but he quickly pointed to the Lorenz quote saying the cuttings on the stomach *could* be self-inflicted, and said that the doctors had no background in forensic medicine. "In my thirteen years of medical practice, I have never seen an exception to this rule [of hesitation marks]."

He sounded sincere and concerned. I asked, "Couldn't the attackers have made the wounds look self-inflicted?" He said it was conceivable, but the issue now could only be resolved by a polygraph. I should go to another state and be examined by both a polygraph expert and a specialist in forensic pathology, he suggested. After all, he noted, "I didn't say you weren't attacked. You may have been assaulted and carved *n-i-g-e-r* yourself for political effect."

Dr. Presswalla told me he had made his report to the police on Friday, and it was he who had instructed them to give me a polygraph. He said he couldn't understand why Sergeant Hayden hadn't told me this.

The phone rang, jarring me. It was Walter Searcy, a local organizer from the black community in Nashville. He insisted that I come to Nashville as a testimony to my truthfulness. We went around and around on this until I finally gave in to him.

The next day I woke up early to see the damage done by the *Virginian Pilot.* "Lapchick's Wounds Appear Self-Inflicted, Examiner Says," proclaimed the headline of a five-column page-1 story.

The story repeated what Peter had told me the night before— "hesitation marks," Presswalla's reason for "stepping forward now," etc. It ran twenty-eight paragraphs before saying that Dr. Amarasinghe stood by his findings that the wounds could not be self-inflicted.

Presswalla said he was waiting for reports from Drs. Amarasinghe and Lorenz before making a "final statement on the matter." If he was, in fact, still waiting, then the police were taking an exceptionally long time in delivering the hospital report I had released to them five days earlier. I was amazed to read a newspaper report quoting unnamed sources which said Presswalla had found "no evidence of serious internal bleeding, kidney damage, liver damage, or recent hernia," even though to the best of my knowledge he had not seen the report nor talked to my doctors.

Then Goldberg and Galuszka set the tone of the debate when discussing the polygraph: "Lapchick refused and *denounced* police, who he said were harassing the victim instead of pursuing the perpetrators."

Not only did I never publicly denounce the police but I am now embarrassed at how naive and reticent I was about their actions.

Next came more from Presswalla: "I have great personal support for Dr. Lapchick's cause, and I don't want to harm him." This was followed by: "Perhaps there is an extra note of caution [in my report] because I have been in an activist role myself."

According to the story, he had not wanted to perform the examination on me because of his sympathy and, when he did do it, he had hoped to "find a graceful way out of the situation" for me.

If Dr. Presswalla thought such statements wouldn't harm me, I wondered what he thought would. If this was his idea of a graceful way out, I wondered what he would do if he were hard-hitting. The answers to such questions were soon to follow.

I was literally sick to my stomach when I remembered that Leonard Sharzer, a noted local surgeon, had examined me in the hospital. It turned out that Leonard was at a conference in Dallas. The frantic search for Leonard began.

Facing my students in my 10:00 A.M. class that morning was terribly difficult. I tried to concentrate on teaching but instead I became unglued. I just couldn't talk about Tanzanian politics.

Karen Gilbert, a good friend who helped me with several programs I ran in the community, interrupted to say that Leonard Sharzer was on the phone. It was the first time I had ever walked out of a class in progress. I didn't hesitate for a second—I had become obsessed with my plight.

Sharzer said he would definitely inform the press that his conclusions supported Lorenz's and Amarasinghe's. As a courtesy he wanted to speak first to Dr. Presswalla to tell him what he was going to say. I admired Leonard for his integrity and professionalism. Now the score was 3 to 1. Certainly the press would now be forced to change its tone.

I ran back to the class and told them, "There is a god after all. A third doctor has just come forth. The truth will soon be known."

I was driven to the airport. Ironically, I felt somewhat sorry for Dr. Presswalla. He would have to swallow hard now with three doctors opposing him. The compassion came from a nagging belief that he was being sincere, that he really believed what he was saying. I thought that perhaps my assailants were so professional that they had carved the "hesitation marks" to discredit me. After all, Dr. Presswalla was a "liberal."

I still didn't realize how deep the waters were as we drove to the airport. Kathy Kent, a reporter for the local CBS-affiliate, approached us. "Will you take a polygraph now?" she asked. I said that I was continuing to stand on my principles.

We were met at the Nashville airport by a dozen or so well-wishers. A press conference had been set up there. The theme of it was that I was in Nashville to refocus attention on the Davis Cup. I didn't yet realize how out of focus things had become. I expected many of the questions would be on the attack and Presswalla's allegations. I gave a detailed explanation.

Finally, one reporter asked, "Why not just submit to a polygraph test to clear up any doubts?" I reiterated my reasons, adding, "In many ways it would be easier to do it, but it would also be easier not to speak out against apartheid. I have taken what I consider to be a consistent moral stand."

I did a lengthy interview with Wayne King of *The New York Times*. He questioned me on my athletic background, if I had kept in condition, etc. When I asked why, he responded that it would be very unlikely that someone who took care of and cared about his body would inflict injuries on himself. I sensed that we had recaptured the momentum, that we could remount the protest against South Africa.

We drove to Don Beiswinger's house for dinner. Don was a

theology professor at Vanderbilt. I again thought of Presswalla, wondering how he must feel.

Walter Searcy, the Nashville organizer, was at Don's with "J.J.," the armed bodyguard hired to protect me in Nashville. It was almost funny watching J.J. dart around the house, checking windows, seating me in exactly the right chair for safety. Some of the pressure was off; I was okay again.

Don asked if we had seen the Nashville papers that day. When he brought them to me, I was devastated. The *Tennessean*'s headline was:

LAPCHICK'S WOUNDS RULED SELF-INFLICTED

The *Banner*'s read:

LAPCHICK WOUNDED SELF, DOCTOR RULES

A TV was on in the other room. We went to see Walter Cronkite's Davis Cup coverage but he had moved to a related item:

> Last week we had a story about Richard Lapchick, the Virginia Beach political science teacher who had planned to protest South Africa's entry in the Davis Cup Match. Lapchick claimed two masked men had assaulted him and carved a racial slur on his stomach. Now a Virginia State medical examiner has concluded that Lapchick apparently inflicted the stomach wounds on himself. Lapchick denied the allegation, but refused to take a lie-detector test.

Everyone was stunned. This wasn't Steve Goldberg reporting but Walter Cronkite. This was the man whom America believed. Someone tried to break the silence with "What was the news about the Davis Cup?" No one had heard it.

Next we were driven to Vanderbilt for my 7:30 speech. J.J., as they say, cased the joint. The only difference was that it was no longer amusing. The balance had shifted again. I didn't feel up to the speech, but I had to give it. Walter Searcy, Bob Lipsyte—

everyone insisted I had to go no matter how I felt. I would rather have been anywhere else in the world as I walked down the steps of the same auditorium where only ten days before I had triumphantly announced that the NLT Corporation had withdrawn as financial backer of the Davis Cup.

That triumph was a distant memory now as a handful of people in the auditorium hissed when I entered. Ninety-five percent may have applauded; most of them were on their feet. But I heard only the hisses. It was close to being the most humiliating moment of my life. I found it hard to believe that all of this had happened in ten days. I knew then, before I uttered a word, that I would soon have to do something dramatic. *I* was the issue in Nashville, not South Africa.

We were back at Don's by 9:30. When Saundra Ivey arrived, she told me that Presswalla had again gone to the press, saying essentially the same thing but now insisting all the injuries were "consistent with self-infliction." He said there was no evidence that I had been knocked unconscious with the file cabinet drawers as I had "claimed." He added that there were no cuts—save a small one on my lip—on my face and no injuries to my chest. A beating such as I said had taken place would have produced such cuts and injuries. Even though, for all practical purposes, this was the same story as had already appeared, it was again to be page-1 news in Virginia the next day. The story would include the statement of my three doctors, which I had simplistically assumed would be the lead, in the seventeenth paragraph. Presswalla had upstaged Leonard Sharzer by issuing his renewed allegations. I suspected that Leonard's call to Presswalla had provoked him to take action.

Presswalla had told Saundra that clinical physicians such as Sharzer, Lorenz, and Amarasinghe were more concerned with treating patients than with examining injuries in the manner he did and were not adequate judges of whether his conclusions were correct.

Presswalla was absolute in his opinions. There were no more "notes of caution" or "not wanting to harm me." He claimed the wounds were "definitely self-inflicted." He told the *Washington Post* that the hernia "was an antecedent. It was not related to the assault." He said although I claimed resulting internal injuries, there was no evidence of them being caused by the beating. He admitted he still had not talked to Lorenz or Amarasinghe, who had made the diagnosis.

He even implied that he had called me on his own initiative Wednesday night, failing to mention that he was returning my call some five hours after I had made it. He told the *New York Post*, "I'm sure this is going to be ammo for the conservative red-neck types to say liberals are pinkos and liars—which includes me because I am a liberal."

The press loved it. During the six weeks that the case received national attention, I was interviewed regularly, mostly by men. The only women who followed it from start to finish were Saundra Ivey, Athelia Knight of the *Washington Post,* and Ianthe Thomas of the *Village Voice.* Interestingly, it was these women who probed most persistently and deeply.

It was, in fact, Saundra's persistence that first raised my doubts about Presswalla's sincerity. For someone who was so definite in his opinions, he made some curious statements to her.

"I feel sure of what I have said based on my experience but another person may have a different opinion. This is why I have suggested he [Lapchick] consult others in this field and show them photographs of his wounds."

He said he would accept my version of events if I passed a polygraph test "administered by a competent examiner. The only person I knew of who could beat the polygraph is a pathological habitual liar and I'm sure Dr. Lapchick is not a person like that. I have never said he is totally lying, but that I see inconsistencies in the story he has given."

Presswalla told Saundra that it was possible that in an "elaborate plot" assailants could have cut me in such a manner as to duplicate the hesitation marks characteristic of self-inflicted wounds. He reiterated that a polygraph was "the crux of the matter now" if he was to accept my version of what had happened. The *Tennessean* printed all of this.

He had told Athelia Knight, "I'm not saying he wasn't assaulted, but there are some medical inconsistencies."

How could a man of science say I "definitely" did something

but would reverse his opinion if I took a polygraph or if another forensic pathologist offered a different conclusion? Could he really believe that someone could be assaulted and while recovering think of carving "*n-i-g-e-r*" on his abdomen for political effect? Did he honestly believe that I had made up the internal injuries when he had my hospital records in hand? Or that my story of the attack was inconsistent? Did he trust his memory so much that he didn't need to take notes that night in the hospital? Or was he relying on the account mistakenly written by Peter Galuszka in the *Pilot?*

It's true Dr. Presswalla had a great deal of experience— fourteen years. It wasn't until March 21—a month later—that the *Ledger Star* pointed out that in his years in America I was only the second living patient that Dr. Presswalla had examined (he claimed he had seen living patients in India and Europe prior to coming to America) and that the other case had had nothing to do with self-inflicted wounds. Presswalla claimed it made no difference in interpreting wounds whether they were examined on a living body or a dead one, and that he had performed thousands of autopsies.

Furthermore, it was not until that weekend that I learned that the term "hesitation marks" in forensic pathology refers only to suicide attempts where a person first superficially cuts his wrist or throat to see how deeply he will eventually have to cut. It had no application at all to a carving such as the one on my abdomen.

Nor did I know that the Cronkite story just preceding the one about me was this: "South Africa has quietly ended segregation on its tennis courts, a move that's expected to result in an end to thirty years of sports apartheid in that white-ruled country."

There was no comment—the story was just accepted as fact, although such South African statements were as common as real change was rare. More than a decade later, South African sports were still segregated. However, on February 24 the one-two punch hurt. First the announcement that South African sports were integrated, then the story that a man associated in the minds of the public with anti-apartheid activities in sports was discredited. Was it a coincidence that Presswalla's first announcement about self-infliction came out within hours of the announcement made in South Africa? It certainly didn't help the next day when the media asked me what I thought of the changes in South Africa. I was not very believable then.

However, I did not know such things that night as I went to bed. I only knew that I was exhausted and humiliated and that I would have to agree to take a polygraph if I was to get the focus back on South Africa.

I met with John Zeigenthaller, the publisher of the *Tennessean,* for two hours the next morning. He recounted problems he had had with a bogus FBI investigation and assured me the truth would come out in the end, that there was no need for a polygraph. Even while he was saying this, I had decided to take a polygraph and had called Zeke Orlinski, a friend in the Washington area, to try to arrange for the polygraph.

The need to do this was again underlined during a TV interview that took place at the Beiswingers'. It was a good free-flowing session but ended abruptly with "Will you take a polygraph?" I replied, "No," since nothing had been arranged. Thirty minutes later Zeke called to say the test was all set for the next morning.

I had abdominal pain all morning and was taken to see a local doctor. It had been suggested that my symptoms sounded like possible spleen damage. The doctor said it was only remaining muscle damage and tenderness. I was actually disappointed. The obsession with proving that the attack had taken place had grown so great that I had hoped he would discover a new injury that Drs. Lorenz and Amarasinghe might have missed.

The local doctor then sent me to a lab for some tests. When the receptionist called me inside, she said, "I want you to know I believe you." I thanked her, but I realized how awful things had become when a total stranger felt compelled to reassure me. As nice as it was, it furthered the obsession—I couldn't wait for the polygraph.

The anxiety and tension built as I flew to Washington. I felt so nervous and upset that I was afraid my emotions would have a negative impact on the polygraph. I was met at the airport by Zeke and Rebecca Orlinski. My tension was not reduced in spite of many reassurances by Zeke, who was a lawyer and former prosecutor in Baltimore. I later called Ron Ellison, another attorney who had actually arranged the polygraph. I was wound tight as a drum, and wanted to take a sleeping pill but was told that it might affect the test—no pill, no sleep.

At breakfast, Ron Ellison tried to calm me. At 10:00 A.M. I went to the office of Bob Niebuhr, the polygraph expert. Ron had been careful in choosing him, as we didn't want any doubts raised. Niebuhr was president of the Maryland Polygraphers Association and was also licensed in Virginia, which we felt was important. In the course of his career he had administered 20,000 polygraph tests. Most important, Bob Niebuhr was in no way associated with the left or liberal political causes.

We talked at length about the case. Having read many of the newspaper articles, Niebuhr said he wanted a friend named Al to assist him in preparing the questions to be asked and in evaluating the results. He was cautious, he said, because he recognized the importance of the test.

We went over the questions. Did you ever lie before you were twenty-one? Did you ever lie for personal gain? There were several control questions such as name, place of birth, etc. The big questions were:

Did you cut that word on your stomach?

Did you want someone to cut it?

Did you arrange for someone to cut it?

Did you know who cut it?

I felt like I was on trial even though Bob and Al were sympathetic to my state of mind. Taking the polygraph was among the most humiliating and nerve-racking experiences I ever went through.

Niebuhr saw that I was convinced that the machine couldn't compute my frenzied emotions. They ran a control series to prove I was wrong. They said to pick a number from one to seven. I picked five and wrote it down. I was told to say no every time as Niebuhr asked "Was it one?" "Was it two?" etc. He went from one to seven, then from seven to one. Then they showed me the charts with marked differences each time I said "no" on number five. I felt more at ease, and we went through all the questions for the third and last time. When the wires were removed from the various parts of my body, I left in the room.

Ron Ellison, Bob Niebuhr, and the mysterious Al met in the other room. They called me back in and asked me who I thought attacked me. I said I couldn't be sure but felt it was either a Klan member or a South African. With this, Bob Niebuhr glanced at Al and then turned to me. "The test proved you were truthful," he said.

I broke down. The emotional pitch had racked me. Bob Niebuhr said the FBI might ask me to take another polygraph test. If they did I would "feel like an old friend was giving it to me," he assured me. He looked at Al as he said it and I finally realized that he must have been from the FBI. Al was not there officially, so I couldn't reveal this at that time. With a tear in his own eye, Al hugged me and said, "God bless you."

On the way to the Orlinskis', I thought that the agony was over at last. I called Andy Fine in Norfolk. He was, of course, thrilled by the result and said he would drive directly over to tell my mother so I wouldn't have to call her. Even Andy was sure the phone was tapped and we didn't want the police to know about the test. I also called my sister, who insisted that I come to New York City. She said a group had formed there that wanted to help me.

Zeke and Rebecca were the perfect people to be with that night. We had met on a charter flight to London and had instantly become friends. Zeke didn't practice law anymore but had bought the *Columbia Flyer,* a dying newspaper he then successfully rebuilt. Zeke and his wife Rebecca shared a marvelous wit. We gorged ourselves on food and drank a lot of wine. The lives we had led up to February 14 seemed ready to be resumed. Sleep was long and deep that night.

The next day I took the Metroliner to New York. Barbara's apartment was half filled when we arrived. Roy Brown, Barbara's first husband, Sam and Helen Rosen, whom I had known for three years, Jack Geiger of the Medical Commission for Human Rights, and Florence Halperin were all there. All were from the New York medical community.

They had read the Bayside Hospital official report and were outraged by what Presswalla had said. They said that the internal injuries diagnosed in the report proved that the wounds couldn't have been self-inflicted. They were even more sure when they saw the "*n-i-g-e-r*" on my stomach. The consensus among them was that Dr. Presswalla had been used by the police to set me up. They felt that as doctors their profession had been misused.

They decided to form a committee and to hire an attorney to investigate. Everyone agreed that Paul O'Dwyer, the former New York City Council president, was the best choice. He agreed to drive in from his country home that night to meet us.

I sensed I was somehow losing control of the situation. Others, who believed either in me or in civil or human rights in general, had taken command of my destiny. So I was reassured when, much to my surprise, my brother Joe arrived.

Barbara, Joe, and I went to Franklin Williams' apartment. He offered us all the facilities of the Phelps-Stokes Fund—an office to use and any other practical help we might need. We liked the idea of the committee and of retaining Paul O'Dwyer as counsel.

We met Paul as planned at 9:30 P.M. He was an impressive man whom I had admired for several years. As president of the City Council he had helped pass a resolution against South African tennis players competing in New York–area facilities. We gave him all the details and he said he would let me know by Monday afternoon whether he would represent me.

We all went back to Barbara's. Jack and Roy had prepared a statement for the "National Committee to Protect Civil Rights." Both the statement and title seemed too broad. We settled on the "Committee for Justice for Richard Lapchick" with a more tailored statement. Paul O'Dwyer had stressed that the word "Defense" should not be used because it implied a defense was necessary. Barbara, Joe, and I stayed up and talked until 1:30 A.M. They were both great. Barbara had been through this and worse with the arrest of her husband Rajat in Uganda in 1968. Joe, a political conservative, had not only never experienced anything like it but I don't believe he thought it was possible for it to happen in America.

Dr. Bernard Simon, a prominent New York City surgeon, examined me early on Monday. He was more thorough than any doctor who had examined me since the attack. His conclusion was that the wounds could not possibly have been self-inflicted.

Momentum was building. I couldn't wait to get back to Virginia with this mess cleared up. I was beginning to miss my students, and I took it as a positive sign that I was able to think about them again.

Bob Lipsyte drove into the city to meet us. It was the first time I saw him in person after thirteen straight days of encouragement and help on the phone. We discussed strategy. Bob felt strongly that we needed a knockout offensive. He said we should announce a $1-million libel suit against Presswalla and the police. Bob argued that simply saying "I didn't do it" would be a page B-10 story while Presswalla's accusations were all on page 1. My only misgiving was the lingering doubt that Presswalla believed what he said. Others suggested that, if anything, the police might have misled him.

Paul O'Dwyer called and agreed to take the case. That evening I was to see Dr. David Spain, the top forensic pathologist in the country who dealt with civil rights cases. The only bad news was that O'Dwyer couldn't go to Virginia until the following Monday, meaning we could not hold our press conference until Wednesday—nine long days away. I knew we had run this risk when we asked someone as well known and in demand as Paul O'Dwyer. Nonetheless, it was frustrating.

Dr. Spain conducted a lengthy examination, having already seen the hospital report. He was critical of Presswalla, reiterating what others had said about hesitation marks only applying to suicide attempts. He said the marks were obviously made to make the letters stand out.

This ended any sympathy I had for Presswalla. While I never reached a firm conclusion about his motives, all the evidence led most of the committee members to believe the worst about him. As evidence mounted, I agreed more and more with them. I wanted to sue him for libel, to make him pay for the suffering he had inflicted on me and my family.

I was honored to be somehow involved with Dr. Spain. He was the man who had done the second autopsies of the three civil rights workers murdered in Mississippi in 1964. He had also done the second autopsy of Fred Hampton, the Black Panther leader slain by police in Chicago, and those of the prisoners killed in the

Attica revolt. Of all people, David Spain knew how medical examiners had been used in the past to bolster falsified police versions of happenings. He had always courageously stood up for the truth.

We took a taxi back to Barbara's. I realized that all was now in place—the opinion of one of the nation's most renowned forensic pathologists, a positive polygraph, the testimony of the three doctors in Virginia and several others in New York. And yet I knew I couldn't return to Virginia in the nine days prior to the press conference; we had been advised that the climate would be too hostile before we released the information planned for it.

I tried to call Lambuth Clarke that afternoon without success. I did reach Del Carlson, who taught political science with me. He agreed to cover my Urban Studies class. I arranged for Jim Brown, the African History professor at Norfolk State, to teach my African Studies class and for Bill Wycoff, a former Wesleyan history professor, to teach my class in Third World Studies. Del, Bill, and Jim all said the climate surrounding the case in Virginia was terrible.

Everyone advised me to get my mother, Joey, and Chamy out of Virginia to avoid retaliation. Bonnie and Phil, my sister-in-law and brother-in-law, offered to drive to Virginia, pick them up, and drive them to my brother's house in Media, Pennsylvania. Eight students offered to remain in the house to protect it.

After two days of working on the committee at the Phelps-Stokes Fund with Shelby Howatt of the Fund and Helen Rosen, we all converged on my brother's house in Pennsylvania on Wednesday night. The plan was for Sandy to fly the children to Florida to stay with her parents on Thursday morning.

Both the children were surviving the ordeal and looked forward to the plane ride. I was pleased that they would be with my in-laws. Sandy's father was the ultimate practical man, politically far more conservative than I. I had waited for the call from him for days after the police request for the polygraph, for I was sure he would want me to take it. He never did; that cemented our relationship.

My mother and I drove back to New York on Sunday morning so we could meet with Paul O'Dwyer. He was scheduled to fly that afternoon to Baltimore to meet Zeke Orlinski and Bob Niebuhr, the polygrapher. He then planned to fly to Virginia on Monday morning. Unfortunately we crossed signals and missed each other in New York.

Finally, O'Dwyer called me at 12:15 A.M. to tell me that he was very impressed with Bob Niebuhr.

I spent much of Monday trying to reach Jack Dici, who did press work for Paul O'Dwyer. He had been assigned the task of setting up the all-important press conference, now only two days away. We knew how much was riding on the conference—everything from clearing my name to getting me back to work at Wesleyan and on South Africa and the Davis Cup.

The matches now appeared set. Vanderbilt had obtained new financial backing. South Africa was still scoring public relations points. Peter Lamb, their "colored" player, was being mentioned more and more in Nashville.

Also getting considerable publicity was the announcement by Piet Koornhof, the South African minister of sport, that tennis and all other sports would be integrated inside South Africa. No one would care—or remember—that almost four years later, the new minister responsible for sport, Mr. Gerrett Viljoen, would make the same announcement to cover for South Africa's first major sports tour since 1978—the Springbok rugby tour of New Zealand and the United States.

With the matches set, the dark, unseen forces I had warned against when I was in Nashville began to materialize. Ads started running in the *Tennessean:*

WELCOME BRAVE CHAMPIONS OF WEST CHRISTIAN CIVILIZATION,
PRO SMALL BUSINESS, AND ANTI-COMMUNIST SOUTH AFRICA

Don Henson, grand dragon of the Nashville chapter of the Ku Klux Klan, announced that the Klan would protect spectators from demonstrators by having between 300 and 500 members present during the demonstrations. When the Nashville police chief said he didn't need their help, a Klan spokesman said it didn't matter since so many Klansmen were on the Nashville police force.

Unknown to me at the time, an officer of the South African Ministry of Information gave a briefing in New York City prior to our press conference. As stated before, news of the so-called Muldergate or Ministry of Information Scandal was just beginning to break in the Western press. In March 1978, we didn't know how bad it would get. But we did know it was bad. By this time I was convinced that the attack and all subsequent events either were engineered by South Africa itself or by their sympathizers in America. To me nothing else could make sense.

The representative of the ministry was asked at this briefing whether or not the Ministry of Information would continue to operate. First, there was Biko's death, the October bannings, and now a major government scandal centering on his own ministry. What good could the ministry do in this climate? The representative said, "South Africa's image is getting better and better. We have already had a number of successes this year." The questioning then went off in a different direction. After it was all over, Richard Walker, the U.N. correspondent of the *Rand Daily Mail,* asked, "What do you consider to be the successes for South Africa this year?" The second success listed was "the destruction of Richard Lapchick."

Richard Walker told me this in late May. I couldn't understand why he hadn't informed me at the time. He explained that it was just so obvious that my "destruction" would be a gain for South Africa that it wasn't worth mentioning.

Yes, these were big stakes. International sports had become South Africa's Achilles' heel. It was clear that these stakes made our press conference on Wednesday increasingly important.

In Virginia Beach, O'Dwyer had met with Dr. Lorenz, Captain Buzzy of the police department, Presswalla, and Wesleyan Vice-President Jim Bergdoll. I was about to call him to find out the results when Helen Rosen informed me that Paul's sister had died in Ireland. Paul would have to fly directly to Dublin from Virginia Beach. When I told Paul the sad news, he asked me to call Jack Dici, his press liaison, to postpone the press conference, which was scheduled to take place within some forty hours at the United Nations Church Center in New York.

When I reached Dici, he replied that the postponement was a

good thing since he hadn't had a chance to call anyone yet! We decided to get additional help in organizing the press conference. A press conference without the press would not do much to get us back on the Davis Cup track.

On Monday night we let Saundra Ivey know about both the formation of the committee and about the press conference, now rescheduled for Friday to allow for O'Dwyer's return. Andy Fine suggested that we also tell Peter Galuszka so he wouldn't feel left out. Sandy called him on Tuesday and read him the release that listed ten of the most prominent committee members. Peter asked if there were any more. Sandy read him some from the master list. Unfortunately, she included Anthony Lewis, the columnist for *The New York Times*. His name had been penciled in for later confirmation.

Lewis had been at a meeting of the Freedom to Publish Committee, convened by Win Knowlton, president of Harper & Row. Of the twelve well-known writers and publishers present, eleven had joined the committee. Anthony Lewis was the only person who did not.

We received a call from him on Wednesday afternoon explaining that he understood why people might have thought he was on the list. He said, however, that his position as a writer for the *Times* meant he had to stay off such committees even if he sympathized with their purpose. Lewis said he had told Peter Galuszka this when Peter called him.

I immediately called Peter to explain. Peter was extremely hostile. "Off the record," I said, "I wanted to tell you what happened with Anthony Lewis." "I'm not talking to you off the record anymore!" he replied emphatically. It was the first time I had talked to Peter since I left Virginia for Nashville fourteen days earlier.

Those two weeks, lengthened by O'Dwyer's circumstances, were the closest I have ever been to "disappearing." We carefully avoided talking to anyone in the media because we did not want the polygraph story to leak out and be lost. We had been told by half a dozen friends that someone called Buzzy Bissinger of the *Ledger Star* had been calling them in reference to a "sympathetic'' profile on me that he was writing. As much as I wanted some sympathy, I was not returning his calls—or anyone else's.

That is why I was both hurt and angered by Peter. I envisioned the next day's headline as "Lapchick Committee a Fraud." Instead, the *Ledger Star* ran "Pro-Lapchick Organizer Charges 'Witch Hunt.' " In Virginia, that was just as bad. Bob Lipsyte was quoted as suggesting two theories. "One, that the police can't solve this case so they're trying to close it; two, that the police are somehow implicated. I'm not saying either is the case, but that's what jumps to mind. It could be that the sixties are back again, and what's scary about it is that people are a lot smarter this time around. This time it won't be a lot of sweet college kids."

The only good news was the resolution passed by the Wesleyan faculty. It said, "The Faculty Association of Virginia Wesleyan College wishes to express its outrage at the attack on our colleague and to affirm categorically its faith in his integrity and truthfulness."

However, one *Virginian Pilot* story was careful to note that three of the thirty-one faculty members who voted did not favor the resolution. Furthermore, it stated that "Lapchick asked the association to issue a statement on his behalf." In fact, Joe Harkey, an English professor who headed the FA, had called to ask what could be done to help.

There were rumors that I would be arrested if I went back to Virginia. Many members of the committee warned me not to return until the day of the press conference. They said that if I were in jail the police could do *anything* to me. In other words if the public believed I was crazy enough to self-inflict internal injuries in the confines of my own office, they could be led to believe that I would do much worse to myself when distraught and humiliated in a jail cell. Andy Fine assured me that I would not be arrested, but the whole situation had become so perverted that I just didn't know what to think.

There were also rumors of the convening of a grand jury to investigate. Presumably such an investigation would be into my account of what had happened on February 14. When O'Dwyer was in Virginia Beach he informed Presswalla and the police that

I had taken a polygraph and that other doctors had examined me. This seemed to squash the grand jury idea. The police began to leak the information about the polygraph.

Suddenly, the Wednesday issue of the *Pilot* quoted deputy assistant commonwealth attorney Scortino as saying, "We considered the special grand jury, but we decided against it because, frankly, there's not that much to investigate." Alluding to the positive results of the polygraph, Scortino said, "You're not supposed to present evidence to a grand jury that you couldn't present at a trial." Was Scortino preparing the public to discount the results of the polygraph that his local police had asked me to take?

He added that any evidence from other doctors—presumably meaning other than Presswalla—would be improper evidence. "You'd get into a conflict of opinions and not hard facts." It sounded as if he had already discounted the further medical evidence that Presswalla had requested. I wondered how the network that seemed to be setting me up was tied together. Did they act in concert? The police, medical examiner, press, now the commonwealth attorney's office. Or was it all coincidence?

That afternoon I had lunch with Pete Axthelm of *Newsweek*. He was the first person from the press to whom I had talked since Nashville. It was good to talk with someone who was somewhat removed from the event and could look at it with more objectivity.

In fact, the whole atmosphere in New York was much different from Virginia, where many people who had been casual friends for five or more years suddenly pulled away from us. Our neighbor who occasionally wrote for the *Beacon,* a local newspaper supplement, told me that it was "assumed" by the editors that I was a communist. After all, I had gone to Cuba and China. What more proof was needed?

In New York, people rallied to our support. This was true of friends and strangers. Many of them had lived through the McCarthy era. We met most through Sam and Helen Rosen, who had virtually adopted us. It was much easier to put our fate in some perspective in New York. We had felt our world was collapsing and there was not much time left; yet by March 9 we had been in our nightmare only three weeks since the attack on February 14. Some of the people we met had suffered far more than we, and had for years. Knowing they had been able to pick up the pieces of their lives helped us to realize that we could as well.

We finally neared the long-awaited press conference. The pressure was building; the press regularly called my sister's apartment where we were staying. The police had seemingly once again leaked the information that I had taken a polygraph. We were asked over and over again by the press if it were true. All I could say was that all would be revealed on Friday.

Bob Lipsyte, with whom I spent Thursday, decided it would be best if we all left the apartment. We started by taping a fifteen-minute interview for National Public Radio's "All Things Considered." Bob and I then cohosted Howard Cosell's class on Sport and Society at New York University, talking about South Africa and how it uses sport for propaganda purposes. Bob mentioned the press conference since these were primarily journalism students. Five actually showed up for it the next day.

Our friendship grew as we spent more time together. Bob challenged me as no one else had. His integrity and sincerity, combined with his sharp wit, always kept me alert. He would often criticize what I said, but I never felt put down. He let me be myself but made me a better person all at the same time. I was glad I was with him on this day.

Paul O'Dwyer returned from Ireland and went directly to his office to meet us at 6:00 P.M. The strain of his sister's death was obvious. Exhaustion had slowed his step.

He said we had three choices for tomorrow. First, we could attack the police and Dr. Presswalla. Second, we could announce a major libel suit against them. Or finally, we could simply present the evidence and let it speak for itself.

Paul said his first inclination had been either of the first two choices. He hated to see authorities get away with abusing the rights of individuals. But he added that his trip to Virginia had caused him to change his mind. If we chose to attack or sue, he warned us, we would be subject to incredible harassment and predicted the climate would be so hostile that we wouldn't be able to continue to live in Virginia. Even after all that had happened, Virginia Beach was home. I knew I wasn't ready to move the family.

Paul added that if we attacked or filed a suit it would mean prolonged agony for our family. I flashed on UPI's Tom Ferraro asking my mother if she thought I had cut myself. I knew that Sandy and I could get through this no matter what. But I also knew that at age seventy-four my mother had already had several years taken off her life. Could I put her through any more?

Finally, Paul said that an attack or the suit could continue to divert the focus away from South Africa and keep it on me.

My conscience was retreating from the direction I had been sure we would choose when we convened that night. For two weeks, we had discussed nothing but an offensive. At 6:00 P.M. there was no doubt in my mind about what I wanted to do. At 7:30 I asked Paul what he would do. "Present the evidence, return as a hero, and carry on the battle." Bob and Sandy agreed. At the time the decision seemed right. Within days, I think we all had misgivings.

As I lay in bed that night I thought of my father's forced departure from St. John's because of mandatory retirement and how he had left with dignity. I had wanted him to fight to stay, but he had chosen to win the victory on the basketball court. In some ways I saw my situation as a parallel—I was choosing to win my point by helping to build the best possible anti-apartheid demonstration in Nashville. None of us doubted that Presswalla would abide by his word and recant after the evidence we would present at the press conference. We were convinced that this ugly episode would be forever behind us.

Chapter 6

Blocked Shot

Friday dawned bright and crisp. Snow was still piled up in the street, the remnants of a terrible winter storm. We drove to the Church Center for the United Nations where the press conference was to be held. It was a familiar place; ACCESS had been housed there during the tennis protests at Forest Hills in 1977. I was still in awe of the glass tower across the street that housed the United Nations, its flags fluttering in the wind.

I met Buzzy Bissinger who had requested some details before the press conference so he could beat the noon deadline for the *Ledger Star*. His aggressive style turned me off. He kept assuring me of his sympathy, and how a few words from me to my friends could help him write his feature story. I decided to have as little as possible to do with him.

Buzzy sat with Peter Galuszka during the press conference. The room was filled with a hundred or more reporters and friends. Paul O'Dwyer began the session by releasing the results and nature of the polygraph test and Dr. Spain's report. I made a statement to clarify why I decided to submit myself to a polygraph after first refusing. The emphasis of both statements was that I could now get on with my work.

Mr. O'Dwyer said that the attack was an "insidious one. It beats anything I have come across in civil rights work and that's a lot." He said that the police were making no apparent efforts to apprehend those who beat me and, thus, had put me in a position of having to defend myself.

Most of the questions focused on Presswalla's motivations. Galuszka and Bissinger were virtually the only ones who didn't raise doubts about him.

The New York, national, and international correspondents were more concerned with the broader story—the possibility of South Africa's involvement in the attack, the motives of the police and medical examiner, etc. We were very careful not to condemn them, much as we wanted to. The Davis Cup was the immediate issue.

Feelings were buoyant and hearts were light as the press conference ended. The tension was broken. Nat Holman, the only living member of the Original Celtics, came over and gave me a big hug. Franklin Williams said, "You just paid South Africa back for what it has put you through."

As the crowd dwindled, Peter Galuszka approached me. He was more cordial now. I remarked that it was all over, that I was looking forward to returning to Virginia later that day. He said that he, too, hoped it was over.

But when I bumped into the correspondent for *The New York Times* on 44th Street, our euphoria became depression. "I have bad news for you," he told us. "I just spoke to the medical examiner and he says he won't change his opinion."

We arrived in Virginia at about 5:00 P.M. Andy Fine and a dozen or so students were there at the airport. It was not exactly a hero's welcome, but I was happy to see them.

The *Ledger Star* was already on the newsstands. At first glance, I thought Buzzy had missed his deadline, for there was nothing about the case in the main section. Then my fears about him were realized. The story was in section B and eight of the first ten paragraphs were on Presswalla's refutations of the polygraph test and Dr. Spain's opinions.

"I am not an expert in polygraphs and have no way of ascertaining what was the significance of it," he stated, and suggested that a medical board of forensic pathologists be appointed to determine if Dr. Spain or he was correct. He then requested that the police release the results of their investigation. I knew this could only mean that Presswalla had seen their report and that it affirmed his conclusions.

Andy drove us home. On the way, we heard the taped "All Things Considered" program and it sounded very good. We arrived at the house in time for the evening news. The local affiliates of NBC and CBS did not even mention the press conference. The ABC affiliate discussed the polygraph but half-dismissed it by adding that it was administered in Maryland where there were no licensing requirements for polygraph operators. I called Jay Moore, the news anchorman, later that evening to inform him that Niebuhr was licensed in Virginia. Moore corrected his mistake on the 11:00 P.M. news. But, as usual, the damage had been done. What began as a day to end it all turned out to be just one more day in the continuing drama.

News stories the next day were mixed. Peter Galuszka wrote a very fair one, extensively quoting from Dr. Spain's report. Part of that report mentioned rope burns on the back of my neck and wrist. Rope burns. The police did not find the rope—that alone should have confirmed that someone had removed it from the office and the building.

I caught an early flight to Nashville where I was to speak at a conference on apartheid. This was the conference that Dennis Brutus and I had tried to communicate about on the day and the night of the attack. I picked up the *Tennessean* at the Nashville airport. Saundra Ivey's article was balanced and, like Galuszka's, appeared on page 1. It concluded with Franklin Williams's charge that South Africa was responsible for the attack. The *Washington Post,* which had sent Athelia Knight to cover the story, printed a lengthy and balanced report on the evidence we presented.

I was picked up and taken directly to a friend's apartment where I was to receive a call from Peter Lamb, the colored member of the Davis Cup team.

We soon realized that someone had tried to break into the apartment through the bedroom window. My friend had already received threats after taking a leading role in the local protests. I insisted that she take some clothes and remain with friends until after the anti-Davis Cup demonstration. She had become one of the primary spokespersons for the protest.

She told me that Peter Lamb had told her that he didn't want to return to South Africa and that he was reconsidering accepting the position on the Davis Cup team.

Even in the atmosphere of fear that pervaded the apartment, I could taste victory. Ray Moore, a white South African tennis star, had already withdrawn from the team after being counseled by Arthur Ashe and, subsequently, Franklin Williams. It would be a great boost to our cause if Peter Lamb pulled out as well.

Lamb's call was a great disappointment. Our conversation was pleasant enough, but he gave no indication of withdrawing.

I was driven along the demonstration route to the site of the proposed rally. I was shocked to see that the rally was to be at the Parthenon, the site of the assassination in the film *Nashville*. Assassinations were no longer only movie themes.

It was good to be at the conference among anti-apartheid activists. It was held at Meharry Medical College, one of the nation's leading black medical schools. The media wanted to ask me about the polygraph test and Dr. Spain, but Dennis Brutus and I had agreed to concentrate on the conference. There was excellent information generated about the reality of apartheid in sport and the false messages emanating from South Africa.

I became faint during the press conference and had to be taken to the office of Dr. Elan, the president of Meharry. I felt too weak to meet the press and John Dommisse, ACCESS's secretary-general, who also attended, brought me to our hotel room.

Sandy called to say how hostile people in the Virginia area seemed to be. She told me of Buzzy Bissinger's follow-up story titled "Lapchick Defense a Media Show." Sandy said she wanted to move away immediately.

I knew things had to be terrible for Sandy to react that way. There were no more flights that evening. Therefore I booked a 9:00 A.M. flight Sunday morning. I didn't want Sandy to feel alone. Several students had arranged a rotating guard schedule so I knew the house was secure, but I worried about her state of mind.

The flight arrived at the Norfolk airport at 12:30 P.M. and I walked to my car. Before leaving Nashville, I had placed a piece of paper in the car door to be able to tell if someone had broken in. There was no need to have done so; the window had obviously been forced open, breaking the window track and leaving it at a sharp angle.

I searched through the engine and under the car for forty-five minutes. I had become so distrustful of the police that I did not want to report it for fear of their saying I had broken into the car myself. Convinced that there were no bombs, I drove home.

Sandy produced an editorial in the Sunday *Virginian Pilot*. It called for a special grand-jury investigation of the case now that "the dramatics of a private investigation had been completed," and claimed that I had denounced Dr. Presswalla at the New York press conference, which was absolutely untrue.

"Of three private doctors who attended him [in the hospital], one conceded that the cuts could have been self-inflicted while another disagreed," the story said. "The deputy state medical examiner for Tidewater, Dr. Faruk B. Presswalla, was emphatic. He said one carving was 'definitely self-inflicted.' Dr. Presswalla, a pathologist with ten years' experience in forensic medicine, went public reluctantly; he too deplores apartheid and sympathizes with the professor's cause."

I began to realize what we were up against in Virginia. I called Charles Hartig, at WTAR-TV, the CBS affiliate. I had been on several of his TV shows and trusted him. Charles advised me to "cool it," that is, to keep quiet for a while so that some perspective on the situation could be gained. He acknowledged that there had been rumors that I would be arrested. The rumors were based on the police report, which no one had seen but many had heard about. Charles added that my taking the polygraph and seeing Dr. Spain had undoubtedly cut short any plans the police might have had for that arrest.

We visited Andrew Fine. He had been upset by the *Pilot* editorial and said he would personally go to the paper to defend me. Andy insisted that I call Hayden about the car break-in, which I did. But before I could complain, Hayden told us that Dr. Presswalla had been very badly hurt by the national attention given to this case, and urged me to hold a press conference, publicly stating my faith in Dr. Presswalla!

When Hayden's "investigators" came Monday, they told

Sandy the break-in was merely one of many car robberies at the airport. They didn't respond when Sandy pointed out that cash and a tape deck were still in the car when I reached it.

I went to see Lambuth Clarke and Dean Wilson on Monday morning. As I entered, two other administrative officers were in Lambuth's office. They left icily, without saying a word to me.

Lambuth said that I was using the college as a platform for my views. He insisted that I was hurting the college in its conservative Virginia community. Lambuth was a nonconfrontational man who did not like to offend people, but he hurt me badly, and it took me some time to understand how disturbed he must have been and how much pressure he had to be under.

Bill Wilson, who was never as warm and easy with people as Lambuth, questioned my priorities. He asked why I hadn't called him to explain that I would be gone for two weeks from my classes.

I tried to explain, starting from the fact that my colleague, Del Carlson, had been fully informed, and that I had left several unanswered messages with Mrs. Baker, Lambuth's secretary, to say I wanted to speak to him.

I could see that nothing was penetrating. Over the years I had always had the feeling that Bill Wilson tolerated me but never that he supported me so I could easily accept his reactions as normal. But Lambuth, who may not always have understood me, had been consistently supportive. I gravely absorbed his attitude.

"The college is my home and its students my family. I would never do anything to hurt it," I said, and agreed to "resign immediately" if he thought it would help. I had a quick vision of a losing coach going to management with such an offer but expecting a vote of confidence. The vision was shattered when Lambuth replied, "You have until May to decide. Don't make your decision today." I knew it was tantamount to an acceptance of my offer.

I had a few minutes before class so I went to my office. Drawers were open and papers were strewn all over the place. I didn't want to touch anything but instead tried to reach Karen Gilbert, who worked with me on our community programs, and Randy Smith, a student who worked with Karen. Both were in my office frequently and I wanted to be sure they hadn't simply left it a mess, although I assumed it had been ransacked. I was unable to reach them before class.

Being back in the classroom was therapeutic. There were not many friendly faces in Virginia, but my students made me feel relaxed. Teaching was a large part of my life and my blood was, once again, running. Pete Axthelm's favorable *Newsweek* column had just come out and several students commented on how good it was.

I finally reached Karen and Randy after the class. They came directly to the office and confirmed that they had not left it like this. We checked the files. The ACCESS and ARENA files were gone, including our mailing lists. I called campus security and Sergeant Hayden. Both said they would investigate, but I have no reason to believe that either ever did.

I stopped by Andrew Fine's house on the way home. He had met with the editors of the *Pilot,* showed them the police photos of the beating, and gone over all the details. Andrew believed they were much more open after the discussion.

He had also called Captain Buzzy of the police department. Andrew had defended the police in several cases and had a good working relationship with them. He asked Captain Buzzy why Presswalla had not retracted his conclusions since I had done what he had asked. Buzzy responded that he was concerned that I would file a libel suit, and admitted that Presswalla had hired an attorney. Andrew explained to Buzzy that I was worried about my family and wanted police help, especially when I was away in Nashville for the demonstrations. Buzzy replied that if I were really so concerned about my family, I wouldn't be going to Nashville.

Andrew asked me if I would agree in writing that we would not sue Presswalla if he retracted his statement. Of course! I assured him.

Bernard Barrow, our neighbor and member of the state legislature, was going to take over the case while Andrew, suffering from exhaustion and the flu, went on a holiday. I went to his house to tell him the plan. As so often before when things looked bright, a phone message from Steve Goldberg of the *Pilot* was waiting to shatter me.

If timing is everything, then Presswalla was a genius. With each shift of momentum, Presswalla came forward to speak to the press. Did Buzzy tell Presswalla about his conversation with Andrew? Or about Andrew's meeting with the editors? Did Presswalla see the *Newsweek* column or Bill Nack's column in *Newsday,* both supportive of me, and, of course, by implication critical of Presswalla? Was it just a coincidence that Faruk Presswalla's written report on the case was given to Steve Goldberg on March 13 when it was given to the police on March 2?

The *Pilot* story, coauthored by Goldberg and Peter, began, "Richard E. Lapchick's shirt was unwrinkled and untorn and every button was in place when police arrived at Virginia Wesleyan College the night he claims he was attacked, a medical examiner's report says. In a written report on the incident, Dr. Faruk B. Presswalla says information about the shirt was provided him by police investigators. He says it helped him reach the conclusion that a racial epithet carved on Lapchick's stomach was self-inflicted."

Goldberg had called me for a reaction on Monday night, March 13, before the story was to appear on Tuesday. I told him Presswalla had never seen the shirt and the police couldn't have thought it important since they told Sandy to take it home, which the official hospital records confirmed that she did.

I told Goldberg that the shirt was still in the bag that Sandy used to bring it home and offered to bring it to him so he could see for himself. He said he didn't need to see it since the police had confirmed Presswalla's report! The shirt had, in fact, been ripped directly down the middle and the reason the buttons looked intact was that they were still in the button holes—fully buttoned.

Presswalla's report said that a Bayside Hospital physician had said there was no blood. Obviously there wasn't; the shirt had been ripped open and didn't touch my body where the cuts were inflicted.

It was a long day; the atmosphere on campus was heavy. Several students whom I was close to shared with me that there was a rumor I had been fired. Did they know something I didn't? I realized after Monday's meeting with Lambuth and Dean Wilson that it was unlikely that I would return next year. Ironically, I had also begun to think that it would be better to be fired than to resign. In that way I would at least be paid a year's salary under American Association of University Professors (AAUP) rules.

I met Dennis Govoni, who had been in the hospital room when Presswalla examined me, in the afternoon. He was upset by the Presswalla report. He clearly remembered the hospital visit, and distinctly remembered my answer of no when Presswalla asked if I thought the attackers were trying to kill me. Dennis also remembered that I said I passed out after the beating on my stomach. He confirmed that Presswalla was not taking notes.

I called Andrew and Bernard. They agreed that Dennis would be an important witness. Andrew said he had spoken to Andy Evans, the commonwealth attorney. Evans insisted that the police had not asked for me to be prosecuted, despite what I might have heard.

Andrew reported he had unsuccessfully tried to reach Presswalla all day to tell him that the police had misled and misinformed him about the shirt. By that time, I had found Mike Mizell, the student who had first noted the carving of N-I-G-E-R in the library. I asked him if he remembered what my shirt was like. Mike confirmed that it was ripped down the middle and hung at my sides, allowing him to see the carving.

Leonard Sharzer, the third doctor who examined me in the hospital, did meet Presswalla that day. Leonard reported that Presswalla was far less decisive than he had been in print, saying that the wounds could have been self-inflicted or the result of an attack. He said he still believed that I self-inflicted the wounds, largely because of the shirt. Leonard said Presswalla was astonished when told the truth about the shirt.

I spoke with Lew Hurst, the highly respected head of the Virginia State Crime Commission. Lew was due to appear in my Urban Studies class. We had been together several times at Wesleyan over the years. I brought him up to date and sought his opinion. It wasn't comforting. Lew indicated that Presswalla's statements, even if retracted, would make it a near-impossibility to bring the attackers to trial.

The Davis Cup matches were only four days away and press interest was growing. Doug Smith of the *New York Post* called to do a story on the reported activities of the Ku Klux Klan in Nashville.

Bill Wilson, a producer on the Cronkite show, called to say that CBS wanted to fly a crew to Norfolk on Wednesday. Several church and civil rights groups had protested that Cronkite had not followed up on the polygraph story.

Tass, the Soviet news agency, called. They wanted to use my case to exemplify United States attitudes toward human rights. I told the reporter I would call him back, not knowing what to do. I remembered that Tass had taken up Harry Edwards' battle for tenure at Berkeley and it had brought results. But Harry was in liberal Berkeley, where Tass endorsement would not be as calamitous as it might be in Virginia. I never followed this up.

Zeke Orlinski called to tell me to get out of Virginia because the police had too big a stake in discrediting me. He hung up and immediately the phone rang again. "If you step foot in Nashville you will never see Virginia Beach again!" a muffled voice warned.

The circus atmosphere—press, police, medical examiners, lawyers, friends and enemies—was alleviated with the late-night arrival of Maggie Kuhn, the founder of the Gray Panthers.

I met Maggie on my 1976 trip to China. I think she was seventy-two at the time. One by one, all the members of the group fell sick under the strain of the constant movement. Maggie, probably fifteen to twenty years older than any of us, kept forging ahead. It was with that spirit that she had built the Gray Panthers into a powerful coalition working for the rights of old people. It was with that spirit that she brightened our home that night.

Maggie gave a speech at Wesleyan the next day. She was sensational. Now Peter Galuszka was with us trying to get a lead on any lawsuit, but I didn't talk to him about anything but Maggie.

That night Bob Lipsyte called to discuss a proposal for a book called *The Last Olympics* that I was contemplating writing. He had talked to several agents and publishers and said there was real interest in it. Bob joked that if I were killed in Nashville this weekend "you would blow the deal and all my efforts would be wasted."

We were ready to go to sleep when Kathy Kent of WTAR called. She had heard rumors that Wesleyan had asked me to resign. The school denied them. So did I. Kathy asked if I was planning to relocate. I answered that such speculation was premature and that I needed to test the climate in Virginia. However, inside I was increasingly certain we would be leaving.

I drove Maggie to her 7:00 A.M. flight and then went to my office. It was the first time I had been in my office in a deserted library since the attack and I went there more to test myself than to do any real work.

After my first class, I went to see Dean Wilson. We had a good open discussion. He remembered seeing a lump over my right eye when he visited me in the hospital emergency room—and suddenly he was a witness. More and more, I saw people not for themselves, but as potential witnesses. Mike Mizell, Dennis Govoni, Niebuhr, Spain, and now the dean: all would testify on my behalf. I wasn't so sure I would have to leave. The mood of relief, as usual, was to be short-lived.

I was walking to my next class when a call came for me in the business office. "If you step foot in Nashville, you won't see Virginia Beach again," a voice said. I couldn't tell if it was the same person who had called the previous night.

I taught my third and final class of the day. My thoughts were more in Nashville than in Virginia Beach, as I tossed over and over whether I should go. I knew I was wasting my students' time that afternoon and didn't like myself for it. I promised myself this wouldn't happen again when classes resumed after spring break.

After class, I reluctantly returned a call to Buzzy Bissinger. He said his "balanced profile" on me was ready and they needed some fresh photos. I told him he had enough photos already, and asked him what he meant by "balanced." He said it was not all good. Buzzy read me a section attributed to an unidentified Wesleyan faculty member discussing my use of my personal "charisma" to sway students. He quoted an unidentified Old Dominion University faculty member, who had supposedly socialized with me a dozen times, as questioning my motives—among other things—saying I controlled the Norfolk press. I congratulated him on his balanced reporting, noting that I did not know any ODU professors well, and had never been with one on twelve or even six social occasions. I was furious. This was the third week he had been writing the story. We were later told that his original draft had been rejected as being too bland. It had certainly been spiced up.

I just sat there in my office for a few moments. The phone rang. I didn't answer it. A minute later it rang again, and I picked it up. The voice said, "Are you going to continue what you have been doing now, nigger–lover?"

I was stopped by Karen Domabyl, the Wesleyan reference librarian, as I left the library. She told me that a man they had never seen before had entered the library and was obviously watching my office. He had told her he was doing research, but he had never opened a book, and had left abruptly after walking around the mezzanine where my office was located. Karen stopped short: she could see how upset I was.

I was trembling as I drove to Bernard Barrow's office to seek his advice. He wrote down the details of the threats and of the presence of the man in the library and told me to call Hayden from his office so he could attest to their being reported. He had his secretary place the call so Hayden know it came from his office. We discussed the pros and cons of going to Nashville, but I knew I had to go. I was much calmer by the time I got home. I had accepted this was the way things had to be.

Chapter 7

Big Rally

It was a rule in our house that we never wake up the children early unless it is essential. But at 6:00 A.M. this morning I went to say goodbye, completely forgetting that they were in Florida! I knew that many friends and some family members felt I had gone too far. Ann Lapchick, my sister-in-law, told Sandy that if she were married to me she would issue an ultimatum: either get out of the movement or lose your family. Others expressed the same feelings.

There I was in Joey's room trying to say goodbye to a child who was a thousand miles away. I had decided to wake him up because I knew it was remotely possible that I would never see him or his sister again.

I had always believed that I hadn't chosen my work in spite of my family but because of them. It tormented me to read about a white cop killing innocent black men in Houston or Cape Town; it tormented me to know that my chances of achieving success in America were directly related to my skin color; to know that the opportunities for blacks on an international level were deteriorating. I wanted to make some contribution, however small, to changing these things so that Joey and Chamy wouldn't be tormented by them; so that Joey and Chamy could really be free.

However, at 6:00 A.M. on the morning of March 17, 1978, standing in my child's empty room, I had to wonder if my being in Nashville was worth the risk. The children were already gone because I feared for their lives. I had even sent Penda, our dog, to my brother's to ensure her safety.

Sandy called to me, "You'll be late. You have to go now." Yes, I *had* to go.

Tom Doyle, one of our rotating student bodyguards, and I were met at the Virginia airport by Sarah Oliver, another Wesleyan student. We were all tense as the plane took off. We had lived in "the South" for eight years, but somehow I felt I was really going to the South now. The Klan would be there in the open, and a tennis team from South Africa would be there as welcome guests. I tried to think of what it must have been like for my father to be driving to Louisville as a member of the Celtics for the first game in the South with the all-black Rens. The Rens weren't welcome in the 1930s, the South Africans were in the 1970s. The world seemed upside down.

Tom broke into my thoughts by describing the man in the library on the previous day and what he had done there. Tom had almost bumped into him in the parking lot. As they stepped back from one another, he had asked Tom where the library was.

Ten minutes later, Tom entered the library and saw the stranger sitting at a table in front of the magazine display, his chair angled toward my office. At first Tom sat down at the next table and then moved over to the table where the man was sitting. He held a folded magazine that he occasionally perused, but primarily he focused his attention on my office.

Mike Mizell came up to Tom in the library after the man had been there for twenty to twenty-five minutes. Tom took Mike aside and described the man's suspicious actions. Apparently in response, the man walked behind the periodical guides desk. Each time Tom looked at him, the man was staring at them.

Mike, never the subtle one, moved toward the periodical guide desk and asked if he was waiting to see me. He answered, "No, I'm here doing research," and abruptly moved to the card catalogue as if to prove that was his interest. But by then he had been in the library for forty-five minutes.

Tom and Mike informed Karen Domabyl about what was

happening and went to get help. The man left in the five minutes they were gone.

Before leaving, he asked Karen about a certain book, went upstairs, and walked past my office. He doubled back past me again, and left the library without a book. Karen watched him walk toward the science building and told Tom about his departure when he returned. Tom dashed outside and saw the man drive away in a brown Cadillac Seville with a tan vinyl roof.

I hadn't said a word for five minutes. When the story was finished, I asked what he looked like. He wore a brown leather jacket, white shirt, brown tie, and black pants. He was white, in his early thirties, about six feet tall with a medium to large build, had brown hair and an acne-scarred face.

I sat quietly for a moment. I didn't know about the acne because of the stocking mask, but the rest of the description could have fit either of the men who attacked me. I tried to be rational, recognizing that it was a description that might fit many men.

I called Bernard Barrow with these details as soon as the plane landed in Nashville. He agreed that the description could be important and assured me he would contact Sergeant Hayden with the information.

We were met at the airport by Mike Mizell, Bob Friedland, and Mary Wells. Mary and Bob were also Wesleyan students who had come down early with Mike to help me.

I taped the "MacNeil-Lehrer Report" that afternoon. Charlayne Hunter-Gault was in the studio and Jim Lehrer was in Washington. The other guests were Bud Collins, the tennis commentator, and Slew Hester, president of the U.S. Tennis Association. I had never met Hester before, although we had exchanged considerable correspondence.

I had assumed that Bud Collins would take a position in support of the USTA, which wanted the matches to take place; however, I was wrong. Hester proved to be very amicable although his thinking on South Africa was, at best, confused. I was impressed by the penetrating questions asked by Charlayne Hunter-Gault. We all felt that the show went very well and served to substantiate our arguments for isolating South Africa.

We drove to the Holiday Inn, where I checked in under the name John Dommisse, ACCESS's secretary-general. I didn't want my name to show up in the register. We had two rooms so several of our student/bodyguards could stay with John and me. A TV bulletin said there were 3,000 demonstrators at Vanderbilt marching in a freak snow storm. Our local efforts were paying off. The demonstrations, which were to be held simultaneously with the matches, were scheduled for Friday, Saturday, and Sunday. The major demonstration was to be held Saturday.

We got to the gym as soon as we could, but the snow and bitter winds had reduced the number of demonstrators to about 500 or 600 by the time we arrived. We were told there were less than 1,000 spectators inside.

We marched for an hour. I was surrounded by Mary, Sarah, Bob, Mike, Tom Doyle, and Tom Hollett, a former student and close friend who had flown down from Washington. The rhythmic chants of the demonstrators let my mind focus on these friends. Whether the threats to me were real or not, they thought they were real and were risking a lot to help me.

As chants of "Sports, yes! apartheid, no! Tennis with South Africa's got to go!" rang through the freezing air, I realized how courageous they were. Their bodies were pressed close to mine to stop a bullet they thought might be meant for me. It was a feeling of dedication and commitment that I had never experienced before and that nothing can ever make me forget. At that moment they made all the Buzzy Bissingers and Captain Buzzys seem irrelevant. If our society was ever to be healed, these would be the physicians. If it would be reconstructed, they would be the architects.

There appeared to be a disturbance ahead of us. Two local demonstration marshalls informed us that our group had been surrounded by Klansmen or what the marshalls believed to be Klansmen. They asked that I leave for my own safety. My thoughts turned to the empty bedroom where I had been preoccupied by such visions twelve hours earlier. What was I doing to my family? "Dr. Lapchick, Dr. Lapchick!" The marshall pulled on my arm, bringing me back to the present. We left immediately and returned to the hotel.

We were joined there by John Dommisse, Lila Miller, and Cary Goodman. Lila and Cary were the first two organizers for ACCESS. The circle of friends and associates was closing. It would be completed within twenty-four hours. We had a quiet evening, sharing a light supper and a bottle of wine. Tom Doyle, Mike Mizell, and Bob Friedland slept in the two rooms with John and me. Unexpectedly, I slept straight through the night, awakened only by a call at 8:30 A.M.

By 10:00 A.M. our rooms were filled with twenty or so people. Another Wesleyan contingent had arrived at 3:30 A.M. after driving through the night to get there. The group made a collective decision that we should not join the march until it reached Centennial Park. The radio informed us that some 6,000 had begun the march to the park.

The plan was for the demonstration to start at the state capitol and march toward Vanderbilt. The NAACP contingent went to Centennial Park opposite Vanderbilt while about 1,000 students went directly to the gymnasium from Centennial Park.

We met the march just as it was splitting up. It was a strange scene that encompassed both generational and ideological differences. The NAACP contingent consisted of mostly black people in their late thirties or early forties—veterans of civil rights marches of the 1960s, marches to protest racism in places like Nashville. But this was a mass demonstration against racism on the international level, and I felt it was a breakthrough.

The student group was racially mixed although predominantly white. They were in their late teens or early twenties and were notably more strident in tone. For them, the action was at the Vanderbilt gymnasium. They wanted to be exactly where the South Africans were. The slogan "The people united will never be defeated" had replaced "We shall overcome."

Raised and nurtured on the civil rights and antiwar marches of the 1960s, I had increasingly been drawn to more direct action in the 1970s. Therefore, I decided I would participate briefly at the NAACP rally and then go directly to Vanderbilt.

Franklin Williams greeted me at the park and accompanied me up onto the stage. I was the only white person up there with Franklin, Ben Hooks and his wife Frances, Dick Gregory, Joseph

Lowery of the Southern Christian Leadership Conference (SCLC), Judge William Booth of the American Committee on Africa, Carl Stokes, Ossie Davis, and Bayard Rustin. To say that I was honored to be in such company would be a great understatement. Dennis Brutus came a few minutes later. I told Franklin that Dennis, of all people, should be on the stage. Franklin agreed and said he would try to include him.

I quickly perceived the importance of the demonstration for the NAACP, speaker after speaker emphasized the need for strengthening the organization. This was Ben Hooks's first big protest as its new executive director. To have agreed to make such a commitment to an African issue was a brave decision for him. A great deal was riding on the day. I began to understand that he wouldn't want to take a chance of spoiling it with a confrontation with the Klan at Vanderbilt.

The spirit of the moment and the tone of the speeches, even if only for a day, recaptured the high pitch of the 1960s. While it was the feeling of the past, it was the substance of its meaning for the future that prevailed. Everyone seemed to pick up on that—students, old people, even the press.

The speeches were forceful, dramatic, and to the point—racism should be attacked wherever it was found. Particularly good were Ossie Davis, Bill Booth, Franklin Williams, and Ben Hooks. Hooks was especially charismatic that day. Dick Gregory, in his own unique way, was not far behind.

About one hour before the rally was scheduled to break up, Walter Searcy reported that the police had just told him that "all hell had broken loose over at the gym." Walter didn't know what this meant or whether it was inside or outside. I was disturbed, especially considering how well the rally was going. We didn't want news of trouble now, only of protest.

As Franklin was starting to speak, he surprised me by stopping and turning to me. "I want to introduce you to the man who first raised the issue of sports contacts between the United States and South Africa," he said. "We might not be here today if it were not for Richard Lapchick. And what was his reward? Thugs sent by South Africa beat him up and carved *nigger* on his stomach. And Richard Lapchick is a white man. How many white heroes do we have? To me, Richard Lapchick is one of them—to me he is a hero. Please stand up, Richard.'' When I did, the 6,000 or so in the amphitheater also stood up and cheered. I was grateful to Franklin and to the crowd. I was most grateful that our victory seemed assured, and that all the work and suffering had been worth it. It was the proudest moment of my life.

By then Dennis Brutus had finally come on stage. Reports from the gym had made us tense but the speakers were among the few who seemed to have heard that ''hell'' had broken loose there. I wondered how Hooks would handle it, when it was his turn to address the crowd.

Ben Hooks introduced me again, this time to speak. So much had been said already that I shortened my speech to simply remind the audience that after the representatives of apartheid left our land there would still be much work to do in other areas of the anti-apartheid movement. I told them that this showing in Nashville would reverberate inside South Africa and would deliver the message that the American people would be tough on apartheid in the future.

Ben Hooks was speaking now, and I decided to hear him from a more protected pocket of the stage. He was worth waiting for. He urged the crowd to disband in an orderly fashion and not to go to the gym. This upset some people who were unaware of what we thought were threatening circumstances. In spite of my original inclination, I decided that in light of threats being relayed to me during the rally I would not go there myself. Hours later we discovered that there had been no problems at the gym. I wondered if the threat against me had also been planted to keep me away from Vanderbilt.

The rally broke up. Everyone felt positive, even amid the clouded circumstances of the police reports. I spent several minutes exchanging stories with Dick Gregory, who has always been one of my heroes.

By then I was surrounded by the Wesleyan contingent. They whisked me into a car to go back to the hotel and then straight to the airport. Everyone sat anxiously in the Braniff waiting area until I actually boarded a plane for Washington with Tom Hollett, my former student and now friend. It was extremely painful to say good-bye as we climbed the elevated ramp. My Wesleyan friends had just given so much. The ordeal seemed over, yet deep down I sensed that my career as a teacher was nearing an end. Even though a final decision had not been made, I knew I could no longer be effective in Virginia and the risks to my family were too great. Still, that would be a tremendous price for me to pay. I was going to Washington so I could look for a new job and find a house.

Even as we flew to Washington we knew that the protests had been extremely successful. We outnumbered the spectators over the three days by more than three to one, and the matches were a financial bust. All the manipulating, all the attempts to discredit me and divert attention from the issue were ultimately wasted.

Chapter 8

Final Buzzer

I spent the next week in Washington looking for a job for the following year. It was a time full of soul searching—what type of job did I want, what could I get?

I went to New York to talk to Gene Stockwell of the National Council of Churches about a job. I phoned home Thursday morning to see how Sandy was. Someone had called her to tell her that there was a show on television about our new home. She turned it on to find a program about a jail.

As I flew back from New York to Norfolk it crossed my mind that people might be waiting to arrest me. Everything was so distorted.

The next day was Good Friday. I got up very early and spent the day writing the proposal for *The Last Olympics*. My concentration was interrupted by a woman on the phone.

"Is this Mr. Lapchick?"

"Yes."

"We are doing a survey. Are you a veteran?"

"No."

"Are you and your wife permanent residents of Tidewater?"

"Yes."

"Are you sure?"

"Yes."

"Do you both have a cemetery plot?"

"No."

"You will need one soon."

Joey and Chamy came home on Saturday; I had already come home. Suddenly our lives seemed much more normal. Joey and Chamy were tanned and beautiful. There was no way to see then the deep scars Joey was bearing beneath his external beauty. That pain would gradually emerge later, but for now all was well. (When we eventually got to New York Joey spent a good part of our first year seeing a child psychiatrist. It took the psychiatrist only one hour to conclude that Joey's aggressive behavior was a defense mechanism. As a then five-year-old, he closely identified with his father. To grow up to be like his father meant that he, too, would be attacked. That is a lot for a five-year-old to handle.)

We tried to pretend that all was well now that the children were home and I was teaching again. However, we were still receiving threatening calls, and we still had people living with us as body-guards. Andrew Fine was still gone and Bernard Barrow had not been able to see Presswalla.

Then, our ultimate vulnerability was exposed. That Friday, at 5:00 P.M., the phone rang in my office. I answered it routinely by saying "Rich Lapchick, hello." The caller said, "Hi, Rich," and I assumed it was a friend.

He continued, "It must be good to have the kids home." By then I knew it had to be a friend since only a few friends and the police knew we had sent them away and fewer still knew they were back.

Then he said, "It may not be for long!" I panicked. "Who is this? Who is this?" I frantically demanded. The only sound was the dial tone.

I immediately called home and asked to speak to Joey. Sandy said she thought he had gone somewhere with a neighbor. I drove straight home without telling her of the call, since I didn't want to alarm her. I was there at 5:30. No Joey. I combed the neighborhood but no one had seen him. I called Sergeant Hayden. He was not there so I told the person who answered to get him because it was an emergency, a possible kidnapping. Sergeant Hayden returned my call two weeks later.

I ran through the neighborhood again. By then it was 6:00 P.M.

and I had to tell Sandy. She was not at all certain now about the neighbors whom she thought had Joey. It had been two hours since she had seen him. We really didn't know these people well. They had lived across the street for only a few months and now they were moving away. Our state of fear even drove us to conjure up thoughts that these people were part of our nightmare.

I went to Bernard Barrow's house, while Sandy remained home to wait for Hayden or his call. There was nothing else to do but wait. As the minutes dragged on, my insides were being torn apart. 6:15, 6:30. Bernard and I walked through the neighborhood again. It was starting to get dark. Joey had never been out of the neighborhood this late. I was becoming convinced that we were about to pay the ultimate price. As we sat there in silence in Bernard's living room I could think of little else but the refrains of unsolicited advice from friends and family that I get out of this work.

My father had prayed when I had polio that if God would deliver me back alive he would do whatever it took to make me whole again. At 7:00 P.M. I found myself offering up the same prayer about Joey. I didn't know what I meant by it. Would I actually stop working in the area of race relations? Would we leave Virginia immediately? Something drastic had to be done. And soon. Every fifteen minutes I called home to hear what Hayden had said or to see if Joey had called. All blanks.

We went outside again at 7:30. It was almost dark now. We stood on the street between the Barrows' house and that of the neighbor whom we hoped had Joey. Cars drove by, their head-lights making it impossible to clearly see who was inside. As none of them stopped, the terror grew. Sandy had joined us, having abandoned any hope of Hayden's help.

I was so distraught as I turned back to Sandy that I was very confused when I saw her starting to run. I turned again and saw the neighbor's car pulling up. Joey seemed to be out of the car before it stopped.

He was in my arms and I buried my face in between his head and shoulder so he wouldn't see the tears. I hoped he hadn't seen the terror and panic on my face. The worst moment of my life was over, but the memories of it may never fade. That was the one price I knew I could never ever pay.

I had arrived at a new low point, having been wrong time and time again for six weeks. Wrong about not going on the offensive versus Presswalla and the police; about the effects of the polygraph and Dr. Spain's report on clearing the deck in Virginia; and especially in thinking that the harassment would end after Nashville.

It was a weekend spent questioning everything; no assumptions went untested. The nightmare with Joey had underlined our vulnerability. With a hostile police force, I knew there would be no safety. With a hostile press, I recognized I could not be politically effective in Virginia. I felt as though the entire community had us in a slowly closing vise. What I needed to know was whether life and work would be better elsewhere. Was all this happening because I was in the South?

This reflective period abruptly ended on April 6 at 9:30 A.M. Ibrahim Noor called from the United Nations Center Against Apartheid. Ibrahim has become one of my very closest friends. As much as anyone else, he helped nurse me back to being a whole person again. But in April 1978, he was Mr. Noor, from the United Nations.

He asked me if I would be willing to come to New York to work for the United Nations for three months. I tried to be cool on the phone but there was no way. As a student of international affairs, as an activist against apartheid, it was almost too good to believe that I would work for the United Nations Center Against Apartheid.

An hour later, I received a call from Nashville. I had been chosen for the Coalition's humanitarian-of-the-year award. That same morning, Pam McAllister called to say that the Federation for Social Action of the United Methodist Church had decided that I should receive their humanitarian-of-the-year award. The contrast in our emotions at 9:15 A.M. and 12:30 P.M. further underscored the mercurial nature of our lives in the recent past. We had run the gamut from despair to hope, from uncertainty to certainty, from painful rejection to warm acceptance. The constant shifting had taken its toll on all of us—our nerves were raw.

Four days later I flew to New York for my three months at the United Nations. I knew I could not return to Virginia for pleasure, that I could not remember that seven and a half of the eight years were very happy. No, this was the South and I was going home to the North. Racism was there, of course, but at least not the racism that deals blows to the body and the mind.

I couldn't know then that those three months would become five years at the U.N.; that the emotional scars were so deep that I wasn't back to full strength until late 1980; that Joey's pain would affect so many aspects of his development. No, all I knew on May 15 when the jet lifted off the ground in Norfolk, Virginia, was that I was on my way home. The relative safety of working for the United Nations was a great security blanket, a warm womb that could protect us physically, emotionally, and financially.

* * *

The womb seemed to explode again in the fall of 1981. The South African Springbok rugby team was set to tour the United States. I became deeply involved in the efforts to stop the tour.

Those 1981 events forced us to see what we had begun to suspect. What had happened in 1978 was not necessarily because we lived in Virginia.

The new trouble began on September 4, 1981, within hours after the city of Rochester became the third city to cancel a game with the Springboks. It looked like the whole tour was about to collapse. Our coalition members were ecstatic when I announced this at our regular weekly Thursday night meeting.

I arrived at our apartment building at 9:30 P.M. feeling very good, only to find Sandy darting frantically about the lobby. Our apartment had been broken into. Valuables, including a camera, watches, jewelry, and cash, were untouched. None of Sandy's, Joey's, or Chamy's things had been disturbed. My things had been thoroughly searched, and, for the most part, ransacked. Nothing had been taken. The nature and timing of the break-in convinced me that it was politically motivated.

The police sent three separate squads that night and they were very deferential. I am sure the facts that I worked at the U.N. set their tone.

Before I went to work the next morning I went to see our new car. We had bought a 1968 Mercedes for $1,000. Sandy had picked it up the night of the robbery. It looked beautiful to me that morning and soothed some of the pain of the previous night.

People at the U.N. were upset about the break-in and the day was spent dealing with both that and the Rochester victory. It was all shattered when Sandy called from Kingston, New York, to say that, as she was driving to Woodstock, the engine of the Mercedes had been destroyed. The oil gasket had apparently been loosened and all the oil had drained out after ninety miles. The mechanic who worked on it said it almost surely had been tampered with by someone. I was frightened.

However, I was not as scared as I was on the following Tuesday when Sandy called to say that our old Volvo had had the grill pried open and the hood was ajar. We had the bomb squad test it, and all was okay. But all was not okay with the Lapchicks. Five days, three major incidents. The last thing I wanted was publicity since I didn't want either the children or my mother to know of the danger. The worst of it was that we were now in New York. We could no longer blame it on living in the South. At least the authorities were more responsive to us in New York.

The events of 1978 and later, of 1981, led me to reflect more on my life, especially my childhood and the various influences in it: the events that took place, both within my family and in the outside world, the influence of my education, of my friends, and of the individual members of my family. The chance to write this book enabled me to go deeply into that period.

Part Three
Growing Up in Sportsworld

Chapter 9

Child of Sportsworld

My father always teased me that I was born under the wrong star. My mother was forty-one and he was forty-five when I arrived, surely not a birth according to the prescriptions of Planned Parenthood. Furthermore, almost at the same moment, the United States detonated its first atomic bomb in New Mexico. It was July 16, 1945. Perhaps the upheaval of the earth during my birth planted the antiwar seeds that grew in me twenty years later.

Sports marriages are never easy and my parents' was no exception. Basketball was my father's life for at least six months of every year. As a player with the Original Celtics and as coach of St. John's, he was as frequently on the road as he was at home. Paradoxically, he was an intensely private man thrust into the public limelight because of his exceptional status as a player and a coach. He hated the attention although he accommodated himself to it well.

At six-five he was the first great "big man" in pro basketball. The teams he played for always won. The Celtics were so good that the American Basketball League broke up the team in 1928 to send players to other clubs. For the previous eight years they averaged 120 victories and only 10 losses each season. He was sent to the Cleveland Rosenblums along with other Original Celtics Dutch Dehnert and Pete Barry. Cleveland proceeded to win the World Championship in the 1928–29 and 1929–30 seasons before it folded the next year due to the Depression.

The Celtics reorganized as a barnstorming team and my father played for them with continued success until 1936, when he became coach of St. John's University. In his first tenure at St. John's, his teams won two national championships and he became one of the winningest coaches in the country.

Used to winning, Joe Lapchick became intolerant of losing. His fame on the court increased his time away from home. My mother, Elizabeth, felt abandoned. She began to withdraw emotionally and became a "basketball widow." Wary of the enormous attention given to her husband by the press as well as the local adulation accorded to all famous athletes, she focused her attention on her thirteen-year-old son, Joe, and twelve-year-old daughter, Barbara. Ironically, my father hated the adulation and looked to his home as a refuge from it. Sensing his wife's withdrawal but not realizing why, he felt he was losing in life.

Both parents viewed my birth in 1945 as a way of renewing that life. They lavished love and affection on me. As I grew older and began to sense the importance of the role I was playing, I felt an enormous burden. By the time I was five, my brother and sister were both in college and rarely at home. My parents' love was so great that I could not let them down. When I did, the guilt was tremendous, though it was always self-imposed. Somehow I thought that if I could be a great basketball player I would fulfill their needs. It was a major misreading of those needs.

But such a misreading was understandable. Joe Lapchick had become the coach of the New York Knickerbockers in the early years of the National Basketball Association. The Knicks had been formed in 1946 as part of the Basketball Association of America, which merged with the National Basketball League in 1949 to become the NBA. There were no blacks in the NBA.

Away from home more than ever with the Knicks, his infrequent moments at home were treasured by me. At age five, I began to be brought to Knick games. In the same year, 1950, he signed Nat "Sweetwater" Clifton, the first black player for the Knicks. Occasionally after the Knick games I would descend into the inner sanctum of the old Madison Square Garden on 50th

Street and Eighth Avenue. I actually *knew* Nat, Carl Braun, Harry Gallatin, Vince Boryla, and all the stars. It was a high-altitude world for a five-year-old. I would do anything to be around it and constantly fantasized about being part of it some-day.

But still something was wrong. For all the glamour and fame, I saw the turmoil and agony my father went through in thinking about each game before he drove to the Garden. Sometimes I would wake up in the night to see him sitting in the chair in my room or hear him walking through the house. He would later tell the press that he lived a thousand deaths in defeat. Late at night, I saw many of them. I always knew when the Knicks lost.

Something else was causing him anxiety: the "nigger–lover" calls. I didn't know what a "nigger–lover" was but I was sure it couldn't be good if so many people disliked him because of it; I did not connect Nat Clifton to the calls. When I was in the locker room, Nat Clifton was "one of the boys." I didn't know that once outside the locker room, he became one of a different set of "boys." What I did see was how each call would eat my father up. My brother and sister were both in college and never knew of this. The only reason I did was because I would unsuspectingly pick up the phone upstairs. In the beginning I would go down-stairs to see my father after the calls. He had invariably retreated to the living room and was doubled over in a chair. He never saw me look in and I never said anything to anyone. It was a secret that I shared with him, although he didn't know that I shared it until I was grown up. The confusion was tremendous. As a five-year-old I wondered what awful sin this man had committed to make so many people hate him. He was soft and gentle to me. What must this other side of him be if so many people thought he was so horrible? I didn't really want to know for fear I might hate him too.

Later, when I realized what the calls were about, my feelings of alienation from the racist segment of American society began to grow. My father was hated because he loved. At last this dark burden was lifted from my mind and placed where it had belonged all along—on the fears and hatred that are bred so profusely in America.

But as I was growing up, I left unexamined the traumas my father experienced. I buried the pain of the hate calls. Neighbors and friends told me how I would follow in my father's footsteps.

Christmas and birthdays brought gifts of basketballs, baseballs, baseball mitts, golf balls and clubs. Neighborhood fathers wanted to teach me to shoot, wanted me to play with their kids. As I look back, the draw and power of the sports experience seems even stronger if more bizarre. They were doing this when I was five, six, and seven years old. I felt such pressure from them. I had to be good. The only thing I couldn't understand was why my own father, who would spend endless hours talking to me, going for walks with me, playing word and board games with me, *never* played basketball with me. Never even *talked* about my playing basketball.

My meetings with the Knicks made each time I picked up a basketball a vicarious trip down the Madison Square Garden court. It didn't matter that when I threw the ball up it barely reached the basket, let alone went in. It didn't matter because I was Joe Lapchick's son and I was going to be a star. Everyone knew it, everyone told me. And I believed it.

I was seven and enrolled at the YMCA day camp in Yonkers. We were playing all kinds of sports each day behind Roosevelt High School where the sessions were held. I was in heaven. However, soon after the camp began I got a high fever and had to stay home. Our family physician, Dr. Ahouse, was out of town so they called a different doctor to see me. Everyone was relieved to be told I had tonsillitis. But when the antibiotics and other medication failed to make me better, Dr. Ahouse came.

A warm, wonderful man, he spent an unusually long time with me and then went into the corner of the room to talk to my parents. I remember hearing my mother say, "Oh, my god!" Dr. Ahouse made some phone calls and an ambulance soon pulled up to our house. With tears in his eyes, my father told me that Dr. Ahouse wanted me to go to Grasslands Hospital where they had special facilities to treat polio. I remember he could hardly say the word as he held me. As sick and half delirious as I was, this moment sealed a bond between us. Captured for the first time was that elusive love that comes from total communication between father and son.

The tests confirmed it was polio. When my brother was allowed to come home from West Point to visit me, I knew the sickness was serious. One day a neighbor visited the hospital with the family. "Do the doctors think he will ever be able to play basketball?" he asked my father. Not if he'll be able to walk, not if he'll be able to lead a normal life, but will he ever be able to play basketball. My father was too polite a man to express the revulsion he felt. I was seven years old. I was not a basketball player, I was a little kid.

I don't think he knew that I heard and saw this happen. The next day he sat by my side and asked me if I wanted to play basketball. I enthusiastically, if naively, said "yes." He told me that all he wanted for me was to have a normal and happy life. He said he had prayed that if God delivered me to him in one piece, that he would nurture me back to health, that he would stop everything else to accomplish it. Subsequently, he gave me years of massages and exercise programs.

I realized for the first time that it was unimportant to him for me to be an athlete. Yet, I knew that now more than ever I wanted to be one. Within a year I had recovered from polio. My father's prayers had been answered. Now I had to make my own prayers come true.

As part of my "rehabilitation," my parents bought me a membership at the Jewish Community Center in Yonkers. At the JCC, I was the tall kid with all the potential. I was always high scorer and leading rebounder on the Comets, a club team. My competition was the likes of John Bonito, Fred Fine, and Alan Carmassin, with whom I remained friends for many years. But none of them played in the NBA, or even in college or high school.

My father was doing more and more things with me now. After Knick games he would take me to Mama Leone's restaurant where he would talk about the game with the press. I recall many evenings there, but one stands out in particular. Still unaware of the significance of Nat Clifton in our lives, I couldn't help but be aware of Jackie Robinson. The national sports press was heavily selling his admission into baseball as an indication that sports was the way out of the ghetto for black athletes; it was to become a widely believed assumption about sport and society. By now I was old enough to take an interest in political discussions at home. I had read about Jackie Robinson. I believed sports was the way out for blacks. The press spoke the truth. I continued to believe this for nearly another decade.

While he never discussed racism in sport, my father freely discussed racism in society. I knew it was something he cared deeply about. The Brown *vs.* the Board of Education Supreme Court decision had sparked a major controversy the previous year (1954) when it called for the integration of public schools. It was a decision warmly greeted by my family.

I was relating to sports and not to politics. Anyway, I had read that they didn't mix. Jackie Robinson was much more real and important to me than the Supreme Court. Therefore, when I had an opportunity to meet him at the Garden one day I jumped at the chance. Some sports writers called him "abrasive" and "aggressive." It was only much later that I realized these were code words for blacks that meant they were "uppity niggers." Jackie Robinson shook my hand and spoke to me for two or three minutes. He was neither abrasive nor aggressive, but kind and thoughtful. At Leone's later that night, a member of the press whose name I've long since forgotten asked his colleague, "Did you see that nigger showboating for the crowd?" The friend nodded his agreement. I was nine years old at the time, and my own sports ambitions soon made me try to put this incident out of my mind. But it stuck with me.

My sports progress was measurable. I was euphoric when in the fifth grade I won the school foul-shooting championship; and the Comets and I were tearing apart the JCC League. I was so happy I barely noticed that my father spent day after day in a malaise called losing. Intensely proud, he was about to resign in mid-season, having heard the rumor he would be fired at the end of the year.

My sports development was so good when measured against my competitors at the Jewish Community Center that I barely noticed that the person I wanted to emulate was bleeding to death under my insensitive eyes. My passion to play sports was so distorting my values that my career as the high scorer among eleven-year-olds at the Jewish Community Center was more important to me than the lifetime my father had given to the sport.

The next year I went to Hawthorne Junior High School. The only way a lowly seventh-grader could survive was by being a good athlete. The competition was better than at the JCC but still I managed to make the seventh-grade all-star team. We were to play the eighth-grade champions. For the first time my father was coming to see me play. He had been rehired at St. John's, and he was more relaxed and not traveling as much as he did with the Knicks. The day of the game I couldn't eat. The way I played I might as well not have eaten the week before. I was awful. My father was incapable of lying so he didn't say anything. I didn't dare ask.

The 1958–59 season, his third back at St. John's, was expected to be my father's comeback year. He had a good team returning plus a sophomore named Tony Jackson, the first black basketball player at St. John's in a number of years. Tony was a poet with a jump shot, and he was to lead St. John's to the Holiday Festival and National Invitation Tournament championships in that year.

Even so, I would hear in private the innuendos from the press and from some other students at St. John's—Tony was lazy, not very smart, shouldn't really be in college. They didn't mention that more than 150 colleges had tried to obtain his services. It was funny that you didn't hear these remarks about white athletes, although my father learned that some of them rarely if ever attended classes—an abuse he and his assistant, Lou Carnesecca, quickly corrected. The misuse of athletes was prevalent almost everywhere in the 1950s and is still the norm at many athletic powerhouses. All of this might have been more important in my mind if St. John's was losing. But winning two championships made it seem less significant at the time.

So I vicariously participated in St. John's success. More important, I grew six inches and became one of the biggest eighth-graders in the New York area. Everyone was predicting I would be six-seven or more. I was good for a slow big man and New

York high school coaches were looking at me. I leaned toward Power Memorial High School. I liked the coach, Jack Donohue, and they always had an excellent team.

Everyone in the family pushed me toward Manhattan Prep, which was on the campus of Manhattan College. It had the reputation of a fine academic school and attracted many of New York City's brightest students. I didn't care that much about being a good student. In my own mind I was convinced I would be a very good player. With hindsight, I now realize that *all* ballplayers believe this; even ones who aren't particularly good overestimate their talent.

In trying to prove my ability I was forced to confront racism for the first time. I had made friends with a few of the black ballplayers who tried out for scholarships at Power Memorial. I was drawn to them because they were ignored by the white players when they were lucky; despised and decried when they were not. I think it was at age thirteen that I was, for the first time, embarrassed to be white.

My new friends invited me to their neighborhoods to play that summer. Those neighborhoods, of course, were mostly in Harlem. My white friends from Yonkers told me smart whites didn't go to Harlem. I didn't claim to be smart but I knew I could play good basketball there and that my days with the Comets and Hawthorne Junior High were past.

It *was* good basketball. However, when I visited my friends' apartments I had to contemplate why I lived so comfortably, as did all of my white friends, while they did not. All of my developing friendships in Harlem were with people who had few of the physical comforts I had come to expect.

What was it about this society that prescribed such antithetical conditions for blacks and whites? I was deeply troubled by what I was experiencing during that summer. And then I remembered Jackie Robinson. Sports would surely elevate these talented players out of the ghetto. The only difference now was that I was not sure I still believed in the sports panacea. I wanted to; I needed to; but I was not sure I did.

Having acquiesced to my parents' wishes, I entered Manhattan Prep in the fall of 1959. I was ready to make my mark on New

York City basketball. I soon learned that freshmen had to pay their dues and I mainly sat on the bench for a good Manhattan junior varsity team. It was one of the better JVs in the city. I became reconciled to my role as full-time cheerleader, part-time player. It was enough for me to send a game against my would-be school, Power Memorial, into overtime with a jump shot. Small things had to carry me then. But I was full enough of myself to ignore the reality of not playing. To be on the team was "manly." I wasn't a boy anymore. To be on the team meant having dates with girls. The two went together. Sport was making my transition to manhood easier.

Manhattan was not the place for a pure jock; at Manhattan, the real "brains" looked down their noses at me. Not only was I an athlete but the curse was already a generation old in my family. For these preppies, sport was the height of anti-intellectualism and was to be avoided. They did, however, have a good biting sense of humor. As we took the floor at our first home game, they unfurled a banner the length of the court that read, "Nobody can lick our Dick."

I was so carried away with sports that I rebelled when my father decided to send me to Europe in the summer of 1960. I wanted to stay in New York and go back to the city's play-grounds. Culture had no appeal. Finally, my mother reminded me that the Olympic Games would be held in Rome that summer. That convinced me to go.

I began to read books about the Olympic Games. What greater honor than to represent your country? What an important role to be an ambassador of peace and understanding. It all sounded so wonderful, so meaningful. Africans, Asians, and Latin Americans could forget the colonial and imperial roles of Western nations. The U.S.S.R. and the U.S. could meet harmoniously. In 1959 it momentarily looked like both "Chinas" might be in Rome. The Olympic Movement was a force for peace.

Seeing Europe helped to challenge my mind—perhaps for the first time. There were no sports to divert me. I wouldn't have imagined that I would ever want to go to an art museum. By the end of the summer I couldn't stay away. Raised as a Catholic, I avoided churches on days other than Sundays. Traveling throughout Europe, I loved to visit the famous and historic cathedrals. Concerts, operas, historical museums. I rarely thought about sports.

Most important was the time I spent with my sister Barbara and Roy, her first husband. They were living in West Germany and we traveled a great deal together. They treated me, the fourteen-year-old dumb jock, like one of their own intellectual friends. We discussed politics. They told me about a senator from Massachusetts in whom they had a lot of faith. I had barely heard of John Kennedy. We talked about Martin Luther King. My friends in Harlem had told me he was their savior, not Jackie Robinson. We talked about Albert Luthuli, the chief of the Zulus in South Africa—and head of the African National Congress.

It was at a friend's apartment that I first listened to the singing of a man with a magnificent voice. I heard about Paul Robeson— all that he had accomplished as an artist, all that he stood for as an activist, and all that he had suffered. I wondered if it could be true. How could I not have heard of Robeson? Why did every European white I met speak of him while no white American I knew did? Blacks in Paris and London seemed to be treated differently from those in the United States. Not understanding then the nature of French and British colonialism, I could not penetrate beneath the surface. I knew that all of the blacks I was seeing could not have been former athletes and entertainers who had made it out of the ghetto. Was Europe a model for America?

I returned to New York on the day school reopened with these thoughts buzzing in my head. I would continue in sports, but now life would have more meaning. I began to tell my teammates about Europe. They were bored. I talked to the girls who hung around the team. They found other things to do. When I talked to the intellectual element, they listened, thinking that perhaps I could be "saved" from the morass of sports. But when they listened, a few teammates and some of the girls began to think I was "weird." "Are you becoming a fag, Rich?" I neither wanted to be saved nor a fag, so I reluctantly focused all my attention on the court again. The reluctance soon disappeared. I was starting on the JV. It was now easy to put aside all that I had absorbed that summer. At the end of the year I was brought up to the varsity along with the other JV starters. I was working hard and I was being rewarded for it. My close friend, Billy Jones, had grown several inches while I had not grown a single inch in two years. Now he was the center and I was the forward—the slow forward. But I could shoot. Also, I was studying more and more and had won the academic scholarship awarded to the three students with the highest scholastic average. My family was very proud. My teammates never even knew.

I was also caught up with my father's team at St. John's. Tony Jackson was a senior now and was paying with LeRoy Ellis at center and Willie Hall at forward. Ellis and Hall were both black. It was probably the most talented college team my father ever coached. They were in the Top Ten all year and at one time were ranked second. They played number-one Ohio State in the finals of the Holiday Festival and lost in the closing minutes. We thought they could win the national championship. They didn't. I actually heard St. John's students asking how could they expect to win with three blacks on the front line?

The second major college basketball point-shaving scandal was breaking. As a pro coach during the first scandal, my father had put together a scrapbook showing how the lives of athletes involved had been devastated. He made each player at St. John's read this and sign to acknowledge that he read it before the season began.

It was the time for the St. John's Athletic Awards Banquet. Tony Jackson, as a three-time All-American, was obviously going to get the MVP award. I was going to attend and sit with LeRoy Ellis. LeRoy and I had become good friends. He was six-eleven from Bedford-Stuyvesant, one of the poorest and roughest areas in New York. Sports did bring LeRoy and me together and thirty years later we are still in touch.

But on this day two men from the athletic department came to our house and asked my father to go with them. He walked back into the house alone and went upstairs. I went up after a few minutes to find him staring at a wall, his eyes full of tears.

The New York district attorney advised St. John's not to give Tony Jackson the award as he was "more implicated in the scandal than you can know about." St. John's had agreed and sent their delegation to inform my father. He asked for evidence but was given none. He said he didn't believe it, that it was unfair to Tony since there was no evidence, no proof. Whom was he willing to believe, he was asked, the DA or Tony Jackson, a young man from the streets of New York?

Later I heard St. John's students ask how could Tony Jackson do this to St. John's after it had done so much for him. I heard others say that Jackson had been given the chance to get out of the ghetto but that he had blown it. They had already forgotten that Jackson had led St. John's to three great basketball years and had brought in many new fans. His presence had been partially responsible for LeRoy Ellis enrolling, and he had helped revive interest in college basketball in New York City for the first time since the scandal in 1950. All that seemed to be remembered now was the battle to get Jackson into the school in spite of his low high-school grades; the battle to keep him eligible during his four years at St. John's. All too easily accepted then, it was never proven that Tony Jackson did anything wrong. Tony, a likely NBA star, was blacklisted by the league.

Six years later he was allowed to play for New Jersey in the American Basketball Association where he averaged 19.5 points per game and was one of the league's best shooters. But the fulfillment of Tony Jackson's potential ended that day in 1961. The sports world had made a scapegoat of him, along with Connie Hawkins and Roger Brown, two other black New York players merely "implicated by the DA."

As has become frighteningly obvious over the past three decades, but especially in the 1980s with the scandalous revelations about academic abuses in intercollegiate athletics, the world of college sport was out of control on many campuses.

But when the scandals started to leak out, the question of protecting the athletes was rarely raised. Undeniably, the athletes who actually took money to fix scores cheated. They were wrong and should have been punished. Yet the primary motive for the behavior of many of the athletic departments was simply to protect themselves. The athletes were back on the streets in almost every case. No surprises. Caught in a sports web of cheating, these athletes took the easy way by joining in the cheating. Just more human tragedy. The reality of the sports world was beginning to sink into me ever so slowly, ever so painfully.

I spent that summer at the Friendship Farm basketball camp just being established by Jack Donohue, the Power Memorial coach. There was a big black kid there who was to begin sophomore year at Power in September. It was the first time I had *lived* with someone who was black. He was shy, sensitive, and very bright. He had difficulty handling the racism of some of the others. As he grew taller throughout the summer, racial barbs became more regular. As he began to dominate, there were no more jokes. But one player "niggered" him to death. I got fed up and intervened. Out of sight of anyone else this player decked me. Ashamed of my fate, I never told Donohue. That particular "nigger" is now known as Kareem Abdul-Jabbar, known then as Lew Alcindor. His baiter is now a head coach at a major university. He probably tells recruits of his "friendship" with Kareem to prove how "with it" he is.

I was getting better and better that summer. Playing not only with Lew, but with four others who eventually started at major colleges, I was averaging 10 points a game for the camp team. My only concern was that I was still five-eleven and was now playing guard. I knew I was slow, but hoped my ability to shoot would compensate. Billy Jones was also there and he was growing and improving.

We both came back to Manhattan that fall with high expectations. His were probably real and mine illusory. We both contracted whooping cough before the season began. Billy recovered in time to make honorable mention All-City. I hardly practiced in the first half of the season and became slower and slower on the court. I started to face the fact that I wouldn't be six-seven, and that being Joe Lapchick's son might not be enough to make me great.

I was spending more and more time with LeRoy Ellis. It was his senior year at St. John's and he was about to embark on a fourteen-year NBA career. Usually we discussed basketball, but sometimes we talked about his life growing up in Bedford-Stuyvesant. Without really knowing it, LeRoy had become my professor of race relations. It meant a great deal to me—and I think to him—when we discussed the poverty he grew up in, the loneliness of being black at an almost all-white school, how hard it was for him to deal with his courses after a poor grounding in fundamentals, and how unfair it had been that Tony Jackson was blacklisted by the NBA. My eyes were being forced open as the 1961–62 basketball season was ending. My personal dream had not quite ended, but my belief in the self-proclaimed verities of sportsworld were being shattered.

My own career seemed to be withering away. Suddenly Manhattan's starting backcourt duo became sick before a game with Cathedral. I had brought Janice, my girlfriend and first true love, to the game so that we could go to a party later. It was her first game. I didn't have time to get nervous when told I would start. I scored 18 points and we won easily. Janice was impressed. So was I.

The next day I went to the Manhattan College trainer because I had injured my foot late in the game. He said, "Coach Connington said you played well last night and he wished you weren't so slow so he could use you more." I knew at that very moment that if my coach said this *after* I scored 18 points, I had no future as a basketball player at Manhattan. Maybe I never really had a future. But now I knew. The funny thing was that it didn't hurt at all. From then on I could play for fun. I came out of the closet as a student and stopped hiding my grades from my teammates.

By 1963 my dreams about sports were dying if not dead. In August, as hundreds of thousands of people marched on Washington, Martin Luther King poetically outlined his own dream. Suddenly my experiences in sport—the important experiences—the nigger-lover calls, the games in Harlem, the experiences with Lew Alcindor, Tony Jackson, and LeRoy Ellis—made King's dream the only dream that mattered to me. LeRoy Ellis, by then a pro with the Lakers, had been the only black man in an all-white sea of humanity at Manhattan's graduation exercises two months earlier.

I was speaking directly to LeRoy and my father when I took the platform as the school's salutatorian. I was supposed to greet the people and say some pleasant things about what our experiences at Manhattan meant to us. I did this, but I also talked about all the work we had to do to make our society well again. I talked about racism and poverty to this relatively affluent white audience. I talked about the responsibility of our generation. Then I took my seat to the polite applause of an otherwise perplexed audience. I looked at LeRoy and my father. They understood. I could go on from there. The basketball dream was dead. Dr. King was about to shape a new dream.

Chapter 10

Stolen Ball

I chose to go to St. John's strictly because I was the last of my father's children. My sister had gone to Barnard and my brother to West Point. I knew that I could go to a school with a better academic reputation than St. John's. But I felt that one of us should go even if it was not among the East's academic elite.

When I arrived at St. John's in September I wondered if I would ever want to pick up a basketball again. I had spent the summer as if I wouldn't, working as a lifeguard at the Tibbetts Brook Park Pool, where my father and brother had also worked many years before. I lifted weights all summer, and I was in the best shape of my life. However, it was not basketball shape. I was a very muscular 190 pounds—almost 20 pounds more than I weighed in my junior year at Manhattan. If I was slow at 170 pounds, I was not anxious to know what I would be like at 190.

I met with Lou Carnesecca. He talked to me as if it was a foregone conclusion that I would play freshman basketball. I think he was being kind, for he definitely knew that I was not going to be able to help *this* freshman team. It had been a great recruiting year. There was Albie Schwartz, a Catholic later to be named to the "Jewish All-American" team, Brian Hill, a smooth ballhandler, Billy Jones, and John Zarzicki, a rough aggressive player in the mold of Jim Luscutoff of the Celtics. They were all very good. But the prizes were twin black towers—Lloyd

111

"Sonny" Dove from St. Francis Prep, and Ed Hill from New Jersey. Both were about six-seven. Lloyd, whose life was to end in a tragic car accident in 1983, was already fluid and proficient at age eighteen. He became an All-American and was named MVP in the College All-Star game as a senior. Ed was raw but as time went on showed perhaps more potential than did Lloyd. With such talent on hand, I realized that Lou was trying to be nice to me. I didn't want to expend all the energy practice would take so I could watch the team from the bench instead of the stands. It did not make any sense.

However, four factors made me decide to play freshman basketball. First, I felt a loyalty to Lou, who was treating me so well. Second, I wanted to be around the team to try to better understand what my father went through every day. He would have little to do with the freshman team, but there would be enough interaction. Third, my withdrawal from playing was not going as well as I had thought it would. I wasn't hooked anymore, but I still liked the taste. Maybe I could have fun playing, since I knew I could not compete with the Doves, Hills, and Joneses. Finally, being a basketball player—even a bad basketball player— at St. John's was an ego trip. It was the first time I would be a player at a coed school and players were definitely having more fun—more parties and especially more women. I was insecure around women, and the protective shield of "athlete" became my sliding board into the social world of St. John's.

St. John's was hardly a cauldron of progressive ideas. Thomas Aquinas was its intellectual mentor, while at other universities the shapers were Marx, Engels, Marcuse, and Sartre. Yet even Aquinas was in the shadows. Sports, especially basketball, was the major topic on campus. Being a jock meant being macho. Being white often meant being antiblack. Overtly, there were few signs of racism. "The [black] boys" and their "foxes" had their table in the lounge. At the time I guess this was viewed as full integration. Blacks and whites were marching in the South, fighting for integration. Little Rock, Birmingham, Selma, Montgomery—the capitals of oppression were being transformed into capitals of resistance.

We didn't have to resist at St. John's. Lloyd Dove and Ed Hill were freshmen there. Everyone assumed the other blacks were also athletes. (No one seemed to know that most were pharmacy and science majors.) Athletes were the right kind of blacks—they knew their place—the court, the table, then home. All was neatly laid out for us.

Some of my "friends" were taking me aside to say that others were "pissed off" because I was hanging around with blacks too much. It was one thing to pal around the locker room together, another to go out socially. If sports was helping blacks out of the ghetto, it was not getting them much beyond the locker room.

I decided that my interest had to go beyond empathy. I read John Hope Franklin's *From Slavery to Freedom* about the history of blacks in America, Martin Luther King's *Stride Toward Freedom,* James Baldwin's *The Fire Next Time,* as well as other books on race. I tried to discuss the things I was learning with my friends, but the basketball season was about to begin.

The team was required to spend one and a half to two hours each afternoon in a study hall prior to practice. George Lee was to have been the star of the team. With his academic dismissal the previous year, everyone knew they could not slide by only because they were athletes. However, "gut courses" were still available and many players took them. There were professors who were enthusiastic fans—we quickly got to know who they were. They wouldn't have much to root for if the star flunked out.

Getting by was a process of self-education, of the athletes informing themselves how to "beat the system." I cannot remember hearing about a coach turning athletes in this direction. The coaches, in fact, seemed more serious about academics than the athletes. With all the revelations about academic cheating in the 1980s I now realize that, by comparison, St. John's was far ahead of the field in educating its athletes, even in the 1960s.

Then, it seemed the whole institution was involved in athletics. After all, the administration chose to build the gym before it built the library. St. John's, like many other schools, used its national sports reputation to attract students and broaden its scholastic capabilities. The system was working—while I was there, St. John's became the largest Catholic school in America.

So now the athletes had to produce both in sports and in the classroom. Without the books there would be no sports. Without sports, there would be no more books. Without athletes, there would be no major sports program. It was in everyone's interest, including the athletes, to keep the athletes eligible to play. So athletes found the courses, they found the professors; they reduced their academic load to the minimum; they found friendly students to "help" them in their work; and they did study, at least during the study hall period. All of this was necessary because the pressures were tremendous. I am told that 90 percent of St. John's basketball players who played for four years have graduated since George Lee's expulsion. According to most estimates, that is almost triple the national average for major sports programs.

At St. John's I was never aware of the additional factor of alumni pressure to win. Since my father was the coach, I am quite sure I would have seen it. However, I had friends in other colleges, as did teammates and members of the varsity, and we frequently heard stories of handsome payoffs from alumni. At the time, most of the money was apparently being given in the Southern and Midwestern schools. One St. John's player had been offered $10,000 a year to transfer to a relatively small school-on-the-make in the Midwest. There were many such stories. Direct payments, clothes, cars, women, jobs for family members. Anything one could imagine. The press seemed to be ignoring it.

Reading my father's scandal scrapbook, as all of us had to do just at the start of the season, I was frightened. I was angry. I knew whom my teammates had to avoid. As I began to learn more about alumni payoffs, about their "support" for intercollegiate athletics, I wondered about the bookmakers on the streets. They were teaching the same values—get what you can. But the bookmakers were more open about it. They were not acceptable. The alumni were "friends." Spending time at St. John's in the 1980s, I see that the alumni gave no "big money," and thus, have a negligible role in the sports program.

We freshmen were ready to play against the varsity in Alumni Hall. We knew we had a good team and could win. The freshmen, however, never beat the varsity. This night was no exception. Our freshman coach was Jack Kaiser, a fine, intelligent man who is now St. John's athletic director. He was also one of the most successful baseball coaches in the country. His philosophy was that the freshmen team would prepare those who would later play on the varsity. That meant Ed and Brian Hill, Jones, Schwartz, Dove, and possibly Zarzicki. Not Lapchick. But all would play that night.

Playing for just the last ten minutes, I didn't do anything exceptional, but I didn't make any mistakes either. Against the St. John's varsity!

The next morning my father said two short sentences to me. "You did well last night. You made me proud." It was only the second time he had seen me play in a game.

Now I was free. I had made *him* proud. I finally realized that although he had never once put pressure on me to play, and in fact had tried to direct me *away* from basketball, the pressure had always been there simply because he was Joe Lapchick. Unknowingly, I had been waiting for this moment.

The varsity started the year poorly but finished strong with wins over Loyola of Chicago, the number-one ranked team, and New York University, our biggest rival. NYU had an excellent team and were solid favorites. St. John's built a big lead at halftime and my father literally ran off the court at full speed. The team was shedding its washed-up label. He knew it—the packed crowd knew it. They were on their feet when this sixty-four-year-old lean tower bolted for the exit. The cheering went on long after he and the team had disappeared into the concrete corridors. The second half was an anticlimax. It never was a game and St. John's won by 20 points.

The future was bright. Most members of the varsity were returning. Despite Ed Hill having to leave school for personal reasons, the freshmen lost only once. And there was the prospect that Lew Alcindor, who as a junior was dominating high school basketball, would come to St. John's. With Lew and Lloyd, the national championship would be within St. John's grasp. My father was a happy man.

The summer of 1964 was another turning point for me. The civil rights movement was in high gear and students from the North were heading south to help in the Voter Registration Drive. Spirits were high. The March on Washington had electrified the nation the year before. Martin Luther King was rumored to be the recipient of the Nobel Peace Prize. Students and activists were organizing sit-ins throughout the South. But the Voter Registration Drive had the most potential. The ballot was power.

On June 21, 1964, three civil rights workers—James Chaney, a black man from Mississippi, and Michael Schwerner and Andrew Goodman, both white men from New York, were arrested for speeding in Mississippi. Local police claimed they had released them six hours later. Their burned-out station wagon was soon found without them. It was six weeks before their bodies were discovered, but the nation knew their fate on June 21.

For me, this event dictated that I could no longer simply read about black history. I had to become actively involved. Over and over I read Martin Luther King's "I have a dream" speech. One sentence kept jumping out at me. "With this faith we will be able to work together, to pray together, to struggle together, to go to jail together, to stand up for freedom together, knowing we will be free one day."

I was ashamed. Ashamed to have seen what racism could do and not act to stop it. Ashamed that I had thought of myself as being "free" because my father had told me he was proud of how I played basketball; that he was free because St. John's had beaten NYU. Ashamed that it took the deaths of three contemporaries to sufficiently shake me to see how much I had to learn, how much I had to do.

That summer the police tried to obscure what had happened to Schwerner, Chaney, and Goodman. It took Dr. David Spain, a medical examiner from New York, to ascertain the brutality of their deaths.

In 1964 the work I could do was at best token. I couldn't go to the South—and frankly did not know if I had the courage to do so at the time. I was working seventy-two hours a week as both a lifeguard in Yonkers and as an attendant at the New York World's Fair. With little time to myself, I went to Long Island or West- chester three nights a week to collect newspapers that could be recycled to raise money. The money was then sent to help with transportation costs in voter registration projects.

My job as a lifeguard was helping to crystallize my vision of racism in the North. All we read about was what was going on in the South. However, the Yonkersites who were condemning the civil rights murders were also complaining that too many people from the Bronx were coming to swim at Tibbetts Brook Park where I worked. The "too many people from the Bronx" was code for "too many blacks." Disdainful of the blacks earlier in the summer, the white bathers were more respectful after a serious riot in Harlem. Fear bred respect. It was a lesson not lost on any of us. March, sing, parade, and demonstrate—do that all you want and get few changes. But destroy property—and sud- denly whites began moving out of your way. Suddenly whites were being taunted and were taking it just like blacks had to for centuries. You could see it at the pool. You could see it in the streets. You could feel it in the movement. The movement was nationwide.

My sister was talking about leaving for Africa, which she did in November 1964. I knew very little about Africa then. The few references to it in textbooks and in high school were to the slave trade and the colonization of Africa, then equated to Europe's efforts to "civilize" and "Christianize" the dark and demonic continent. South Africa—Christian, civilized, industrialized, and rich—was portrayed as the hope of the continent. That summer I didn't quite understand why this great hope was being suspended from the 1964 Tokyo Olympics. If they were Christian, civilized, industrialized, and rich, then why shouldn't they play? The press condemned the decision, arguing that it was wrong to "mix politics and sport." Most stories explained why. Generally one paragraph near the end referred to the fact that South Africa was expelled because some nations, led by the Communists, felt that it was a racist country. My curiosity was aroused and I began to read about South Africa. The fact that my sister moved to Africa increased my desire to learn more and more. It was in the realm of sports that my education about apartheid had its origin. Many years later I would remember that and try to use it to educate others.

Our family was turned inside out in a matter of hours after my father's annual trip to St. John's to sign his contract. He had always signed one-year contracts. St. John's had been good to him. It had hired him in the 1930s when his playing career was ending. He always said he didn't even know *how* to coach then. And it had rehired him when he resigned from the Knicks. St. John's was about to pay him $12,500 for the 1964–65 season! Yes, St. John's was family. He loved the game and St. John's for letting him play it. But they stole the ball that day.

What he wanted to do most was to help lead it to a National Collegiate Athletic Association (NCAA) title—the national championship. He wanted to give this to his school before retiring. He knew it could be done if he could recruit Lew Alcindor that year. He liked Lew personally very much. Joe Lapchick, the first great big man in basketball, knew what Lew was going through. I counted Lew among my friends. It would be great to see Lloyd and Lew on the same team. There would be no stopping them.

As he was signing the contract, Father Graham, the athletic moderator, said something like, "Joe, we've been proud of our association with you. You've made a great contribution to the school. We hope that your final year will be a great one." He assumed this meant his final year with Alcindor. Of course, it would be a great one. Then they explained to him—for the very first time—that St. John's had set mandatory retirement at sixty-five. Joe Lapchick was devastated.

When I left him in the morning he was buoyant. When I saw him that night he was a defeated and lonely man. I told him we could fight this through the student body. He said no, a rule was a rule. If it had validity, then exceptions should not be made. He called my brother, Joe, who was superintendent of schools in Aspen, Colorado. He told my father that, in general, it was a good rule; in Graham's position, my brother would have done the same thing. For every great teacher over sixty-five there were ten bad ones. Sacrifices had to be made. He only wished it wasn't my father. It was the midnight of my father's life. The man who had spent a significant part of his life fighting for others would not now fight for himself.

He convinced me at the time he was right. The word spread quickly on campus. I remember Lynn Burke, the Olympic champion turned St. John's cheerleader, coming up to me. She was very upset and wanted to do something. Everyone wanted to do something. Protest at St. John's had not been a major activity. I was pleased to see it might be a possibility. On that day, however, I told Lynn that it would upset my father.

Jack Donohue, the coach of Power Memorial High School, and more importantly, the coach of Lew Alcindor, came over to our house that night. He was an outgoing man with a good sense of humor. But that night he was very serious. I had never before seen him like that. He wanted to talk to my father alone. I had never before been excluded. Something had to be very wrong.

Jack Donohue had been asked if he would be interested in being the assistant basketball coach at St. John's. When Lou Carnesecca joined the staff in the 1958–59 season, my father and the athletic department promised him the head coaching job when my father retired. That job had been taken. Jack as assistant coach? St. John's was a powerhouse again. He could move from there into a good head coaching position. Why was he so serious? This effusive man was so timid. Why? At first, my father couldn't understand it. Suddenly, he couldn't miss it.

He asked Jack if St. John's mentioned Lew Alcindor when they brought up the subject of the job. Yes, they had. What a scenario. One of the most renowned figures in the history of sport, the last of the "pioneers" still coaching, was to be mandatorily retired to make room for this high school coach to become an assistant coach. Lew Alcindor would come with Jack. Joe Lapchick would go home with a $100-a-month pension.

It didn't even make sense. First of all, Jack idolized my father. That is why he was so timid that night. I don't think he would have seriously considered the job because of the pain the circumstances would cause my father. Second, even if he would have considered it, St. John's had offered him several thousand dollars less than he was making at Power Memorial. You didn't have to be a wizard with business figures to know that this did not make sense.

Most importantly, St. John's knew my father had a good relationship with Lew Alcindor and with Jack. Maybe they could have considered hiring Jack as an assistant in addition to Lou. Perhaps that would reinforce any decision by Alcindor to come to St. John's.

What they didn't know and what no one knew except Lew himself, was that Lew Alcindor didn't trust Jack Donohue. As Lew related it in a story in *Sports Illustrated,* Jack had told him he was "acting just like a nigger" at the halftime of one game. For Lew, that was the end of Jack. Jack explained that he was only trying to stir him up to get him to play more aggressively; that he had no racial intention. But for Lew, that was the end of Jack.

When I read this, I wondered how many good players had been destroyed by unthinking statements made in the heat of combat by unthinking coaches. Alcindor was strong and could overcome it. How many didn't?

Many years later, Lew Alcindor, now Kareem Abdul-Jabbar, talked about the possibility of being traded from the Milwaukee Bucks to the New York Knicks. Peter Vescey, a reporter for the New York *Sunday News,* asked Kareem why he wanted to return to New York after he had chosen to leave it for UCLA in 1965. He replied:

> I will say that the only reason I left New York was because Joe Lapchick was forced into retirement at age sixty-five. I wanted to play for St. John's and Mr. Lapchick but for whatever reason he was squeezed out.
>
> I really liked the man and I found I could relate to him as a human being. I used to see him during the summers at camps and he'd never pressure me in any way.
>
> I remember he'd tell me stories about when he was young and the people in his neighborhood used to gawk as this tall, skinny kid passed by. They'd call him the gypsy. He went through the same things I went through a generation before.

My father had been dead for several years. He didn't know this. Nor did he know that exceptions to the mandatory retirement rule were made after he left. Maybe St. John's finally recognized the cruel effects of the rule. Maybe it was merely the fact that there was nothing to be gained by invoking it.

I could not sleep that night. It was still a month before practice began, but that night my vision was of a packed Madison Square Garden. St. John's had just won their fourth NIT championship and my father was being lifted on the shoulders of a sea of humanity. What a glorious sight. But it was only a vision.

Without any encouragement from my father, mild protests took place on campus over his retirement. There was a petition, a couple of rallies. Lloyd Dove took the podium at a rally on academic problems at St. John's. He talked about the injustice of my father's situation. He talked about how much more Joe Lapchick had to give to St. John's. He asked "if the administration could do this to the best-known person on campus, what could it do to others?" I will never forget Lloyd for that. Not only was he a ballplayer—and athletes never dared to challenge the system in those days—but he was a black ballplayer. It took great courage. Yet, I will also never forget the reaction of some in the audience. No comments had been made after any of the white speakers sat down. But when Lloyd finished, I heard a group of students saying how disloyal he was to St. John's; several claimed that he was inarticulate. This "boy" belonged on the court, not at a protest rally.

Without my father's encouragement, the protests had no force. The opening of his last season ended the students' rebellion but initiated my father's own form of silent protest. He was coaching his heart out, and it almost gave way. Unknown to anyone but his physician and myself, he had two mild heart attacks during games that season. But he couldn't be stopped.

St. John's got off to a great start, including a 75–74 comeback victory over number-one ranked Michigan in the Holiday Festival final. After the tournament each game on the road meant a farewell ceremony for my father. They were all very touching. They were also very frequently followed by a loss. My father attributed the losses, at least in part, to the ceremonies. How could the team fight hard against a school that was being so nice to the coach?

Fortunately, there were no ceremonies in Madison Square Garden during the NIT. St. John's was seeded next to last, yet won the first three games.

St. John's played top-seeded Villanova for the championship, and beat them. For the team, for the crowd, for all New York, it seemed like Joe Lapchick's final game was a crusade. My vision had become reality. Joe Lapchick was riding that sea of humanity. The Garden was in pandemonium. It was the proudest moment of my life. Half of the people must have been in tears. The headline in the next day's *New York Post* was "Joe Lapchick Walks with Kings." He always had. Within a few months he had turned his dismissal from sports into a moment of pure joy, and his tears into his triumph.

Before the end of the season he had been discussing other coaching jobs. He had one offer from the pros and another from the college ranks. I think he probably would have accepted one if he hadn't won that day. But the win simply made him say, "What a way to go!" His intense pride had almost killed him that season, but the victory had made the pain worthwhile.

Chapter 11

Inside Out

_____

My last two years at St. John's were ones of increasing political and intellectual awareness. It was a time when the Vietnam War and the racial situation in America were crying out for change. At Berkeley I would have been a moderate. At St. John's I was a radical. In the real world, I was probably a liberal.

The irony of my father's mandatory retirement was that I was able to have much more time with him. We would sit and talk late into the night. He wanted to know what I thought about the Vietnam War. For him, the war might have meant losing me and that was enough for him to be against it. The geopolitical situation was not the issue. He didn't want me to fight. We watched Muhammad Ali "debate" William Buckley. At the time they were saying Ali was mentally incompetent but that program showed how bright Ali really was. When he was reclassified by his draft board, Ali said, "I ain't got no quarrel with them Viet Cong." In my senior year of college I was the sports columnist for the *Torch*, the school newspaper. I wrote of Ali's courage to stand up for what he believed. My father thought it was the best thing I had written. White students told me it was scandalous, unpatriotic; I was mixing politics and sports. Black students said thanks.

We both read and discussed the *Autobiography of Malcolm X* that spring. My father had always disliked Malcolm X while he was alive, believing the press portrayals of him as a violent, white-hating man. The book was a revelation for both of us. Martin Luther King was still the sun, but Malcolm had become respectable. We were learning together.

In my last year at St. John's I was physically there but felt emotionally removed from it. I shared an apartment with Vincent Ferrandino, probably the most serious and, perhaps, the brightest student I knew at St. John's.

During this time I spent many evenings with Lloyd Dove. We had seen a good deal of each other that year. He was having a great season, leading St. John's to a 23–5 record and an NCAA bid. Lloyd was intelligent and sensitive. He was considered quiet and shy by most students, but this may have been because they were whites viewing a black man in an all-white environment. I had quite a few opportunities to be with him and his black friends, and among them he was a different man.

One evening Lloyd and I went to hear some jazz in Greenwich Village. It was 2:00 A.M. before we headed back to Long Island, and we were both a bit high. I asked him to stay over at my apartment. For twenty minutes he thought of every possible excuse not to. I asked what was really wrong. It was difficult for him to answer, but he finally blurted out that he had never slept at a white person's house before.

Lloyd Dove, sophisticated, intelligent, handsome, All-American Lloyd Dove had never spent the night at a white person's house and, when finally faced with the choice, was apprehensive. I cringed. During my four years at St. John's, I had spent some of my best moments with Dove—double-dating, drinking, listening to music, and sharing feelings. Looking back I think I would rather have been with him than anyone else on campus. Yet here was the bottom line—he was black and I was white. Because of that difference, Lloyd was apprehensive about staying with me.

As on previous occasions, my consciousness of being white swept over me. No matter how close we had become, Lloyd couldn't forget that I was white and, therefore, a possible racist. I am convinced that he didn't believe I was, but there was that hesitation—a self-protective internal mechanism telling black people not to trust white people, not to let the defenses down. I was stunned, and hurt, but in the silence that dominated the end of the ride, the world became more clear to me. That world saw this black man as a jock. As long as he remained a jock, it was color blind. Off court, whether at a white social gathering or at a protest supporting Joe Lapchick, he was invisible. Ralph Ellison, the author of *Invisible Man,* was right.

In the quiet of the car I decided that knowing, studying, and raising money for good causes was not enough. There was too much at stake. I didn't know *what* I would do or *how* I would do it, but I knew then that a major part of my life would be devoted to actively searching for ways to change society. My brother insisted that I was a naive dreamer. Although we were miles apart politically, I had to wonder if he was right.

Lloyd stayed at my apartment that night. We consumed a few more drinks and fell asleep in our clothes at about 8:00 A.M. Poor Vincent. I am sure he must have thought we had had a wild night when he found our bodies strewn about the living room in the morning.

I went home so I could discuss the previous evening with my father. He was sympathetic but not surprised. He mentioned a friend named Bob Douglas whom he knew from his days with the Celtics. They had shared a similar conversation in the late 1940s. Appraising my needs that night, he told me to study—to prepare myself for whatever path I would choose.

Joe and Elizabeth Lapchick had just faced a severe test. Both were Catholics—my mother was devout. Thus it was difficult for them in 1966 when my sister, Barbara, announced that she was divorcing Roy, her Jewish husband.

But the true test came when Barbara introduced her new husband-to-be, Rajat Neogy, a prominent Ugandan literary figure whose parents were Indian. I have known innumerable "liberals" who have balked at sexual relations between the races. For them, any form of integration was positive as long as that sexual boundary was not crossed.

As well as I knew my parents, I did not know how they would react. My father and I watched the sunrise as we talked about Barbara and Rajat. In 1966, such a relationship was virtually unheard of in polite middle-class white society. Then we reached the bottom line. He asked me if Barbara loved Rajat and if they were happy together. I said it seemed so. "Then that's all that should matter," he said. My mother had already given her blessing.

Bill Russell's book *Go Up for Glory* was published in 1966 as Russell's fabulous career with the Boston Celtics was in its final quarter. He would still help the Celtics win more championships, and he had already been a member of the Olympic team and participated in two NCAA championships as a collegian at the University of San Francisco. His Celtics teams won the NBA championships in nine of his first ten years and he was chosen the most valuable player four times by fellow players. He had done everything right in basketball. He should have been lionized.

He should have been—but Bill Russell was black, outspoken, and intimidating. *Go Up for Glory* was, perhaps, one of the first honest sports stories, and these were difficult times to be honest. Protest against the war was threatening all the "yes, sir" people in society, yet Russell criticized America's "yes, sir" mentality. Blacks were rioting in city after city. Respectable black leaders were supposed to calm the waters. Russell wrote about having to confront the conditions that had caused the riots. He wrote:

> The relationship between the white and the Negro is most often represented by the police—the symbol of authority . . . most Negroes look on the police as the white man with a badge, the symbol of the white man's authority. The policeman becomes a natural enemy. . . .
>
> But it is the people—the whites and the Negroes—who inhabit the battleground day after day and night after night who are the true warriors. Their voices must be heard.

Russell also tackled the sports empire. He told story after story of racism, of quotas in the NBA, of racist fans, players, and coaches. He even discussed the humiliating segregation of the U.S. team's domestic tour prior to the 1956 Games:

> It was a hurting thing. Not desperate. We were men. We had experienced it before. But . . . it was another scar, another slice.

We were representing our nation in the largest sports event in the world. But in our own country we were not equals as citizens.

My father and I both read Russell's book early in 1967, and when I had finished, I told him—for the first time—about listening on the upstairs phone when he was receiving the "nigger–lover" calls. I told him that I had been frightened for him; that I had been afraid to ask him for fear I would also hate him if I knew his terrible secret. I informed him of how many times I had been called a "nigger–lover" for befriending blacks. There was a spontaneous yet enormous emotional release. We both accepted the relief of relinquishing our shared secrets. No words passed between us. We understood each other's pain.

The publication of Russell's book was followed by a public outcry. Critics said that he was only able to write the book because of basketball; he was another ungrateful black man. Russell withstood the attack and grew stronger. But he was, in reality, protected by his dominance as a player. If K. C. Jones, for example, a black teammate of Russell's on the Celtics, had written that book he might never have played again. Russell was just too good; the NBA could not afford to dump him. Sports was supposed to be the great equalizer for blacks. Now it was being described as a racist reflection of a racist society.

My father, for the first time, began to open up about his own racial experiences in sport. The Tony Jackson case bothered him more than any other. He mentioned the early days in the NBA, and the signing of Clifton. But it was when he recalled the all-black "Renaissance Five" (commonly called the Rens) that I became most interested. All my life I had heard that the Original Celtics were the greatest team of all time. Now he told me that the Rens were as good as the Celtics by the early 1930s. What had happened to historical accuracy? This was new information for me.

My father admitted that he knew nothing about black people let alone black athletes prior to his contacts with the Rens. Raised in an immigrant family, he had all the apprehensions about competition from blacks shared by other immigrants early in the twentieth century.

The difference was that he was able to have years of contact with the Rens. They played against each other, traveled to the same cities, competed in front of crowds ready to attack these audacious barnstormers, and finally confronted the stereotypes that each held about the other. At first, the Rens couldn't fully trust the Celtics while the Celtics couldn't fully understand the Rens. Time changed that. However, time moved slowly.

All the Celtics knew was that the Rens could play them even, yet they saw the differences in lifestyle. The Rens traveled in a large bus purchased by Bob Douglas, their founder-owner, so that they could avoid confrontations in hotels, restaurants, trains, and public buses that wouldn't allow blacks. There were some towns where they couldn't be seen by day. They couldn't eat, wash, or even purchase gas in some places. When they could find hotels that would take them, they were usually bug-ridden. On the court they faced hostile white fans, yet they played the game straight and with dignity.

Joe Lapchick found it impossible to even share a drink with Douglas in some places. They integrated arenas in several cities, most notably by playing the first interracial game in the South, but they couldn't socialize together outside of New York and a very few other cities.

For years my father was oblivious to racial slights. He finally asked Bob Douglas about them in New York during the off-season. Douglas replied, "Joe, I can't go where you can go. I'm not going to subject myself to rejection and humiliation." They talked for hours that day and my father realized that previously, in spite of admiring the Rens for years, he had never really learned anything personal about them or about Douglas. It had shocked him that, perhaps subconsciously, he had chosen to ignore the racism around him. My father told me that the talk with Douglas was pivotal in his life—a life he vowed to change.

I had been accepted into a masters program in African Studies at the University of East Africa in Uganda. That is where I wanted to go, but I didn't want to leave the country for long because of my father's health. I chose instead to enroll at the graduate school of international studies at the University of Denver, where

I would major in African Studies. However, Barbara and her new husband invited me to come to Uganda at least for the summer. I hoped that visiting Barbara and studying even briefly at the University of East Africa would show me how to proceed with my life. It only showed me how much I had to learn.

This was Uganda prior to Amin. 1967 was a beautiful time to be there. Barbara ran the Nommo Art Gallery and Rajat was editor of *Transition,* an influential literary magazine. Both the gallery and the magazine were showplaces for talented Africans, so I was exposed to a wealth of African art and literature. Sitting in their house and listening to Rajat, Barbara, and their guests was a living classroom on Africa. Kampala was an intellectual capital and it seemed as though I met every important African writer and scholar that summer. They included Ali Magrui, the African scholar, and Paul Theroux, the well-known writer. It makes me ill to think of what Idi Amin did to this beautiful and rich land.

While I had countless extraordinary experiences, two above all have stayed with me. The first related to sports. I hadn't played basketball in two years yet I was drawn to a tucked-away court on the university campus. I was able to talk to the African students in the classroom but outside I was a social outcast. I was not only white, but a white American. Not only racist, but also colonialist. This wasn't a problem with Rajat's friends, but it was with the students. They had seen too many patronizing Westerners who wanted to "help the natives."

I watched the Africans play basketball, day after day in the melting sun. Bad as I was, I knew I was better than the players I was seeing. After all, I had trained for fifteen years while they were obviously newcomers. I had vowed to stay away from sports a few months before, but I was so frustrated by the alienation I was feeling on campus that I had to play. I hated being stereotyped.

What irony! Here I was almost on the equator in blazing heat. Now I was the white man trying to break into African society by playing basketball. It seemed ridiculous but I was desperate. It worked. We played together. We drank beer together. We talked sports and, here in Uganda, sports really did open a door, at least for me.

The second thing I brought home was the African students' perceptions of black Americans. Black pride was rising in urban American cities. Part of that pride was a cultural identification with Africa and Africans. I quickly learned that in June 1967 it was not a two-way flow. I was abruptly stopped the first time I naively referred to an African as "black." "We are not blacks, we are Africans. Blacks are Americans." I was surprised and taken aback. They did not identify with American blacks at all. In fact, the students criticized black Americans for allowing their oppression to continue. It seemed that they felt African independence movements could be analogous to a black revolution in the United States. I disagreed with their analysis just as I would disagree with Andrew Young ten years later when he tried to compare the civil rights movement in America with the struggle against apartheid in South Africa. I unsuccessfully tried to explain the difference in the situations. What was important was not that I disagreed but that this *was* their analysis.

Perceptions changed one July morning. "Black revolt in Detroit" was the headline in *The People,* a Ugandan newspaper. Racial outbursts, large and small, had spread through urban America in the middle sixties. But Detroit was the bloodiest—41 dead and 347 injured—and costliest in terms of property. There was $500 million worth of damage. Some 5,000 inner-city residents were homeless. But what was most meaningful for the African students was that there were 3,800 arrests.

They believed that this was the start of a black revolt, a black American independence movement. The first American magazines to reach Kampala called it a riot—spontaneous and unplanned. The students didn't believe it for a second. American blacks, they felt, were taking control of their destiny.

We spent much of that summer dissecting Detroit and its aftermath. What was nonviolence? When did a riot become a revolt? What was the future of revolt and what were its consequences? Whatever the nature of the conflict, it was apparent that, once again, violence in America was leading to social change. The men who ruled America could listen to Martin

Luther King, applaud and go to their white suburbs and forget. They could not ignore a Detroit and would rush to take prompt action to quell the riot/revolt. White Americans seemed seized by fear of a reign of terror; black Americans, to their African brothers, seemed equally seized by a vision.

I left Africa and arrived in Denver still searching for ways to participate, ways to contribute. I marched in all the antiwar demonstrations but knew there had to be more. I was away from St. John's, away from sports. The academic demands were enormous. I was reading five to seven books a week on subjects such as international economics, African studies, political ideologies. I met Sandy on my first day there. She was a graduate student in art, an apolitical woman and very different from my deadly serious, highly competitive, very political fellow students.

Professors began to give me direction. George Shepherd taught African studies; Ron Krieger trained us in international economics; Steve Hunter interpreted diplomatic history. All three were political activists in the antiwar and civil rights movements. They demonstrated that one could be an academic activist. That seemed to be what I should do—teach, work with my students to get them involved, and be an activist myself. All seemed to be settled by the third quarter. I was confident as a student and, for the first time in my life, had a concrete concept of what I would do. Additionally, Sandy and I decided to get married in June.

Then one April evening my confidence crumbled. Martin Luther King was assassinated in Memphis. I was all at once filled with sorrow, fear, and rage. I called home for comfort, but there was none. It was a weepy conversation. The apostle of nonviolence, armed only with moral courage, had met—inevitably, perhaps—violent death. As inner city after inner city erupted, I began to see that revolt just might be underway. I feared for the U.S. for I believed that sustained violent revolt by black America could lead to only one thing—massive retaliatory repression against blacks.

Mostly, I hated America—that is, white America. For King, the philosophy of nonviolence could only be effective if it pricked the conscience of a moral society. This society seemed to have no conscience and was not moral to this twenty-two-year-old. In Asia, we were killing Vietnamese by the thousands to save them from Communism. In Memphis, we had killed a black leader trying to make things better for his people. I wanted to get out. By midnight I decided I would leave the country and join Barbara and Rajat in Uganda. Then I realized that I could afford to go to Africa, get my degree there and work *because* I was white and had the money. Most blacks in Denver or New York cannot pack up and leave.

By 4:00 A.M., I decided to stay and fight. By eight in the morning I had written to Wilt Chamberlain, then playing for Philadelphia, LeRoy Ellis, who was playing for Baltimore, and a host of other professional basketball players whom I knew. I wrote to Jim Brown, the great football player and social activist. I wrote to Coretta King. The idea that I was proposing was to form an organization called PRIDE that would help to introduce black and African history and culture courses into the curricula of high schools around the country. While the time for the idea was ripe, I did not expect a serious response. Then Wilt and LeRoy endorsed the idea. Brown, through John Wooten, his associate, wanted to meet me in Cleveland. I began to see the potential linkup between sports and politics at close range. With the athletes' endorsements, I was able to get Walter Mondale, Jacob Javits, and Hugh Scott, then Senate minority leader, to join PRIDE's advisory board.

That year saw several other linkups between sports and politics. It had been announced in November 1967 that a number of black athletes would boycott the 1968 Mexico City Olympics to protest racism in American society. The efforts were being organized by Harry Edwards, a former athlete then teaching at San Jose State. Harry, along with Jack Scott, was to become one of the major shapers of the oncoming athletic revolt.

In February 1968, South Africa was readmitted to the Olympics when the International Olympic Committee (IOC) met in Grenoble, France. The reaction was instantaneous. All African nations except Malawi announced they would boycott. They were joined by most developing countries from Asia and some from Latin

America. The Socialist nations threatened to pull out. With the potential for racial violence already illustrated by the assassination of Martin Luther King and an attack on IOC President Avery Brundage's hotel in Chicago by blacks, the IOC voted South Africa out again in April.

In both cases, the media criticized the attempts to mix sports and politics. It gave extensive coverage to black athletes like Jesse Owens, who opposed the boycott, and to Brundage, who continued to insist that politics had no influence on the IOC's decision to bar South Africa.

I returned to New York at the end of May before the wedding. Most of the daily discussions were of what I would do in the future and about PRIDE. After my New York friends had a bachelor party for me I arrived at our house in Yonkers weary from too much to drink. Sandy called and said, "Did you hear? Robert Kennedy was shot last night in California." Suddenly sober, my body became rigid, my mind became numb. I couldn't believe it.

At the time I was an RFK supporter and thought he was our best hope for real change in America. We had recently met on his campaign stop in Cheyenne, Wyoming. We briefly discussed PRIDE, the concept of which had been endorsed by all the presidential candidates except Nixon. He told me how much he admired my father and wished me luck. I could still feel his firm, reassuring handshake.

My father had been keeping a vigil all night. For him RFK was the hope to end the war, to heal the cities, to bring peace to the world and to the country. It was too much to take. When would it all end?

I tried to postpone the wedding date. Not only was it scheduled for the night Kennedy was to be buried, but it was to be held in Rockville, Maryland, just outside Washington. Tent City and the Poor People's March were in Washington. Kennedy would be buried in Arlington. But Sandy's parents insisted that the wedding be held as planned, and I acquiesced.

I went to Cleveland to meet Mayor Stokes, Jim Brown, and John Wooten on Monday morning at the offices of the Negro Economic Union, which had been cofounded by Brown and

Wooten. But Stokes remained in Washington after Kennedy's funeral and Jim Brown was in Los Angeles. So Wooten and I met to talk about what the Negro Economic Union was doing and what PRIDE hoped to do. We felt that Cleveland might become a test city for the introduction of black history and culture courses in the schools.

Aside from the business aspects of the meeting, I left with a real understanding of the faith of a large part of the black community in the Kennedys. John Wooten, a serious, astute man, talked about looking forward to the Kennedy children growing up and entering politics. In 1968, it seemed like a long time for the black community to have to wait. The black community is still waiting.

Whether it was inspired by or fearfully reacting to the potential of a black Olympic boycott, *Sports Illustrated* published a five-part series by Jack Olsen called "The Black Athlete: A Shameful Story" in July (discussed in detail in Chapter 13). It was the first investigative report I had read on how pervasive racism was in professional and intercollegiate athletics. It confirmed all that I had come to believe about the nature of sports in America, and seemed to add fuel to the controversy about any black role in the Olympics.

Lew Alcindor, along with UCLA teammates Mike Warren and Lucius Allen, had already boycotted the Olympic basketball trials. Up to that point I had not known what to think about the idea of a boycott. However, I respected Lew's judgment enough that I began to support the idea. My father strongly disagreed with me on this, although paradoxically he respected Lew Alcindor more than ever for his decision. He knew it was a decision based on principle and my father thought Lew had made a courageous personal sacrifice.

I watched part of the Olympic Games with my father in New York. Any illusions I had had about the Olympics had been destroyed a long time ago. The pre-Olympic "ceremonies" in Mexico City included a three-day student riot in which thirteen were killed and hundreds more injured. Striking students claimed that the incredibly high cost of staging the games was a national disgrace.

While the boycott itself had been called off, everyone knew
something would happen. The goals of a total boycott were
expressed in the simple gesture of two young black men. When
Tommie Smith and John Carlos raised their clenched, black-
gloved fists on the victory stand, they eloquently expressed what
white America had tried to ignore: sport, like society, was racist.

The importance of that gesture became evident in the ensuing
reaction. White society was quick to punish Smith and Carlos
immediately in Mexico and for many years after as both became
unemployable. The sports establishment, from Avery Brundage
on down, did everything it could to pretend nothing had changed.
In response to a question about how the Olympics could survive
as long as politics continued to become more and more a part of
the games, Brundage replied, "Who said that politics are becoming more and more involved in the Olympics? In my opinion this
is not so. You know very well that politics are not allowed in the
Olympic Games."

However, that memory of Smith and Carlos on the victory
stand would not go away. It became *the* Olympic picture. Everything had changed. Black athletes were vigorously speaking out.
And my father, initially spurred on by Bill Russell's writings,
resumed telling me of the forms of hate he had encountered in
sports because of his racial views.

Suddenly horror visited our own family. We got the news that
my sister's husband, Rajat Neogy, had been sent to Luzira Prison
in Uganda. The date was October 18, two days after the Smith-
Carlos raised fist salute. We could no longer think about the
Olympics, the Rens-Celtics saga, or about the integration of the
NBA.

Rajat had been charged with sedition. The charge stemmed
from his printing a letter to the editor in *Transition,* the magazine
he edited, that said that Uganda should Africanize the courts,
that is, the judges should be Africans. The trauma lasted for five
months.

The case was clearly racial and political. Rajat was an Asian
Ugandan. By 1968, Asians had become scapegoats for all the ills
of Ugandan society. The trial became an anti-Asian showpiece
and, in the process, Rajat had his Ugandan citizenship revoked.

When the jury handed down its verdict, Rajat was ruled innocent. But the mental anguish for my sister continued when he was rearrested at the conclusion of the trial. Knowing that all mail would be opened, she sent a letter back to us with friends. Her baby's nursemaid had turned out to be a police informer. Now Barbara was unable to sleep because each night she listened for the nursemaid's steps that signaled the arrival of the police car to collect the day's information. Joe Lapchick, who said he died a thousand deaths in defeat, was dying once more through the suffering of his daughter. My mother and father drew very close together during this period. The weight of the horror was finally lifted when Rajat was released in the spring of 1969. He and Barbara rushed to leave Kampala and all they had there before President Obote could change his mind and rearrest him. It was over for all but Barbara and Rajat, who had yet to work out their private nightmares and inner fears. More than twenty years later, Rajat still has deep scars.

*   *   *

The events of the previous four years had a tremendous impact on my father. Joe Lapchick had been known as a man who shaped the destinies of others. He had tried to instill pride in being self-disciplined and honest, and pride in being able to accept victory and defeat in the same way.

The press described him as a humble and self-effacing man. An event in the last full summer of his life underscored this. The Maurice Stokes NBA All-Star benefit game was being held at Kutscher's Country Club.

There were mobs outside the arena when my father arrived. At six-five his head was way above the crowd. No one else in line was connected to the game. He could have signaled Kutscher's employees at the gate, said "excuse me," and gone right through. In spite of wanting to see Lew play against Wilt, he refused to use his influence to go ahead of those who had arrived before him. If you didn't know him, this almost seemed absurd. The first great big man of basketball refused to use his fifty-year-old reputation to obtain a seat to see two of the greatest big men square off. As my father told a reporter that night, "It wouldn't have been right. These people have come a long way to see the game and if I had forced my way in, one of them would have been turned away." He never saw the game.

I spent two weeks at home during the 1969 Christmas holidays. The events of the 1960s were forcing my father to look at the dark side of his life; to acknowledge to himself the cumulative effect of the series of racial incidents he had encountered in sports. In the course of our conversations, it became even clearer that his lifelong friendship with Bob Douglas had been pivotal for what my father did in race and sport. I hated for that Christmas vacation to end. As much as I thought I knew my father, I was learning more and more. I was about to move to Washington where I was to do research for my Ph.D. thesis on the racial factor in American foreign policy. Being so close to New York, I felt I would continue to learn more about him.

Back in Denver to prepare for the move, I met Dennis Brutus at a reception in his honor. Dennis, as I've already said, had suffered for years because of his efforts to end racism in sport and apartheid in South Africa. This meeting took place less than a week after I left my father. Dennis and I talked nonstop for four hours, finally finishing at 3:00 A.M. Race and sport—I couldn't get it out of my mind. I decided to submit a new dissertation proposal, this one on the politics of race and international sport. I never went to sleep that weekend and finished the new proposal early Monday morning.

The proposal was approved and we canceled our plans to go to Washington. Three weeks later I was in London where I did the bulk of my research. By the time I returned to begin teaching at Virginia Wesleyan College, my research had shown to me that racism and politics in sport were not products of American society but were global in scope.

My mother came to visit in Virginia on August 4, 1970. She was unpacking when we received a phone call from Monticello, where my father worked at Kutscher's. He had had a heart attack while playing golf. The doctor said we should come right away. We drove straight through the night, arriving at 6:30 A.M.

My father was in the intensive-care unit. My mother went in first. Because of the rules, I had to wait one hour before I saw him. His spirits were good but you could see that his body had taken a terrible beating. We joked with a nurse about allowing our dog, Blivit, my father's constant companion, into the room to sleep under the bed. He complained that we had driven there "for nothing." He repeated this when my brother Joe arrived. But he lit up with a broad grin when told that my sister was flying in from Greece, where she and Rajat had been living since fleeing Uganda.

My father seemed to be doing better and there was hope. I was at the hospital most of the day. He was talking about going home. He couldn't wait to see Barbara. She was due in Monticello at about 8:30 that night and he asked that she wait until the next morning to see him.

Suddenly I heard a commotion in the corridor. The door swung open, and the intensive-care unit took on a cocktail party atmosphere. Five or six people entered. One man talked to a nurse on duty. I was incredulous. She looked at me and shrugged her shoulders as if to say "What can I do?" The people, one of whom was carrying a small dog, stood around my father. The man introduced himself as one of the principal owners of the hospital. He said how proud they were that Joe Lapchick was with them and that they wanted a photograph with him. They got it.

Joe Lapchick, a man who sought privacy but was denied it throughout his life because of his fame in sports, was even to be denied it now. Late that night, he took a turn for the worse. By 7:45 A.M. on Monday he was dead.

We were called at 7:15 about his condition. My sister and I rushed to the hospital at 7:30 in the hope of snatching one final moment, one last touch that would have to last a lifetime. We rushed into the intensive-care unit to see his body wrenched across the table with his legs dangling off one end and each arm floating over a different side of the table. His face was frozen in pain. Barbara, who had traveled thousands of miles, kissed him tenderly.

I met with his attending physician in the corridor. He told me they did everything they could, that he was sorry, and then tried to explain the mass visit on Sunday.

They were bracing for a lawsuit. But this was Joe Lapchick,

the man who had fought battles for others. Our family would never have allowed the last moment of his life to precipitate a legal battle. He would have been very unhappy.

His death was widely covered by the media. We would go home late at night to see clips of him speaking on the news. We couldn't let go. He was still with us. Hundreds of friends came to the wake in Yonkers. St. Denis's Church was jammed for the funeral. Television crews were there. The stories kept coming. All emphasized my father's qualities as a human being and the contribution he had made to basketball and to his community.

On the last night of the wake I noticed several black men staring at the drawing of my father above the closed casket. The same men were seated together at the funeral and stood together at the burial. I walked over to introduce myself and to find out who they were. The first man I went up to said, "I'm an old friend of Joe's. My name is Bob Douglas." They were the remaining members of the Renaissance team. I was deeply touched. Mr. Douglas took me in his arms.

Part Four

Teamwork: The Rens and the Original Celtics

Chapter 12

Caged Superstars

When men commence to make money out of sport, it degenerates with more tremendous speed and inevitably results in men of lower character going into the game.

Dr. Luther Gulick, 1898

As the new century dawned, America discovered a new diversion. It was conceived by James Naismith, who had been hired by Dr. Gulick to invent an indoor winter sport for the Young Men's Christian Association (YMCA). It was not meant to be a sport for the masses but a genteel sport by which the Y-types could keep physically and morally fit during the frigid winter months. It would keep the young men busy with a civilized outlet for their excess energy, teach discipline, and above all, strengthen the YMCA's ability to mold them into the upright Christian image that was to be imbued and projected among the elite.

But basketball was also being played on the streets, especially in immigrant communities. There it became a contact sport, which it has remained until today, despite denials that this is the case. In 1894, the YMCA published a series in its *New Era* magazine entitled "Is Basketball a Danger?" It pointed out problem areas such as increased jealousies and rivalries, the loss of interest in class work, rowdyism among spectators, and, finally, rivalries caused by unfair officiating. Four years later, before it could reach its international network, basketball was thrown out of the YMCA. Men of conscience like Gulick gave up, as boys of "lower character" took up the game.

Compared to today's sport, basketball as played in its infant days in the Y was very crude, with peach baskets serving as the nets, irregular floors, and balls that sometimes bounced and sometimes didn't. But compared to street basketball, playing in the Y was pure luxury.

Never dreaming that it would become a fifty-year professional career, Joe Lapchick played street basketball in the Hollow in Yonkers, New York. "Teams" consisted of as many of the children from the Czech community as would be on the streets and want to play. A street team could have three to ten boys on it without anyone caring. Naismith's "Rules for Basketball," published in 1892, said, "The only limit to the number of men that can play is the space. If a great number of men wish to play at once, two balls may be used at the same time, and thus the fun is augmented though some of the science may be lost. . . . As many as fifty on a side have been accommodated." Rules about numbers were confusing anyway, as basketball was officially being played with seven, then nine, then eight to a team.

Discarded soccer balls were always prize finds, as they were stuffed into a cap and used as a basketball. Baskets were another matter. Usually, throwing the ball onto the roof of a shed was a goal. At a young age, strength to reach the roof and not accuracy was the key.

When they were ready, young boys joined the bigger boys in weaving around moving ice wagons. Passes had to go under the bellies of the horses. Tossing the ball between the legs of the walking horses was a score. Wagon operators were very angry at the games, as the children frequently startled and upset the horses. It gave operators great pleasure to see the children slip on the "gifts" left behind by the horses. Frances Lapchick could never understand why her son smelled so bad until she happened by a "game" one afternoon. There was no supper that night for young Joe, who didn't want his father to know that he spent his time playing instead of working to supplement the family's meager income. There were four sisters—Anne, Emily, Frances, and Florence—in addition to brothers Ed and Bill. As the eldest child, Joe was expected to help with the family's finances. Although life had gotten better for the family when the elder Joe Lapchick became a trolley motorman (after careers as a coal miner and hat finisher), they were still poor by any objective standards.

Young Joe opted for bed that night, but was back on the streets the next afternoon. He made a deal with a friend who agreed to keep a separate set of playing clothes at his apartment. Joe never had the tell-tale odor and Frances thought he had reformed. This arrangement worked well until the day when Joe went to his friend's house and discovered that his mother had found Joe's clothes and burned them. Playing on the streets was over, but it didn't matter. At twelve, Joe was 6 feet 3 inches tall and weighed 140 pounds and was playing indoors for the Trinity Midgets and Public School Twenty.

The philosophy of the so-called sports reformers underwent a dramatic change. Men like Dr. Gulick, who tried to freeze out immigrant children at the YMCA, now became advocates of bringing them in. As the American industrial machine grew and capitalism adjusted to the changes, it became obvious that immigrants and their children would be valuable as crucial labor cogs in the industrial wheel. Team play would yield a cooperative spirit, loyalty, self-discipline, self-sacrifice and group control. Gulick himself became a leader of the Playground Association of America and helped found the Public Schools Athletic League in 1903. Cary Goodman, in his book *Choosing Sides,* argues convincingly that the organized play movement which began during this time was designed to acculturate immigrant children to American capitalist ideas. The playgrounds, settlement houses and forms of supervised recreation were to be training grounds for the inculcation of the American dream and the American spirit.

For young Joe Lapchick that dream was close enough to touch. He had been a caddy on a golf course every weekend since he was nine. One advantage of being so tall was that he could pass for the requisite twelve years of age for caddies when he was only nine. He carried bags for many top golfers, for Christy Mathewson, Fred Merkle of the New York Giants, sportswriter Grantland Rice, and entertainment personalities such as Al Jolson and Douglas Fairbanks, Sr. At dusk each Saturday and Sunday he himself would play. He was also learning to play baseball and was the water boy for the top local baseball team. He was convinced that his dream would be realized by playing either baseball or golf. Meeting these celebrities and seeing their wealth fired that dream. He could taste it. He would do anything to realize it. All he wanted was success.

In 1914 Joe had to leave school after the eighth grade. He went to work for the Ward Leonard Electric Company in Bronxville, New York, making 15 cents an hour for a 10-hour day. He played sports each night and on weekends.

Beginning in 1915, Joe used to hang out at Lou Gordon's sports shop in Yonkers. He listened intently to all the stories of the athletes so he could pick up pointers. Gordon, noting his size and interest, sent Joe to see Jimmy Lee, who managed the Hollywood Inn basketball team. The Inn was a private athletic club for affluent businessmen. It sponsored a team which was made up of former high school stars. Lapchick recalled the times:

> I shall never forget the afternoon that I entered the sporting goods shop. I had never thought of it before but the suggestion stuck and I went down and tried out. Even then I was 6 feet 3 inches tall. I was skinny as a rail and quickly proved I was the greatest floor man ever to be in the game. I did this by remaining most of the time flat on my backside.
>
> I got broken up a good deal. Arms and ankles were cracked and dislocated, and for a season or two I was quite miserable. But finally I began to catch on to the tricks and was able to take care of myself. In those days, brute strength and the ability to take it and dish it out were the chief requisites.
>
> Players then were admitted roughnecks. If a man began to show too prominently in a game, his opponents ganged up on him and tried literally to break him in two, frequently with considerable success.
>
> I have had as many as a half dozen jerseys torn off me in one game, and I remember one night when three opposing players picked me up and threw me into the fifth row of chairs.

There were no coaches or training as we know them today, so Joe began his own training program to improve his coordination. He would go behind the Alexander Smith carpet mills at night. He ran and ran, forwards and backwards, practicing starts and stops, directional changes, and pivots. It began to pay off when he joined the professional Bantams, who played in the Hudson Valley. He was paid $5 per game minus expenses. "I netted the grand total of $15 the first year and $18 the second year."

However, this wasn't so bad during the war years, as money and everything else was scarce while Americans went to war to make the world safe for democracy. But it was only a white world which had secured that safety. Blacks fought in the war in large numbers with distinction. But when they returned home there was great disappointment and the realization that life had gotten worse for them instead of better.

The Klan, playing on the knowledge that there wouldn't be enough jobs for all returning soldiers, stood up for jobs for the white soldiers. Within a year after the war ended, membership in the Klan had increased from several thousand to one hundred thousand. It operated in the North and Midwest and spread its particular brand of terror as never before. There were seventy lynchings in that year. Ten returning soldiers were murdered. Eleven blacks were publicly burned alive before the eyes of men, women and children. In the summer of 1919, there were twenty-five race riots. But the mood had changed; the riots were characterized by blacks rebelling against whites, not whites attacking blacks. Blacks resisted and showed new self-respect and determination. They had a sense of togetherness and unity in the urban communities which was little known in the rural South.

Whites were also disillusioned. Wilsonian idealism had lost much of its appeal after the war. The public was in the mood for withdrawal. In foreign policy this meant isolationism. At home, it meant perhaps the first term of "benign neglect." Warren Harding was elected president on the basis of his call for a "Return to Normalcy." This meant refueling the industrial engine, consequently pitting blacks against immigrants in the competition for industrial jobs, increasing racism. There were two things that weren't so normal. First, many blacks were now proud and resistant. Second, the economy became so hot that even the poorest people seemed to be doing better. The masses became absorbed in the pursuit of prosperity and wealth. Immigrants and blacks alike felt they were doing better. Left alone, life was just fine.

It was in this context that professional basketball took off. It was a place where the public could seek escape. Pro players became relatively rich men. Between 1918 and 1922, Joe Lapchick, the man who had earned a total of $33 in the previous two years, was making $75 to $100 per game. He was playing on four teams in four leagues at the same time: the Visitations in the Metropolitan League, Holyoke in the Western Massachusetts League, Schenectedy in the New York State League and Mt. Vernon in the Interborough League. Needless to say, he couldn't play in all the games of each team, so he, like other rising stars, put himself up on the bidding block. Whoever came up with the highest bid won the services of young Joe Lapchick for the night. By playing owners off against each other, he successfully increased his market value from $5 a game in 1916 to twenty times that in 1918. With no income tax, Joe Lapchick was rich for an immigrant boy. Not only could he touch that American dream, he almost owned it now.

Players of the same class would gather in New York's Grand Central Station. Honey Russell, Elmer Ripley, Dave Wassmer and others met there to discuss which team they should play for that night. The owner's agents would likely be there to bid. Then they would board the train for Schenectedy, Holyoke or wherever.

The men also discussed the game, but never in terms of who won or lost. The question was "How did you do last night?" It was a triumph if you personally scored more points than your opponent; otherwise, it was a defeat. Obviously there was no room for team loyalty in such a system. Winning was a personal victory not to be shared.

Bill Hoffman, a sports columnist for the *Yonkers Herald Statesman*, described Joe at the time: "What a basketball player—and what a 'brute.' The feminine trade will just adore him." Sports groupies did not just appear with Joe Namath; there were always women around for the sports celebrities. This became especially true for Joe Lapchick after he bought a big car. It was a time for heads to swell. He would cockily drive to an arena with his date, get out and throw his equipment bag in the air. Whichever kid caught it entered the arena with Joe and carried his bag. It was a great break for the kid who would both meet a star and save the fifty cents admission price.

While Joe was playing for some good teams, Schenectedy was not the Original Celtics. And Joe Lapchick was not Horse Haggerty. Horse was the burly, aggressive center for the Celtics, who began to remind Joe of his more humble origins. Lapchick said Haggerty would beat opposing centers down with his bruising play: "It would take me two weeks to recover after playing against Horse."

The Celtics were founded in 1912 by Frank "Tip" McCormack to play for the Hudson Guild Settlement House on New York's West Side. The Settlement House, like others around the city, was doing its part in the organized play movement in getting kids off the streets. McCormack organized the Celtics to play on what was known as the "dance hall circuit." Promoters knew they couldn't draw enough fans just to see a ball game, so dances were held before and after the games to attract more people. In 1916 they transcended the neighborhood and became the New York Celtics. McCormack went off to fight in the war and returned to find that Jim Furey had taken over the team, along with its name and several of the original players. When the team became professional in 1918, only Pete Barry and John Witte were left from the first Celtic team. Hart, Goggin, Mally, Calhoun and the McCormack brothers were gone. When Frank McCormack sued Furey over the use of the team's name, Furey agreed to call his team the "Original Celtics."

The team played at the Central Opera House and later at the 71st Regiment Armory on Park Avenue and 34th Street. In 1920, Furey signed Johnny Beckman and Dutch Denhert. With Beckman, Denhert, Barry, Haggerty and Witte, they were a formidable team. Beckman was a real fighter on the court. He was a leader and was considered by many to be one of the best scorers in Manhattan. Denhert was solidly built and would become one of the game's first innovators; he invented and then perfected the pivot play. Pete Barry, a member of the first Celtics team, was its master strategist. He was credited with being the smartest player on the court and was one of the finest rebounders in the game, although he was only 5 feet 11 inches tall. Haggerty was the enforcer. He was so strong and tough that no one wanted to mess with him. Witte was the "coach," a term used loosely at the time. The coach's main job was to get the players out of the bars in time for the game.

By 1921, the only real rival was Tex Rickard's Whirlwinds, who played in Madison Square Garden. A three-game series with the Celtics was set up. The Whirlwinds, whose stars were Nat Holman and Chris Leonard, easily won the opener 40–27. The Celtics won the second game 26–24. The rubber match was canceled because the promoters claimed they feared violence from the fans. It was more likely that they were hyping the fans for a bigger payoff in 1922. It was not to remain a rivalry, however, because Furey signed Holman and Leonard to play for the Celtics. Holman, from an East Side tenement, was later to be considered perhaps the greatest player in the 1920s. He could shoot the eyes out of the basket, especially from the outside. He averaged nearly ten points a game for the Celtics—a figure almost unheard of in that period. While playing, he earned a physical education degree from Savage Institute and then coached at City College of New York.

In 1922, Furey revolutionized the game by signing players to exclusive one-team contracts for guaranteed salaries. This allowed a stability that never existed in pro basketball. It created the first real "basketball team" in that sense.

In 1922 the Celtics lost two of three games to the South Philadelphia Hebrew Association team, also called the "Wandering Jews." Their star was Davey Banks, who Furey then signed to play for the Celtics. Banks, only 5 feet 7 inches tall, became the fastest member of the team, and was also a great shooter.

Joe Lapchick began to outplay Haggerty, although Horse still won the physical battles. He punished Lapchick more with each game as he saw what was the inevitable end. Furey signed Lapchick in 1923 and he replaced Haggerty.

He didn't fit in right away: "I was only a beginner in the type of game the Celtics played. I was frustrated because of my ineptness, and the resulting anger which shot through me every time I made a mistake was no help. I had been bred to the theory of individualism, whereas the Celtics were devoted to a team effort."

But it was only a matter of time. In those days there was a center jump after each basket. At 6 feet 5 inches tall, Joe Lapchick nearly always got the Celtics the ball.

By the time he learned what he had to, no one could beat the Celtics. Joe Lapchick had realized his dream and reached the top of his world. He earned $10,000 the first year and $12,000 soon thereafter, making him, along with Nat Holman, the highest paid player in the land.

It sounds unbelievable today, but in his first year (1922–23) the Celtics record was 193–11. In the next year, it was 204–11. In 1924–25, they traveled 150,000 miles and were 134–6. In 1925–26 they won 122 and lost only 7 times. They were playing everywhere east of the Rocky Mountains, drawing huge crowds. Ten thousand people jammed Madison Square Garden and an incredible twenty-four thousand came to a day/night double header in Cleveland on February 22, 1924.

The greatest money was to be made as a touring team like the Celtics. But by 1925–26, the owners in the new American Baskeball League refused to play against the Celtics, forcing them to join the league in the 1926–27 season and to cut back their touring. They won the "world championship" in the next two years while compiling a 236–15 record. Bringing the team into the league backfired on the owners, as fans lost interest because the Celtics dominated the league. The Celtics were about to be dissolved.

The Celtics did not know the world north of Central Park. Harlem was swelling with blacks who had been migrating from the South for several decades. Racial tensions increased after the war as city after city experienced riots. Those white residents of Harlem who were still there left soon after the war as Harlem became America's black capital city. The black press discussed racial injustices, called for change and served to unify blacks in

Harlem. It was like a magnet for black writers, musicians and actors. The spirit of black defiance that was growing in the post-war era was being reflected in the emergence of new literature. A fresh, clear vision of social, economic and political freedom was being expressed through culture.

The Harlem Renaissance was under way. Black theater thrived. There were musical reviews and serious music as well. But it was the writers who had the greatest impact. Claude McKay, one of the many Jamaicans who had come from the West Indies to New York, was the Harlem Renaissance's first great writer. Countee Cullen and Langston Hughes followed. The Twenties were a period of high black culture.

To be sure there were blacks who were not so defiant and willing to give the white man what he wanted. One of Harlem's most famous night spots was the Cotton Club which catered to an exclusively white clientele. There, black art was tailored for white taste and therefore seriously compromised. It was near the Cotton Club that the Renaissance Casino Ballroom opened in 1922.

Bob Douglas was born in Jamaica in 1882. He arrived in the United States four years later. Douglas labored as a courier and porter for almost a quarter of a century in New York, but his love was always basketball. He was thrilled by the rise in popularity of the sport and dreamed of having his own team. Just as Joe Lapchick didn't know where his dream would lead him as a young boy, Bob Douglas couldn't have known that the opening of the Renaissance Casino Ballroom would start him on his way and that once begun, his team would join the Celtics as one of the only teams to be inducted into the Basketball Hall of Fame.

Douglas was in contact with some of the better black players in the New York area. However, while everyone bid for the Celtics and the better white teams, Douglas knew the extent to which racism in America would limit his chances of success. He needed a place to call home court. The opening of the Ballroom cracked the door. He became manager of the Renaissance Casino Ballroom and started a team in 1922. Douglas named them the "Rens" after the Renaissance Casino. Like the white teams of the era, they played on the dance floor. The team did well against weak competition in the early years. The money was coming in and Douglas signed James "Pappy" Ricks in the 1925–26 season. Ricks was a great shooter and the Ballroom filled up more and more after his arrival. Clarence "Fat" Jenkins and Eyre "Bruiser" Saitch joined Ricks. Jenkins stood only 5 feet 6½ inches tall. Like Davey Banks of the Celtics, Jenkins looked like a midget when standing next to his teammates. However, Jenkins was the team leader and captain. Douglas gave him control of the offense. Saitch added size at 6 feet 1 inch and was very agile on the court. Saitch was also one of the first black tennis stars and twice won the National Negro Tennis Championship.

With these three stars, the 1925–26 season marked a turning point. Unofficial records show that the team won 81 games while losing only 17. Word of the Rens began to spread. Promoters suspected that confrontations of white and black teams would draw crowds. They were right, and the Rens began to play the white teams and win consistently. They continued to prove their artistic value as well as their financial value over the next two seasons when they went 84–19 and 111–20. They were playing regularly against the Celtics and caught the attention of the sports world by splitting a six-game series with the world champions in 1926–27. They would not match them this well again for several years, but they had made a point. The press called them the "Colored World Champions."

The Celtics found themselves without a financial backer. In a column he wrote for the *Yonkers Herald Statesman,* Joe Lapchick said,

> There was no backer or money man. On the first page they (fans) may have noted the demise of one James Bugs Donovan, who was shot full of lead on the west side of New York due to his operation in the beer business. He had quarreled with his erstwhile partner and was an obituary figure within two weeks.
>
> Bugs Donovan was the owner of the Celtics though the Celtics supposed their owner was a man interested in real estate. We attended the wake and our boss's body was a mess—they must have used old fashion cannon-balls on him.

It should be noted that prior to Donovan, the Celtics "owner" was a department store cashier. The Celtics sometimes had to go to the store to collect late payments. They were having too good a time to wonder where the money was coming from until they read that the cashier was indicted for embezzling $190,000. The Celtics then suspected that some of this was their money, but it was too late.

In 1927, league owners, who originally boycotted the Celtics to force them to join the league, now plotted to get rid of them. Fans were losing interest as other teams simply couldn't compete with the Celtics. The owners tried everything to subvert the Celtics. Pete Barry was told that a family member had a serious illness, so he went home and missed a game. Johnny Beckman disappeared before one game; he had been a temporary kidnap victim. Davey Banks was not admitted to the arena one night. Nothing worked, and the team continued to win. The owners decided to break up the team.

The owners understood the importance of ethnicity to the fans. Thus, Nat Holman and Davey Banks, the two Jewish stars, were given to the New York Hakoahs. It seems ironic that the game which today has become a black-dominated sport at the highest levels was so successfully played and sometimes dominated by Jewish players in the Twenties, Thirties and Forties. Stereotypes prevailed. Ed Sullivan, later to be a great TV star, wrote in his column, "Sports Whirl": "Holman, Jewish star of the Celtics, is a marvelous player . . . Jewish players seem to take naturally to the game. Perhaps this is because the Jew is a natural gambler and will take chances. Perhaps it is because he devotes himself more closely to a problem than others will." Davey Banks was known as "the Rabbi" according to writer Lank Leonard in his column entitled "Tall Pole and Little Jew Shine Brilliantly for New York Celtics." The "tall Pole" was Lapchick, who was Czech.

Lapchick, Denhert and Barry went to the Cleveland Rosenblums. In effect, they became the "Rosenblum-Celtics" after they won the league championship in 1928–29 and 1929–30. The Celtics would regroup and barnstorm the country after the season ended. The high-living style continued unabated since the team made the same salaries as when they played in New York. The Celtics traveled first class in Pullman cars on the train, stayed in the best hotels, and ate at the best restaurants. The camaraderie and fellowship was remarkable. They really were a family that nurtured and protected each other.

Bob Douglas continued to expand his family and the Rens became more and more successful. The pieces continued to fit together. In 1929 Douglas got his big man for the center jump. Charles "Tarzan" Cooper, 6 feet 3 inches tall and 220 pounds, was brought to New York via the Philadelphia Colored Giants. Cooper was born in Newark, Delaware in 1907. He went from a Philadelphia high school to the Panther Pros in 1925, and then played for three years with the Giants. Joe Lapchick, whom the white press acknowledged as the greatest center of his time, said that there was no doubt that Cooper was the best by the early 1930s. John "Casey" Holt and Bill Yancey, a star in the Negro Baseball league, also joined the Rens. Against stiffer competition, they went 120–20 in the first year that the six played together.

While the Rens were making almost as much money as the Celtic players, their lifestyle was a reflection of the racial realities. Their tremendous financial success inspired promoter Abe Saperstein to found the Harlem Globetrotters, the "clown princes of basketball." In an interview in *Sports Illustrated* just before his death in 1979 at age ninety-six, Douglas said, "Abe Saperstein died a millionaire because he gave the white people what they wanted. When I go, it will be without a dime in my pocket, but with a clear conscience. I would never have burlesqued basketball. I loved it too much for that."

For Joe Lapchick, the early games against the Rens were life and death struggles on the court. Much more importantly, he experienced the consequences of racism for the first time. In spite of the radically different lifestyles off the court, the Celtics and Rens built a shared brotherhood on the courts. As the two best teams in the country, everyone was out to get them. The players today would barely recognize the game.

Games were usually played in dance halls so crowds could be increased by the lure of dancing before and after the games. To accommodate this, the floors were highly waxed. It was very difficult to run without slipping on such courts, so both the Celtics and Rens developed a passing game that became their trademark.

Bounce passes were discouraged because the balls used were so inconsistent; they were just bladders covered by leather. You never knew which way the balls would bounce or if they would bounce at all.

The name "cage" or "net" game originated when many courts were surrounded by a rope or wire "net" or "cage." The intention was to keep the ball in play as there were no out-of-bounds lines. However, the nets were often used to pin the ball and the opponents.

Sometimes games were played in church basements. There would be pot-bellied stoves at one end. Players had to be careful not to get burned on the stove. There were often posts in the floor of the court in such basements. Running opponents into these concrete "picks" was the origin of the term "post play." Inexperienced players were often victims of the play and incurred serious injuries.

Injuries were especially common early in the season as there was no such thing as a training camp. You had to play your way into shape. Old timers claim that today's players pamper their injuries. While this is surely a disputable point, one has to understand how rough the sport was and how old timers had to keep on playing despite injuries if they were to make a living. Elmer Ripley once knocked out Joe Lapchick. Although he had a deep gash on his left forehead, stitches allowed Joe to play. Two weeks later, an elbow opened up a large gash over his right eye. He played for six straight nights, getting new stitches after each game to replace those that were knocked out. On the seventh night another elbow fractured two ribs. He never stopped playing. Lapchick wrote, "If you complained about anything, you were gutless."

Beckman was the Celtics "doctor." His prescriptions were based primarily on the theory of "survival of the fittest." If you were strong you survived. If you were weak, you could be crushed. If you admitted to a weakness, you became weak.

One night Lapchick's arm became painfully swollen. He could barely raise it and went to see the doctor: "Becky, I don't think I can play tonight." Beckman gave Lapchick his famous guilt-producing stare and said, "What's the matter, no guts, you yellow-livered louse? Who do you think is going to get the tap for us? Since when does a basketball player run on his arms?''

Lapchick played and ruptured a blood vessel. The arm became black and blue from the shoulder to the wrist. Beckman told Lapchick not to play and to see a real doctor. Lapchick replied, ''To hell with you, I'll play.''

On another occasion, Lapchick's arm became badly infected by scratches. Beckman placed a steaming hot towel on his arm, soaked it, pulled off the scabs, and poured a bottle of whiskey over the open wounds. Lapchick played the next night with an arm that was green and with pain such as he had never experienced before. Many years later he described this to a real doctor who, slightly horrified, told him it was a miracle that he didn't get gangrene and lose his arm.

The basketball players' uniforms helped prepare them for the battle. They wore padded pants, knee guards and elbow guards. They wore sweaters not only to warm up but to stay warm; most arenas were not heated. As a testament to the importance of the Celtics and Rens, the Rome, Georgia, *News Tribune* announced that the gym would be heated for them—a rare occasion. Uniforms were worn game after game. The only light they would see was during game time. Ultimately, they were to be discarded and replaced—never washed. This unsanitary practice, combined with the cheap green dye used in the uniforms, was a frequent cause of infections for the players. Basketball shoes were of such poor quality that they frequently wore out during a game.

Officials were not highly thought of by either the Celtics or the Rens. They frequently took the side of the local team. Lapchick said:

> The umpire at that time was a joke. No one, least of all the players, paid the slightest attention to him. If he tried to assert his authority in any way, the players would curse him out; and if he still proved officious, they'd run into him and knock him flat.

Horse Haggerty once got so angry at a local referee that he knocked him out. After the game, Haggerty was attacked and beaten by a local gang. That taught the Celtics never to move alone.

The fans also went after the referees. Between spectators and players, the ref's white shirt would sometimes be covered with blood by the end of a game. Police protection for the ref was often provided. A referee named Chuck Solodare had his neck broken during a game and was hospitalized for nineteen weeks.

The problem of refs and fans was different for the Rens. Eric Illidge, the road secretary of the Rens, told *Sports Illustrated,* "In all those years, the referees gave us nothing. Sometimes we had to fight just to stay alive." In a game with the Goodyear Tire Company in Akron, Ohio, Wee Willie Smith was hit with "a vicious elbow during the game and Smith broke the offending player's jaw right there on the spot." The player's name was Schipp "and evidently he didn't like colored people."

The referee threw Smith out of the game but said nothing about Schipp, who had started the action. Illidge argued with the referees that both should be ejected. The coach of the Goodyear team agreed. The refs refused to continue. Illidge recalled: "That's when all hell broke loose. We had to form a circle in the middle of the floor and fight back to back. I had my pistol out and Fat Jenkins pulled out the knife he kept hidden in his sock. We were ready to fight our way out, but the riot squad came and saved our lives."

The fans were also rough on the players. While the manager watched the promoter to be sure he didn't run away with the money and the "sixth man" watched the time-keeper to help him remain objective, fans near the net would stick hat pins into a player's backside or burn him with a lit cigarette. Fans who were out of reach of the court threw cigarettes and cigars through the net. Bottles were thrown at foul-shooters. In industrialized towns, fans threw small store bolts at out-of-towners or shined mirrors to reflect the lights into the eyes of the shooters. In coal towns, miners would wear their helmets to the games and shine the lights into the eyes of the visiting team.

The abolition of cages and nets gave fans a field day. They could shake the backboards of the visitors to throw off shots. Fans ran out and tripped the players. When the Celtics played in a northern Michigan town, a fan attacked Nat Holman while he was dribbling up the court and landed a solid punch to Holman's head. The spectator became the town hero.

The fans, opponents, referees, injuries, inconveniences—none of these were very important. The Celtics and the Rens were self-contained families. They were the best in their business and had enormous pride in what they were accomplishing. Basketball was their whole way of life. The members of these teams knew each other better than they knew their parents, brothers and sisters, wives or children. When they were together on and off the courts, life was secure emotionally and financially. It was a high life for men of such humble origins.

Chapter 13

On the Road

The high life came crashing down with the onset of the Great Depression, as the American Dream suddenly ended in an American Nightmare. The gyrations of industrial machinery began to slow. Consumer goods were now outside the reach of the growing poor. The ranks of the tramps and unemployed swelled. Suicides skyrocketed. The bellies of more and more Americans cried out for food. With so many rural Americans sucked into the temptations of urban living, slums sprouted everywhere. The greed that fueled the Twenties made the Thirties harder to accept. If the spirit of the country had not died, it was certainly on its deathbed.

While the Depression was undeniably tough for everyone, it was especially hard on blacks. In the urban areas, they were the first to lose their jobs, while in the South they worked for almost nothing. There was nothing for them to fall back on. By 1934, 38 percent of the black population was unemployed and considered to be incapable of self-support; this compared to 17 percent for whites. Their relative economic prosperity had been snatched away by the Depression. The Harlem Renaissance, which had been so inspirational, effectively ended in 1930 as it became harder for artists to sell their work.

Sports historians write today about the Celtics and the Rens in the Thirties as if little had changed. Sportswriters at the time continued to mythologize sport—it would go on and so would American life. While fans weren't losing interest, it was becoming harder and harder to pay the admission price.

The Rens tried to keep playing out of the Casino Ballroom. The "Rosenblum-Celtics" tried to stay alive in the league. Based on the theory that dwindling fan interest was based on a stagnant style of play and seeing the "same old players," the American Basketball League abolished the famed pivot play and instituted a rule that each team must carry two rookies. But owners blamed the fans and the players just as industrialists repeatedly blamed softened workers. The press trumpeted the reflection of society as viewed from the top.

When Max Rosenblum decided to withdraw his championship team from the league, he proclaimed that his dedication was to the game and not to making money. He said, "I have placed my wholehearted efforts for many years into the promotion of professional basketball in Cleveland—a promotion upon which there was never based any intention of profit."

Playing for the dance-hall crowds was no longer possible for the Rens. Almost simultaneously, the Rens and the Celtics decided that their survival was based on barnstorming across the country. The Rens got into their bus and took off. The remaining Celtics bought themselves a Pierce Arrow for $125 and followed. Each team cut itself adrift from the familar in search of emotional and financial solace from the Depression. Emotional relief came; financial comfort never really followed.

The formula was simple. First, all the overhead expenses were to be cut down. That, of course, was easier for the Rens, who didn't have that many to begin with. Second, the teams would play anywhere they could obtain a guarantee—with sharply reduced expectations. Third, they would play local teams and try to hype interest in the match-up as if it would be a real barnburner even if the local team was terrible. Finally, in big cities they would match up against each other and exploit the black-white conflict with the media and the fans.

It was a conflict that the proud Douglas was willing to exploit, but on his own terms. He knew, as did the Celtics, that it was a gamble. The Harlem Globetrotters had become white America's image of what a black basketball team should be. As long as blacks were clowns, tricking rather than outsmarting their opponents while speaking barely recognizable English, they were allowed to succeed. This was especially true if the profiteers of this showmanship were whites like Abe Saperstein, owner of the Globetrotters. The players were merely his field hands.

After all, this was the heyday of *Amos 'n Andy,* a radio show that whites loved and blacks despised. Freeman Gosden and Charles Correll were the Sapersteins of radio. These two white men, whose voices portrayed the black pair, exaggerated every stereotype white Americans had about the blacks. Amos 'n Andy were the Globetrotters of the airwaves—they succeeded by trickery, conniving and breaking all the rules.

Douglas said that what he wanted to offer was simply good basketball. The Depression-era match-ups between the Rens and the Celtics were classics on the court even if there was some artificial hype off the court. Both Douglas and Lapchick believed it was the greatest basketball rivalry ever seen. Neither would claim that his team "was the greatest team of all time," although many called them that. In fact, Lapchick called the Rens the best team of the mid-Thirties, while Douglas said the Celtics were the best prior to that time.

The Celtics wouldn't be rich anymore, but they would still be together. Max Rosenblum decided to back the Celtics, who still used Cleveland as a home base in deference to the Rosenblum patronage. But it was no longer that great 1920s unit. Lapchick, Denhert, and Barry came from the Cleveland franchise. Nat Hickey and Davey Banks rejoined them. Carl Husta, who had played for Cleveland, joined the barnstormers. He was a smooth shooting guard who had his basketball beginnings in Kingston in the New York State League. For $75 a month, he set up the chairs, drew the court lines, played the game, showered, and then returned to join the orchestra for which he played the drums. So the Celtics, even the Depression-era Celtics, were the big time.

Joe Lapchick said, "We looked at the time romantically. We were going to survive, overcome and still be the champions. But, the truth was, we were becoming old men." The aging Celtics played without Holman and Beckman, their two best shooters from the Twenties. The new rigor of their lifestyle made it still harder to meet their old standards. However, they still had that spirit and belief in themselves, and their competition was rarely up to even this somewhat antiquated version of the glory team.

The Rens were another matter. First, they didn't lose any of their players. They were younger than the Celtics and were used to a lifestyle which denied sleep and normal bodily comforts. Most importantly, they completed their roster with the addition of the powerful Wee Willie Smith. Standing 6 feet 5 inches tall and weighing 225 pounds, Smith was an imposing figure on the court. Ironically, he came from Cleveland, which the Celtics called home. In other times, he might have joined the Celtics and allowed them to continue as unchallenged world champions.

Instead he became the capstone for the Rens' "Magnificent Seven." He was the perfect complement for Tarzan Cooper since hostile opponents could never gang up on both big men. The whites accused Smith of being a "dirty player." Lapchick said it was just the opposite: "He was big and strong. Refs frequently ignored it when opponents roughed up Smith. It was when the game got out of hand that fights started. I never saw Smith start a fight." With Smith and Cooper getting the ball; with Ricks and Yancey shooting uncannily; with Jenkins controlling the pace and Holt and Saitch ready to pitch in, the Rens dominated basketball for the next four years. They won 473 games and lost only 49 during those four years. At one point, they had won eighty-eight consecutive games. No white or black team could consistently beat them. Only the Celtics could beat them, but by the 1933–34 season even they could not win the season's series.

The formula for success of both teams became the formula of survival. The Rens always lived an unpretentious style on the road out of necessity. They usually had to sleep in their bus because they were denied hotels. They traveled by bus because many forms of public transportation wouldn't have them. They ate on the bus when restaurants refused to serve them. Segregation may have been the law in the South, but discrimination was the accepted practice in the North. Life worsened for the Rens only in the sense that the road became endless in the Thirties and there was less money to put on the bus. However, their basic lifestyle outside of New York was quite the same.

The sports press wanted America to think that the life of the Celtics was the same high life they had enjoyed before the Depression. The champions had to be an example of reward for hard work and persistence. A column written by Bobby Norris in Macon, Georgia, in January 1935 was typical:

> Naturally, the champions must stop at the finest hotels and travel in style. Not entirely for the sake of appearance but for the comfort that is necessary to sustain their perfect physical trim all season. They are an expensive lot. Joe Lapchick, who serves as coach and boss of the crew, once was recognized as the highest salaried star in basketball. He was pulling in $10,000 per season then.

The Celtic promotional materials exhorted fans to "forget the Depression and have a good time."

Both teams were playing almost every night and twice on Sundays. The managers who booked the games were not masters of geography and were just as likely to arrange for back-to-back games three hundred miles apart as they were to arrange them for nearby towns.

By driving all night, the teams saved the expense of hotels. Even if there was no time to eat, the Celtics would always pack in a case of 3.2 beer. Denhert told a reporter, "The malt tonic, taken in judicious quantities, gives us something to wear off in games." This was a real indicator of the times. The Celtics were always a hard-drinking crew. When they had traveled in style before the Depression they didn't have to be refreshed in their car.

Life without hotels and Pullmans and without much leisure time or money was certainly less fun than it was in the Twenties. Moreover, packing six to seven large men in a car, night after night, was taking its toll on their aging bodies. In 1934, the average age of the Celtics was thirty-four. Most of the players had trick knees, charlie horses, sprains, bad backs, colds or all of the above. Their ankles swelled up after sitting for hours in the car. Usually two men would be assigned the night's drive. It was not uncommon for gas station attendants to mistake the Celtics for gangsters when they pulled up in their big limo late at night. But at least they were sure of getting gas; the Rens, on the other hand, had to learn which towns sold gas to blacks.

The players learned to compensate for each other on the court. Those who had driven the previous night were on the court less and were expected to do less when they played. Columnist William A. Spring of the *Yonkers Herald Statesman* praised Lapchick for pacing himself:

> It is the effortless ease with which Lapchick works that makes him a master of the art. After his 200th game, no doubt, he realized that all this running around got him nowhere. Basketball players who tear around the court like so many deer really are not traveling at all, and accomplish about the same thing as a six day bike rider who pedals around and around and never gets out of the same square block.

He didn't realize that they had no choice. In 1934, for example, the Celtics played on Christmas night in New York City. They piled into the car and drove all night through a blizzard, arriving in Johnstown, Pennsylvania, at 6 P.M. without sleep. They gave a clinic from 7 P.M. until game time at 9 P.M. Exhausted, they coasted and were losing 51–49 with ninety seconds left. Lapchick called time out to say that they should play all out. They won 56–52.

The previous year, they had played eleven games in ten nights. Their bodies aching and their tempers short, the Celtics lost a game to the Yahoo Center Five. They were about to graciously accept defeat when an opposing player told the Celtics that they should retire and not drag down their glorious traditions. Lapchick was furious and called Nig Rose, their booking agent, at midnight. "Get us a game with these punks as soon as you can. We'll play them anywhere and for nothing." The match was set for two weeks later. The Celtics were confident, so Lapchick told the player who had derided the Celtics that this would be the Celtics' last game if they lost. The cocky opponent nodded his appreciation for Lapchick's newly acquired wisdom. The Celtics won 61–8.

The Celtics traveled to Baldwyn, Mississippi, in mid-January 1934. According to Rose, the Celtics' car stalled some eighty-five miles outside of Baldwyn. The players pushed the car for several miles while unsuccessfully trying to jump-start it. They finally hitched a ride in a cattle truck and arrived at 7:30 for a 7 P.M. game. They looked terrible and played even worse. With seven minutes remaining, they were losing 26–7. The fans were screaming—not with joy for the locals' apparent victory but because they believed the Celtics were deliberately losing the game. The Celtics could barely walk, let alone run. Losing, although never welcomed, was more acceptable at that moment even though it had been a great year. They were 50–1, having lost only to the Rens 44–40. A record of 50–2 wouldn't be so bad under the circumstances, but the cries of fix from the fans ignited them, and the Celtics outscored Baldwyn 19–1, only to lose 27–26.

Once again Lapchick called Rose. There were no open dates and a number of upcoming games with the Rens. They were to play the Rens in St. Louis on January 31, in Evansville, Indiana, on February 1, and in Dayton, Ohio, on February 3. On February 2, they were to oppose the Earle (Arkansas) Cardinals in Memphis. Lapchick told Rose to make it a doubleheader. They beat the Cardinals in the opener 33–20. Baldwyn came on the court knowing the Celtics had not had a day off since December; geography told them that the Celtics couldn't have slept between St. Louis, Evansville, and Memphis. Nevertheless, Baldwyn could only watch with awe as the Celtics won 40–27. The pace never let up. The Celtics played thirty-two games in twenty-eight days. This included a tripleheader in Nashville one day, an afternoon game the next day in Indianapolis, and a game that night in Dayton.

The Rens had much the same fate, since duress and exhaustion could lead to inconsistent play and irate fans. But it was always more dangerous for them because they were a black team in a white world. The Rens took off for Chicago after an easy game in Wisconsin. They had the next night off and looked forward to some relaxation in Chicago, one of the few cities where they could stay in decent hotels. They used such cities as bases when they were scheduled to play in towns where they couldn't stay.

The bus broke down and the Rens pushed and shoved it for almost ten miles in the ice-cold Wisconsin winter. They finally got to a town with a railway station. Their night off was spent in the station as they couldn't find food or hotel rooms. The morning train brought them to Chicago in time to play that night. Their minds were present but their bodies were back on that Wisconsin highway; they lost. The spectators were sure they had intentionally dumped the game and stormed the court. They had to escape through a back door and get a police escort to the station. It was neither the first nor the last time the Rens fled from a belligerent white crowd under police escort.

Another episode in Akron, Ohio, has already been mentioned. Akron had also brought bad luck for the Celtics, who approached the town on a foggy night for a game with the Firestone Tire Company team. Nat Hickey was driving when he spotted a freight train through the thick fog. Hickey slammed on the brakes, but they didn't hold. Carl Husta and Davey Banks jumped out of the car as it careened wildly over an embankment. The car landed on a lower road. Hickey was too nervous to move. Lapchick and Denhert went back to discover Banks unhurt in a snow drift and Husta nursing his newly bruised back on the icy pavement. The Celtics won that night all the same.

On another occasion they traveled to Butler, Pennsylvania, from Pittsburgh after six weeks in the South. It was a bitter cold night. One of the tires blew out, the brakes froze and the carburetor developed trouble. It took five hours to travel the thirty-four miles to Butler. They arrived in a frozen state, greeted by an impatient crowd that had waited one and a half hours for them. The arena manager insisted that they start without warming up.

Butler scored the first nineteen points and led by twenty-three at the half. The Celtics sent for a bottle of Scotch and allowed it to warm them up. Relying on Lapchick to get the center jump after each basket, the Celtics scored twenty-nine straight without Butler getting possession of the ball. Nig Rose called it a performance that had never been matched. The Celtics weren't convinced it was worth the price their bodies paid. But complaining wasn't part of their style.

Hearing reports of an impending blizzard, the Celtics arrived early for a game in Webster, Massachusetts. The poster on the arena announced the game for the following night. They checked their route book and, sure enough, they were booked that night in Westfield, Massachusetts—some fifty-four miles away.

By then the blizzard was in full-force. They called the Westfield promoter to cancel the game. His arena was filled with anxious fans and he refused, informing the Celtics to get there however they could. They stopped at each town to call and plead with the promoter. He wouldn't listen. Arriving at midnight, they drank a bottle of brandy and beat the locals before a packed arena.

In spite of all the hardships, the owners loved the Celtics' dedication and willingness to sacrifice. In February 1934, Nig Rose discussed the Celtics' current methods of operation with a reporter from the *St. Louis Post,* contrasting them to teams in the old professional leagues. He said that previously there had been too much luxury overhead. Referring to the possible reestablishment of a pro league, Rose said:

> When it does return it will have to be on the basis established by the Celtics—that of a sensible budget. Extra fare trains and Pullmans, high priced hotels, $2 luncheons and all that sort of stuff will have to be squeezed out. The sport can't stand that sort of overhead. The Celtics have solved the transportation and living problems and that will set the standard for a revival of professional basketball on a reasonable expense basis.

The Rens and the Celtics promoted themselves and made their managers' jobs easier. They both knew that, for different reasons, fans wouldn't want to see them badly defeat a local team. Before the game, reporters would be told to expect a close battle. After the game, they would be told how much the team had improved. All the while, the Celtics and the Rens were carrying their opponents to make them look good.

The Rens tried to avoid fights because they added nothing to the game and might make white spectators antagonistic and threatening. The Celtics had their own code of conduct for a physically aggressive opponent. They would concentrate on him by blocking him out of the play and having his man shoot all the shots until the coach had to remove him.

In the fall of 1935 they played a local all-star team in Ohio. The All-Stars used brute force in every play. The Celtics called time-out and the fans were sure they would reciprocate. Pat Herlihy tipped the ball to Paul Birch, who threw it to Banks. He scored *for Ohio*. Herlihy repeated this on the center jump. The crowd went wild. They did it again after a beautiful display of Celtic ball-handling wizardry. The Celtics were very serious and shook hands. Ohio, suddenly enjoying a two-point lead after the Celtics had scored six for them, was humiliated, and the rough-house tactics stopped.

Lapchick explained the philosophy to a reporter:

If a team is reasonable with us and does not rough us and try to take advantage of the fact that we are pros, we'll let them down easy and make a good show of it. Occasionally, though, we run into a team that gets too enthusiastic and we have to put the pressure on.

A short time ago, for instance, we were playing in a certain southern city. At the half we were leading by only one point. The team came back in the second half, apparently thinking it had a chance to win, and started out roughing us up unmercifully. Furthermore, the referee was accommodatingly blind to their tactics. I called time-out and we decided to settle it then. We won by 53 points.

Of course, there's no fun in that because when you're playing for blood the crowd doesn't particularly enjoy it. After all, we must entertain them so they'll come to see us next year.

Once they played the Indiana Omars in Indianapolis. One of their players began to take underhand shots from forty to fifty feet out. Chris Leonard, the best man on defense, couldn't contain his laughter when he saw this man's technique. He never went near him until it was too late, and that man scored six baskets to help the Omars win.

Ed Sullivan, then a sports columnist for the *New York Graphic*, later went over to the manager to get the player's name and was told, "Homer Stonebreaker." Sullivan, apparently feeling this was as funny as his technique, laughed and asked his real name. "Homer Stonebreaker" was again the reply. The Celtics had a rematch with the Omars in Cleveland. Leonard was all over Stonebreaker who never scored a point. Leonard scored 12 points and the Celtics won easily.

Professional athletes respected players who could compete in more than one sport. The Rens had several pro baseball players and a tennis champion on their team. Lapchick had played pro baseball and golf. Lou Gehrig toured each winter with an All-Star team under his name. He came into the dressing room before a game with the Celtics and pleaded, "Please don't rub it in tonight." The Celtics assured him that this was not their intention. With five minutes left and the team down by 3 points, Lapchick called time-out and said, "Let's go!" Gehrig's All-Stars won by two. After that, the Celtics decided to put the game away first and then let their opponents score.

The Celtics and the Rens both possessed a balance between enormous pride in themselves and compassion and respect for their adversaries. They wanted to win but not to destroy. Lapchick called the felling one of "quiet fierceness." A column by Wirt Gammon in January 1935 illustrated this. The Celtics had asked how Adolf Rupp's Kentucky team had done. When told that Rupp had sent his first team back in with the score 66 to 19, Gammon wrote, "Lapchick registered genuine disgust" and said,

> Why does coach Rupp do things like that? I just can't understand it. Those coaches are all in the same boat, have the same problems. I can't understand why they can't appreciate each other's position and not jeopardize each other's jobs.

The Celtics never complained about ethnic references to them in the press. It was another way to promote fan interest. The Celtics were also called "the Shamrocks" and more rarely, the "Irish." The *Atlanta Constitution* ran an article by Jimmy Jones in January 1934:

> The Celtics are a colorful crew, too designed for crowd appeal. Denhert is a Dutchman; Lapchick a Pole or something; Davey

Banks is Jewish; Barry and Herlihy are Irish and Hickey is a
French Canadian. They are reinforced this year by Carl Husta.
Husta must be Hungarian since there are no nationalities left.

The scientific method was not one of Mr. Jones's tools of
inquiry. Denhert was German and Lapchick was Czech. Hickey
was from Hoboken, New Jersey. Even in 1934, there were several
nations left to choose from besides Hungary for Husta. The
Birmingham and Chattanooga newspapers referred to Herlihy as
"a new Jewish star," "the Jewish luminary," and a "scintillating
Jewish product."

Lapchick wrote of a treasured ethnic moment for the *Yonkers
Herald Statesman:*

> An incident I shall always remember happened after a game in
> Chattanooga. While dressing there was a great rumpus outside the
> door. Pushing aside all opposition was a burly Irishman, who
> opened the door and said: "Glory be praised—Shamrocks." Leon-
> ard grasped the situation and introduced everyone thusly: Barry as
> Barry, of course, Banks as O'Brien, Denhert as O'Flynn, Holman
> as Shaunessy, and me as Flavin. A big smile beamed across his
> good–natured pan and he cried, "Oh, me buckies 'tis glad I am to
> see some faces from the old sod!"

Fans also came because of the team's ability to perfect their
own game and to create innovations that would revolutionize the
game. The Rens were pat in personnel while the Celtics were
changing some. Paul Birch joined them to replace Pete Barry who
retired at age forty-one. The powerful Pat Herlihy played more
and more for Lapchick. Even with the changes, the Celtics had
basically played together even longer than the Rens. They knew
each other's moves inside out and could anticipate where their
teammates would be without seeing them go there. Reporters,
fans, coaches, and players all agreed that no one could handle
the ball better than the Celtics and the Rens. Even when the
games got rough, they were graceful on the court.

And there can be little doubt that they were the greatest
innovators the game has ever seen. The Celtics originated the

switching defense, the give-and-go offense and the pivot play under game conditions, usually after building up a big lead.

Before the switching man-to-man defense, players judged their performance solely on the basis of how many points they scored in comparison with the man they guarded. This was all a logical outgrowth of the team concept of the game that Lapchick had so much trouble adjusting to when he joined the Celtics:

> The Celtics never practiced so I couldn't figure out how they were switching. I was always in somebody's way and my teammates were getting picked off right and left. They were angry and told me how dumb I was. But I couldn't understand. Then Johnny Witte told me, "Joe, it isn't how many points you score or how many times you get us the tap. We know you will be great in those areas. But to be a member of the Celtics you have to also contribute without the ball." That helped me to understand. The team was the thing. We were five green shirts playing together and not five individual performers.

Lapchick described Dutch Denhert's discovery of the famed pivot play:

> We were playing one night in a game that was a total walkover. Denhert walked under the basket, turned his back on it, and began to kid the other team by receiving a pass and throwing it back to the player who had thrown it to him.
>
> Suddenly one of our team, receiving a pass from Denhert, found himself completely unguarded. This happened again and again and we thus saw that what Denhert had conceived as a joke was really a powerful offensive threat. We began to study it until we worked out the swiftest possible manipulation of the ball.

The Rens perfected all these plays. In addition, Tarzan Cooper and Wee Willie Smith are credited with the invention of the double-pivot play in a game in St. Louis in 1933. With the game safely in hand, Smith moved in front of Cooper. They passed the ball back and forth from the pivot line. Smith batted the ball back over his head to Cooper who then batted the ball to players around the foul line. The newspaper story said they "knocked the patrons out of their chairs and befuddled the opposition."

The crowds dwindled. However, wherever the Celtics and Rens played each other, every coach within a hundred miles would bring his team to see the masters teach their trade. There were always dozens of yellow school buses outside the arena. When the Rens played the Celtics in St. Louis in January 1934, more than one hundred fifty teams came to witness the master teachers of the era. When they played other teams, they did not always have the energy to teach during the whole game. They would play as the Celtics and as the Rens for enough of the game to both assure victory and show the fans how the game was supposed to be played. However, when they played each other, there was no time to innovate, no time to rest. They respected themselves too much to do anything short of playing the entire game as if it was the last minute of a close encounter.

It was easier for the Rens to do this in the Thirties. The Rens were in a period of heady ascent, while the Celtics were making their last stand. Lapchick and Denhert were playing less and less. Barry was forty years old. Lapchick talked seriously to a reporter in Waco, Texas, in 1936: "No, we don't disguise our ages. We think that's in our favor. Paul Birch, who joined us only this season, is twenty-three. We sorta watch out for Paul—watch his morals and so on—he's so young."

Gradually all the Celtics realized that being legendary was not the same as being immortal. Playing in Buffalo for $100 before one hundred twenty people was not the same as it used to be. Ironically, it was the Celtics and not the Rens who began to try everything to fill the arenas. They held clinics before almost all the games to assure that at least local players and coaches would attend. They added new men like Herlihy and Birch. They even persuaded W. L. Stribling, then boxing's number one heavyweight contender, to join the team on a southern tour only three weeks before he was to fight Max Schmeling for the championship. As a rule, they drew fair crowds in the North and Midwest and good crowds in the South.

Famed singer Kate Smith backed the players' salaries in the mid-Thirties. Her patronage promoted fan interest for a while.

This was especially true whenever she attended the game. She brought the house down when the Celtics played the Young Men's Hebrew Association (YMHA) at Duquesne University's gym. With the Celtics ahead 39 to 18, she was introduced between the third and fourth periods. Kate Smith, even then an impressive figure, announced, "May the best team win." Even the YMHA team couldn't contain their laughter.

The Celtics started new antics on the court. With Denhert only able to perform a few pivot plays and Lapchick a few palms, the burlesque began to entertain the fans. They used the hidden ball trick when Herlihy put the ball under his shirt. They passed the ball to the referee.

But it was Banks, the lightning-like wisp of a player, who became the real clown. He would sit in the stands while the team played defense. He would flirt with women spectators. Sometimes he took popcorn from children and sat courtside to eat it. Then he would call for the ball with popcorn blowing everywhere. Pat Herlihy would lift Banks onto his shoulders for jump balls. When Banks shot the ball, he would sometimes fall to his knees to pray while it was in the air.

The crowds loved all the tricks. Many believed that the Celtics were better at them than the Globetrotters at this time. After all, the Celtics weren't paying refs and the opponents to make them look good as Abe Saperstein was doing. Even so, the Celtics weren't happy that they had to do these things to survive. They loved the game too much to make a joke of it and soon after they were forced to do so, Lapchick and Denhert quit. The fun was gone, and now what that Yahoo Center player had said about quitting before they destroyed the Celtics' honor and glory struck home.

Earlier in 1933, Lapchick had told a reporter:

Some of us are getting older now. We pack and jam ourselves somehow into a big automobile going from city to city, playing somewhere every night. It's a terribly hard life, but I don't believe you could prevail on any one of the boys to quit it. Basketball is in our blood. We love the game, we always have and we always will.

But much of the fun of the old barnstorming days is gone. It has become a hard racket now and the fun of the thing is lacking. There was a time when backers fought each other to underwrite the tours. Crowds have fallen off and the backers are unwilling to take a chance. So we players underwrite it ourselves and make the tour on our own account.

During those last years, games with the Rens were the only thing that brought the Celtics back to their best days. Each match-up was like the Super Bowl in the minds of the players. Nat Holman sometimes rejoined the Celtics for these big games.

The white press, which rarely mentioned the Rens in the North and never mentioned them in the South, now paid attention. These writers had already dubbed the Celtics the greatest team ever. The Rens could only call themselves "Colored World Champions." But this was hard to explain when the Rens won the series with the Celtics in 1933–34, the same year they had won eighty-eight straight games.

For many spectators, the match-up was black versus white. If there were any "incidents," the fans were ready. It was a test of racial pride. For the players, the match-up was the chance to test who was best. Over the many years of the series, the Celtics won most of the games. Losing the series to the Rens in 1933–34 was a first, although the Rens had previously come close when they split the 1926–27 series. The Rens had some scores to settle, but it was never easy and the Celtics began beating them again in 1934. It was a war on the court. Bob Douglas told me, "We always played in a war, but often it was a race war. When we played against most white teams, we were colored. Against the Celtics, we were men. Over those last years a real brotherhood was born out of competition and travel."

However, the Rens had much to be bitter about, as recognition from the press was hard to win. Even when they had it, a subtle racism could be read into most of the stories in the white press. Words seemed carefully chosen to protect the stereotypes. Thus the *Dayton Herald* of February 5, 1934, described "the shifty Renaissance Five" versus the "matchless Celtics." Blinky Horn in his column called the Rens "the Sepia Squadron" and wrote that the "Rens clowned and grinned their way through a combat with a local colored team last night." Of the Celtics he wrote, "They come as near to being the poetry of motion as it is possible in basketball."

Sid Keener of the St. Louis *Star Times* wrote of the "Renaissance tossers" and the "Celtic shooters." The Rens were "lightning fast," the Celtics "steadier and more accurate." Others wrote that the Rens "outmuscled the Celtics" or that the "Celtics outsmarted the Rens." Most of the stories granted some throwaway line like "the Rens represent among their own race the greatest in the court game." They were still the "Colored World Champions" playing the real World Champions. The press was very free in questioning Dutch Denhert, who, aroused by his Celtic pride, made statements like "They have a great bunch of players but we generally succeed in outsmarting them one way or another and they are inclined to let down when you get ahead of them." The white Celtics were smart, steady, accurate and graceful poets. The black Rens were shifty, strong, and fast grinners. The media, after all, was serving the nation. The nation it served was white.

The press made their competitiveness seem like a bitter personal rivalry rather than heat generated by the battle of the giants of the game. Stories before the games repeatedly predicted fights. When fights occurred, it was generally the Rens who were blamed. A typical account appeared in the Brooklyn *Times Union* on April 6, 1933:

> Pat Herlihy was the innocent victim of an attempt at peacemaking. Willie Smith of the Rens . . . and Nat Hickey locked up arms on a play near the sidelines and just as it looked as if blows were to be struck, Herlihy stepped in and locked Smith's arms in the hope of averting trouble. The other players rushed in and separated them and just as they stepped apart Smith let a right fly that dipped Pat on the chin. Pat, being Irish, decided that peacemaking wasn't in his line and tried to return the compliment. . . . A moment later Herlihy and Smith were in a tangle and before they could be stopped the crowd surged out onto the floor.

Note that Herlihy was a peacemaker because he grabbed opponent Smith's arms. It was fine for him, as an Irishman, to fight back against the ungrateful Smith.

Another especially rough game was reported before a home-town crowd of seven thousand five hundred in Cleveland which the Celtics won 44–34. It was noted that "all the grips and holds commonly believed to be only in the wrestler's stock and trade and not a few hefty punches were shown by the fighting-mad cagers." When fights didn't happen they wrote about the number of fouls, as if it were the same thing.

There were many fouls. But it must be remembered that in those days a player was not ejected because he exceeded a certain limit. After a key game in St. Louis in January 1934, Denhert said, "We're bitter rivals and they'd give a right arm to knock our ears off. Naturally, when they turn basketball into football, the Celtics must fight back." Forty-six fouls were called. Banks had committed twelve violations and Smith eight. After the game Banks said, "Those Rens are too tough for experiments and trick plays. We have to play all out."

Perhaps that game typified the series. According to the St. Louis papers, whoever won would break the series tie and be the champion. The two teams were labeled "bitter enemies" and fights were predicted. The Celtics were 60–2, having lost to the Rens 44–40 and to the Baldwyn, Mississippi Athletes. The Rens were 45–1. Their loss was delivered by the Celtics 44–36.

A huge crowd of 8,513 came to see them play. Some one hundred fifty high school teams attended. The Rens got off to a fast start and led 33–29 with less than five minutes left. However, the Celtics rallied to win 38–35.

The next day the papers reported that the series would continue. Each pre-game story said that the series was tied and that game was for the "championship," but the series seemed to go on forever. The next night in Evansville the posters announced:

CELTICS (World's Professional Champions)
versus
NEW YORK RENAISSANCE (World's Colored Champions)

Under the "Seats for Colored" heading, the promoter promised that "as usual there will be a section reserved for colored people." After a Celtic doubleheader in Memphis, they played the Rens again on February 3 in Dayton, Ohio. All the Ren-Celtic games were billed by the local papers as being for the "World Championship." The Celtics won in Dayton 42–39.

The Celtics seemed to be in high gear and good form in February 1934. The northern press asserted that they were on top of the basketball world again after these key victories over the Rens. The Rens were almost never mentioned in stories about the Celtics in southern papers. On February 18, James Saxon Childers of the Birmingham (Alabama) *News-Age Herald* naively asked Joe Lapchick if the Celtics were the greatest team in existence. Even after the recent wins, Lapchick responded, "No, the Renaissance, the Negro team, is the greatest basketball team of the day. Over the years we have beaten them 6 to 1, but recently they have beaten us. I believe they can do it again." Douglas later said that this type of acknowledgment meant a great deal to the Rens. It was especially important that it came in the South, where the Celtics and Rens played the first game between blacks and whites in Louisville, Kentucky.

Dutch Denhert still wouldn't let go. The 1933–34 series ended in a virtual stand-off. It was a new year in 1935 when he was interviewed by Harry Martinez for his column "Sports from the Crow's Nest." Denhert seemed to acknowledge the greatness of the Rens and yet attributed part of their success to ex-Celtics:

> They're a fine team all right, but they haven't beaten us so much, only about 25 percent of the games we've played against them in the past 10 years. They have been in existence about 10 years and in the beginning of their career, we beat them regularly. But they stuck together so long that they began to learn how to play the game well, what with some of our ex-players coaching them. And then it was they who gave us hard fights.

The series that year was also a stand-off. The Celtics were in Chattanooga and Wirt Gammon of the *Chattanooga Times* asked Lapchick if he thought the St. Louis Americans were the next best team after the Celtics:

> The Rens and the Celtics are far ahead of the rest of the pro basketball field and have been for years. They (Rens) are our closest

rivals. Every year we play a long series with them for a sort of unofficial world championship. When the returns are added up at the end of the season we were always ahead—except two years ago when they had a slight edge.

Lots of cities clamour for a game between us and when they want it badly enough we give it to them. But it is nothing like one would think. There is no time for putting on a show for the fans. The going is rough with everyone bearing down every minute. The fact that each team knows the strong and weak points of the others very well results in the contest being a very bitter and rough game.

A month later the Celtics played the Rens in St. Louis. The Rens led the series 5–4 and this was reported to be the last game of the series that year. The arena was so crowded that the game started at 9:20 P.M. instead of the scheduled 8:30 P.M. time. It was very rough going with forty-seven fouls called. Lapchick, who was playing less and less against other teams, played almost the entire game. He and Pat Herlihy had seventeen fouls between them. Tarzan Cooper had seven. The Celtics pulled away at the end to win 50–41. The series was tied again, but it wasn't over; the teams drove to Kansas City for a game the next night "for the world championship." Such championship games proliferated as both teams relied on the rivalry to pay the bills. The season was even extended into April. They played in Saratoga, New York and the Celtics prevailed 49–44 after outscoring the Rens 11–2 in the closing minutes. The *Saratogan* described the game: "Both teams were out for blood and the spills were frequent. Players from both teams suffered minor injuries, cuts and bruises."

While this series kept them going, it was becoming harder and harder for men like Lapchick and Denhert to go on. Lapchick was married to Elizabeth Sarubbi in 1931 and had two small children. He began to feel like he knew none of them. His home was Cleveland and the road. From November to April he might spend two to three days in New York where he could be near his family in Yonkers. He couldn't quit because he didn't know what else he could do besides play basketball.

The Celtics compromised and moved back to New York. Without the Rosenblum patronage, there was no necessity to be in Cleveland. So, with the agreement of the players and Kate Smith, Lapchick and Denhert came home.

Joe's wife was happy; she had felt forced to live with her mother and father during those years. At twenty-seven, she had married late for those times. Living at home, even though she was married, made her feel like the proverbial old maid. She was sure that his return would help relieve the burden of raising two small children by herself.

It didn't work out. No matter where one called home, the only home for a barnstorming team was the road. Now, without the support of her parents, it was even harder for Elizabeth Lapchick to raise the children. The crowds grew smaller still, and what little fun and excitement had remained was gone. Lapchick knew it was over for the Celtics. They could still rise to the moment in head-to-head battles with the Rens, but it would take days and sometimes weeks for Lapchick to recover from the bruising play. This made him unable to play much, if at all, against other opponents. The same was true of Denhert. While players like Birch and Herlihy were exceptional athletes, the fans wanted to see Lapchick and Denhert.

In January 1936 the Celtics played the Rens in St. Louis. It was the same type of game as always—hard fought, bone-crushing, and exciting. Forty-nine fouls were called. The Rens led the series 5–4 before the game and the Celtics tied by winning 51–41. It should have been a great moment. Davey Banks, Herlihy and Birch were ecstatic. But Lapchick and Denhert knew the only statistic that counted. In 1935, 8,500 had come to see them. Now it was 3,400. The series was dying and the death of the Celtics would surely follow.

At this time Lapchick was asked by Father Rebholz, the Athletic Moderator at St. John's University, to succeed the great "Buck" Freeman, coach of "the Wonder Five" at St. John's. Lapchick jumped at the opportunity, although he was afraid he would not know how to coach or how to talk to university men with his eighth-grade education. But it was a way to stay in the game he loved. Nat Holman had successfully made the transition at City College. So life on the road came to an end for Lapchick. New York would really be home.

Birch, Herlihy and others continued to play under the name "Celtics." But writers and fans marked 1936 as the real end of the Celtics' dynasty and domination. The time had come to mythologize them, to embellish the already rich legends.

The timing could not have been worse for the Rens, who were reaching their peak in 1936. They would go on playing and even occasionally be called "world champions" by the white press, but without the Celtics to be measured against, it was an empty accolade. They played on into the mid-1940s, adding such stars as John Isaacs and "Pudgy" Bell. In 1939, they won a tournament for the world title by beating the Harlem Globetrotters and the Oshkosh All-Stars.

Harder still for Bob Douglas was the unending recognition given to the Globetrotters. Then Rens dominated the sport for a decade as pure basketball players. Individually and as a team, they were incomparable. Yet the fans and the press adored the Trotters.

Bob Douglas fought for the dignity of his team and its individual black stars. He never compromised them as black men just as they never compromised themselves. Some said he paid them more than he could afford and bought that well-fitted bus so they wouldn't have to endure the rampant racism on every street corner in America. Yet the press called Abe Saperstein "the Jewish Abe Lincoln." The press made the Trotters into the living proof that America allowed blacks to "make it." The Trotters were purportedly showing America and the world how sports could help overcome racial prejudice. The media portrayed them as a high-living, highly paid team taking their happy message from city to city and country to country. The Globetrotters, unlike the Rens, received enormous press coverage, drew large crowds, and eventually were the subjects of a movie and a television cartoon show. The message they brought, of course, was exactly the one that Bob Douglas desperately avoided, even at his own financial expense. The Trotters were, quite simply, white America's acceptable image of blacks—lazy, lackadaisical, and inept, able to entertain with their bodies without threatening whites.

For many, it was just as disillusioning to find out that the "Jewish Abe Lincoln" was no more a racial emancipator than the original model himself. The Trotters were woefully underpaid, lived the lifestyle of the 1930s Rens and Celtics even into the 1960s, and, worst of all, were the subjects of derisive if humorous thought by the hundreds of thousands of whites who would watch them play. When the time was eventually ripe for blacks to join the NBA, it was none other than the great emancipator himself who tried to stand in the doorway to block them.

As the Thirties faded into the Forties and Fifties, life for the old Rens became more difficult. Everyone remembered the great Celtics. The Trotters were still going strong, shuffling from station to station. The individual Celtics had, for the most part, gone on to better things. Pete Barry coached Kate Smith's Celtics. Dutch Denhert coached the Detroit Eagles to pro titles in 1940 and 1941 and also coached the Sheboygan, Wisconsin, team. He also owned a bar and grill in New York. Johnny Beckman coached Baltimore in the American League. Lapchick and Holman became as famous as coaches as they were as players.

But it was quiet obscurity for most of the Rens. Tarzan Cooper, the greatest center of the Thirties, was typical. He left the Rens to paint houses so he could have a steady income. Legends in the black community, few whites remembered their greatness or, for that matter, that they existed at all. The media buried them while it breathed life into the Globetrotters.

However, the Rens were suddenly rediscovered in the 1960s as cities began to burn. Douglas, embittered because the press seemed to deliberately ignore the Rens, was wary of the new attention. A bright, racially aware man, he wondered if this acknowledgment was a symbol of progress or an easy way to diminish white guilt for having denied blacks in those days. He wondered where these people who enshrined the Rens in the 1960s had been the previous forty years.

The years no doubt make memories softer and the times seem better then they were. Events are embellished and become fact.

Legends and myths become mixed. The Celtics and the Rens were and are legendary. The passion and love they shared for the game may not exist in the world of sports today. In spite of the struggle for survival and the intensity of the rivalry between the Rens and the Celtics, new meaning in life grew out of those times. Certain moments, long forgotten by everyone else, helped sensitize Bob Douglas and Joe Lapchick to black-white relations.

A month before his death in 1979 at age ninety-six, Bob Douglas told me, "I read about what happened to you in Virginia. It was awful, but I was glad to learn about what you were doing. It didn't surprise me. I always said the acorn doesn't fall far from the tree. Joe Lapchick was my best friend, in or out of basketball." Joe Lapchick used to call Bob Douglas his teacher. They had learned together.

The learning was acquired slowly for Lapchick until that conversation in New York which followed so many deferred invitations to Bob Douglas. Until then he had assumd that being around and playing with blacks was enough to break the psychological barriers that existed between blacks and whites. When Douglas kept saying "Not tonight" to Lapchick's eager invitations to join him for a drink, Joe Lapchick never thought anything of it, assuming that Bob must have had other plans. Lapchick had never given much thought to the indignities suffered daily by his black contemporaries. Never having really socialized with blacks, Lapchick didn't know that some places wouldn't allow blacks to have that drink. He couldn't have imagined that for Douglas it would be even worse to go to a bar where he would be served but where white patrons would render him numb with their icy stares. He never knew that if Douglas had stayed to have that drink, he often would have had to get on the bus and leave for one of the cities where the Rens could spend the night. Joe Lapchick didn't realize how much he didn't know about Bob Douglas.

The New York conversation had shaken Joe Lapchick. He was disgusted with what he learned. He wondered why he hadn't learned it before. It was just as instructive to Lapchick some twenty years later when he mentioned this conversation to Douglas to learn that he had forgotten it. Profound, meaningful, perhaps life-changing for Lapchick, the conversation wasn't even recalled by Douglas. Douglas was used to talking occasionally to white men—reporters, players and fans—about the conditions suffered by blacks. He saw surprise and sometimes even concern in their faces. But he also saw them turn and walk away untouched.

But Lapchick was always sensitive to the hurt felt by others. He wanted to protect his family and his friends. It was he to whom his brothers and sisters turned when they were in trouble. Many of his players would later say that this was the reason for his success as a coach. He was not a master strategist or great technician of the game. But people came to know that he genuinely cared about them. Players felt tremendous loyalty to him and that personal loyalty was a major motivating factor for them on the court. His life with the Celtics had taught him how to relate to people, to make the individual believe that he had a part to play in the larger whole whether on the team or in society. Before his last game at St. John's in 1965 for the National Invitation Tournament Championship, his players were in an emotional uproar to win it for "the coach." One of the stars, Ken McIntyre, was asked by a reporter how he felt about Lapchick. He said, "I believe in him. If he asked me to run through a wall, I would only ask, which wall?" When he died five years later, his last team acted as honorary pallbearers. Bob Douglas was there. He saw it. He knew what Lapchick stood for. When he had given him his first lesson on race in New York, Joe Lapchick was just another white man who happened to be a basketball star.

Once the Depression started, the Rens and the Celtics had shared a more similar lifestyle. As crowds dwindled in their traditional game cities in the North and Midwest, the Celtics moved south. The crowds were bigger, the gate receipts fatter and the weather warmer. The warmth was attractive as it allowed the increasingly injured bodies of the Celtics to heal faster—or, at least, to make them think that they did.

There had never been a professional game in the South between blacks and whites. Lapchick began to suggest to Douglas that the Celtics and the Rens play there.

Douglas's initial response was that there were enough hostile white crowds to face in the North. Douglas knew that they didn't stop at shouting "Nigger, nigger" in the South. They lynched blacks. In the year the Rens were founded, the NAACP had initiated a campaign to get congressional legislation passed to punish the crime of lynching. In the years he had lived in the United States, the NAACP estimated that 3,436 people had been lynched by mobs, mostly in the South. A newspaper in Tennessee had invited local townsfolk to come out to witness the burning of a "live Negro." Three thousand responded and watched. Douglas said it might be one thing for two black teams to play against each other. But, as much as he loved beating the Celtics, he didn't want to beat them in the South. For Douglas, the cold of Wisconsin must have appeared much more appealing than the type of warmth that might await his team in Alabama and Mississippi.

Eventually, faith and courage rose up and the game was set for Louisville, Kentucky. Both teams were a little apprehensive and tentative in their play. Used to being rough with each other, they held back that night. No one had suggested it, but it happened nonetheless. There were no incidents and Lapchick later said that the fans seemed to enjoy the quality of play. After all, even an apprehensive and tentative game between the Rens and Celtics was better than an all-out game between any of the local teams. Lapchick realized that something significant had happened that night. The game itself was enough of a breakthrough; after the game, the two teams returned to business as usual, with the Rens sleeping at a local black college while the Celtics stayed in one of Louisville's best hotels, the Depression not withstanding.

Many of Lapchick's most important experiences of this type took place in the South or in places where racial struggles were rarely won. Douglas also sent the Rens on southern trips to give impoverished rural blacks a chance to witness the Rens.

Local promoters were not always terribly honest. The Celtics' usual deal was a guaranteed flat fee or a percentage of the gate. For most of their playing days the latter was more profitable; the Celtics would always try to monitor the counting of tickets sold since payment took place in cash on the spot. There were a few times when the local promoter vanished with the money or could not meet the guarantee. On at least two occasions, the Celtics walked off the court when it appeared that they were being had. Douglas had told Lapchick about having received more than one bad check. There was a simple rule that everyone agreed to—cash in hand or no game. It was easier for the Celtics to enforce than the Rens.

Lapchick frequently handled the Celtics' business affairs on the road. Such was the case in one of the first contests with the Rens in St. Louis, a town where in the 1930s "integration" was a dirty word. The crowd was a big one. Lapchick was pleased when he was given an envelope with the cash but he noticed that the envelope marked "Rens" was very thin. After he counted the money he asked about the other envelope. The Rens were to be paid by check. Lapchick called over several members of the Rens and Celtics. They agreed that the Rens would get the money and the Celtics would accept the check. From the look on the face of the promoter, Lapchick was sure that his expenses for the game had just doubled.

Over the years, Lapchick developed great respect for the Rens' road secretary and business manager, Eric Illidge. After the ice had been broken with the Louisville game, others in the South followed. Illidge and Lapchick were to appear on a radio program together in Alabama to promote a game. Illidge was already in the studio when Lapchick arrived. Lapchick was shocked to find out that Illidge had to use the service elevator when he came to the studio. The studio manager, of course, thought he was being liberal for interviewing a black and white together. He thought nothing of the indignity caused to Illidge but was speechless when Lapchick chose to ride back down in the service elevator with Illidge.

The two businessmen also broke the ice in Evansville, Indiana. The Rens had a last-minute cancellation of a game there against a local team. Eric Illidge finally asked the local promoter, Mr. Grubbs, what the problem was. Grubbs admitted that an Evansville reporter told Grubbs he would have to leave town if he ever brought a black team to Evansville.

Illidge asked Lapchick to assist him in convincing Grubbs to go ahead with the game. Grubbs finally got up his nerve. A good crowd watched the Rens run up a 10–0 lead by repeating the same play five times: Wee Willie Smith tapped the ball to Cooper who sent a screaming pass to Yancey for the easy score. But five times in a row? The Evansville coach called time-out. Illidge listened to the team in their huddle. The Evansville players did not know who to guard because "all the niggers looked alike."

These incidents were important, but there was so much more to learn. After Lapchick went to St. John's, the contacts were fewer but were always meaningful.

Lapchick was saddened to watch the Rens in decline in the early Forties, to hear about players like Tarzan Cooper painting houses instead of coaching. Tarzan lay dead for days before his body was discovered in late 1980. James "Pappy" Ricks, the master shooter, had his career shortened by his taste for liquor; Douglas blamed it on his inability to handle the money he made. Casey Holt had it better for a while after he became a member of the New York City police force. He was off-duty when a friend asked him to investigate a robbery. When uniformed police arrived and mistook him for the thief, Holt was killed before he could estab-lish his identity. One has to wonder if he would be alive today if he was white; would the officers have assumed he was the thief? Wee Willie Smith drove a bus in Cleveland and then did janitorial work for the schools. He never recovered after his son was killed in a car accident. Smith later had his leg amputated and hardly resembled the man he was in the 1930s.

The way the story was told, the Rens had little education and no skills outside of the arena. Therefore, their fate was to take up menial jobs when their playing careers ended. Aside from Nat Holman, the Original Celtics also had little education. Yet Witte, Denhert, Barry, Beckman, Hickey, Holman and Lapchick all had coaching careers and years of glory. Banks owned a lumber company, Denhert a bar and grill, and Herlihy a baking and confectionary business. Their fame, as individuals and as a team, grew. Lapchick saw that the only blacks who became popular heroes other than the Trotters were Jesse Owens and Joe Louis, who humiliated the Nazis for America. The Rens had none of it. He saw what was happening. He just didn't know what he could do that would make any difference other than to his friends and family.

Chapter 14

The Nets Fall

It is ironic that Lapchick's coaching career was launched by two referees who recommended him to St. John's Athletic Moderator, Father Rebholz. Dave Walsh and John Murray told Rebholz that Lapchick would be a natural. As a player Lapchick had a reputation of being a "referee baiter" with little respect for the early breed. An incident in Nashville in 1935 made him rethink his position.

The local opposition was stretching the Celtics to the limit and Lapchick believed the refs were assisting the locals. He blasted them after each call. One ref stopped the game and took Joe Lapchick aside saying, "I heard so much about the great Joe Lapchick and was really looking forward to meeting you tonight. I'm sorry that I met you. All you are is an animal."

Lapchick went into the dressing room after the game, concluded that the ref was right and returned to apologize. He never stopped protesting the calls of referees, but after the Nashville incident he realized that most refs were professionals trying to do a job.

Lapchick built a great reputation as a coach at St. John's. However, it was not an easy transition for him. Although he was nominally the coach of the Celtics for the six previous years, this meant driving the car, getting the players out of saloons in time for the game, and keeping track of the money.

"I was scared stiff at the idea of speaking to college boys, let alone coaching them," he confessed. On the first day of practice the team gathered around their new coach with great expectations. Lapchick realized that he had no idea what to say, so he instructed them to practice shooting. Three days later they were still shooting when Jack Shanley, the captain, asked, "Coach, don't you think we should try something else?"

The coach said they should scrimmage and divided them into teams. He escaped to the top of the bleachers so Shanley couldn't question him further. He thought it also made sense because:

> I had read that a coach should get up high and look down at his team. So I walked back and forth at the top of the bleachers in the old De Gray gym for the whole preseason. It was the beginning of my insomnia. I couldn't sleep because I was being paid for nothing. The only reason we did well was because the captain and a few other players managed to get along without any help from me. A faculty member asked one of the players about me and was told "Lapchick stinks." I was told to throw him off the team. I couldn't because as far as I was concerned the boy was absolutely right. That season was a nightmare.

Lapchick sought help from Clair Bee at Long Island University and Nat Holman at City College of New York (CCNY). But it was Father Rebholz, the man who hired him, who gave Lapchick the confidence he needed in himself. Lapchick tried to resign first as baseball coach and then as basketball coach after the season. Rebholz said he wouldn't accept the resignations and that Lapchick would be a certain success in both sports.

Lapchick began to analyse the Celtics' style of playing the game in order to teach it at St. John's. As success mounted, he said, "I was never afraid again." St. John's was consistently invited to the National Invitation Tournament (NIT), the oldest of the postseason championships.

They won the 1944 tournament with such stars as guards Hy Gotkin and Larry Baxter, center Harry Boycoff, and Fuzzy Levane. Both Levane and Boycoff were pros after the war. Hy Gotkin became a lifelong friend of Lapchick.

The next year Boycoff, Levane and Baxter all were in the army. Although invited to the NIT as defending champions, St. John's was seeded seventh in an eight-team field. It was a great field featuring three of the best big men of the era—Bob Kurland of Oklahoma A & M, Don Otten of Bowling Green, and George Mikan of DePaul. Otten played in the NBA until 1953 while Kurland and Mikan were voted into the Hall of Fame. Mikan, of course, dominated pro basketball for a decade with the Minneapolis Lakers.

St. John's made it to the finals against heavily favored DePaul and Mikan. Lapchick was known as a nervous coach and this game, which turned out to be one of his greatest victories, was also one of his most embarrassing moments as a coach. St. John's was ahead by five points with the second half about five minutes over. It appeared as though the heavy underdogs might win. When George Mikan fouled out, Joe Lapchick passed out. He regained consciousness ten minutes later when St. John's had a 12-point lead and had sewed up the championship. "I dealt a helluva blow to coaching strategy that night," he joked.

While Lapchick was complementing his fame as a player with an illustrious coaching career, the college game flourished. The slower, more methodical and rougher pro game was alienating fans who were increasingly turning to the college games. In addition to those mentioned, Lapchick developed other St. John's stars such as Dutch Garfinkel, Howie Vocke, Bob Tough, Bill Kotsores and Dick McGuire.

In the meantime, a new pro league, the National Basketball League had formed in 1937 with mainly midwestern teams. It adopted many of the college rules and went after college players, landing such stars as John Wooden and Red Holzman who went on to become famed coaches after their careers ended. The league was very unstable and dwindled to four franchises during the latter years of the war.

However, the end of the war and the signing of George Mikan breathed new life into the league. Mikan played for Chicago that year and they won the championship. In 1947–48 he joined the Minneapolis Lakers and they won the championship, easily defeating the Rochester Royals in three out of four games. The

Lakers then played in the last "World Tournament," where they were stretched to the limit, narrowly beating the Rens, 75–71. Thus, as late as 1948, with an older team of less publicized stars, the Rens were still near the top of the basketball world.

It was a year of great hope for Douglas and the Rens. Branch Rickey of the Brooklyn Dodgers baseball club had signed Jackie Robinson to play for the Montreal Royals in 1946. Rickey signed other black stars like Don Newcomb and Roy Campanella. It was sad to see that the great old stars of the Negro leagues weren't being signed. But the big breakthrough came as Robinson started the 1946 season with four hits, including a home run. He never let up and in 1947, after all the years of forced exile, blacks were in the major leagues in baseball. Douglas was sure that the new rise of pro basketball would mean integrated league teams.

An equally important sign to him was the creation of the Basketball Association of America (BAA) in 1946. He saw this as the big league. Ned Irish, who had done so much to popularize college basketball, was behind the New York franchise. Walter Brown was in Boston. Teams were also located in Washington, Philadelphia, Cleveland, Chicago, St. Louis, Detroit and Pittsburgh among others. These were big cities with large black populations.

By 1947–48, the second year of operation, four of the original eleven teams had folded. But Douglas saw this as an opportunity to bring in the Rens. Moreover, Ned Irish had signed Joe Lapchick to coach the New York Knickerbockers.

The league owners met in Philadelphia in the fall of 1947. Bob Douglas could taste victory; he bought a new car and drove to Philadelphia for the meeting. On their agenda: the admission of the Rens to the league. Bob Douglas recalled the day with Bruce Newman of *Sports Illustrated:*

> I'll never forget that day as long as I live. . . . They invited me to sit in on their discussion before they voted. I remember that at one point an Italian fellow from Providence stood up and said the league could get along fine without us. Then Joe Lapchick, who was with the Knickerbockers, got up in front of his boss, Ned Irish, and said, "I may lose my job for saying this but I'd play against the Rens any goddam day. To me they're the best."

Douglas was asked to leave the room before the vote was taken. Leaving with confidence, he was stunned when he was informed that the motion didn't pass.

Joe Lapchick and Douglas shared time together after the meeting. Bob Douglas was despondent. Emotionally scarred, he was convinced that the door might be forever closed to blacks in the game he loved. Lapchick told Douglas that had it not been for their conversation in New York almost two decades earlier, he would probably never have stood up in that meeting. That conversation had helped create a consciousness about race that few others of his time shared. It was then that Bob Douglas told Lapchick that he couldn't recall the conversation. He had had so many similar ones without any expectations or results.

By 1947, however, Douglas knew Lapchick was different. Douglas had heard people tell him that Lapchick was anti-black since his St. John's team was all-white. Douglas pointed out that there were virtually no blacks playing at predominantly white colleges. Critics said Lapchick joined an all-white pro league. Douglas said it was really the only major league and that the National Basketball League, which by then had Dolly King playing for Rochester, was not as significant.

Douglas told Lapchick of these charges and said that he always chewed up anyone who made them. Although he had forgotten the earlier conversation with the man who was then just another white man who happened to be famous, his respect for Lapchick had grown tremendously as he saw Lapchick prove himself time after time.

Lapchick was relieved that Bob had brought this up. He had heard the charges but said there was no way to deal with them other than to persist in the pursuit of his principles. While he could do that, hearing them always made him sick. Here was a man who felt he truly believed in equality in an era when not many did. He felt that Nat Holman was of the same mind, but few others were. He wondered what possessed people to say such terrible things.

Douglas said to him:

Joe, in all our years together, I have always enjoyed our relationship. I must admit that I usually thought the basis of it was the love of the game that we had in common. I never could fully trust you or any white man. My black heart told me that if I was together with two white men and we were told that only two of us could live, it would be the whites who would survive. Whites would always choose whites. I knew you were very different, Joe, but today, for the first time in my life, I know there are whites who would risk everything for blacks.

My father told me about this conversation when I came to him to relate what had happened to me on the night Lloyd Dove stayed in my apartment. Like him, I had thought that I had as full and totally trusting a relationship with Dove as he had thought he had with Douglas. He had thought that years of playing together, eating together and standing up together meant there were no barriers. I too had thought that my years of friendship with Lloyd had left no barriers. Yet there I was in 1967 making that total breakthrough for the very first time like he did in 1947.

Joe Lapchick was no crusader. He didn't plan to stand up in that meeting. But when the situation arose, he knew he could do nothing less. Although he failed, he gained solace from the fact that Bob Douglas, at last, had completely understood his real beliefs.

Lapchick considered resigning from the Knicks, but ultimately believed that it would not serve any purpose. On the contrary, he believed that he could be instrumental in breaking down that wall against color. But the league would have to stabilize first.

Douglas didn't want to go on and turned the Rens over to Eric Illidge. The National Basketball League (NBL) lost four of its best teams to the Basketball Association of America (BAA) before the 1948–49 season. Rochester, Ft. Wayne, Indianapolis and George Mikan's Minneapolis teams all switched leagues, leaving franchises like Waterloo, Oshkosh, Sheboygen, Hammond and Anderson in the NBL. When the Detroit franchise folded a third of the way through the season, Illidge was offered a replacement franchise in Dayton. However, a boycott by the fans destroyed any chances of success and Illidge took a large personal financial loss as the NBL moved close to collapse.

The BAA, strengthened by the addition of the new franchises

in Minneapolis, Ft. Wayne, Rochester and Indianapolis, was becoming a big league operation and 1948–49 proved to be a good year. George Mikan led Minneapolis over Coach Red Auerbach's Washington Capitols for the championship.

The leagues merged before the 1949–50 season and formed the National Basketball Association (NBA). The NBL franchises such as Anderson, Waterloo and Sheboygan couldn't make it. So as the 1950–51 season approached, only major cities with major arenas were left in the NBA. The time for racial integration had come, although there were still obstacles.

Abe Saperstein, sensing the imminent integration of the NBA, began lobbying against it. At first, he told league owners it would be bad for blacks, just as major figures in the Negro baseball leagues had argued that integrating the major leagues would hurt black baseball players a few years before. After all, he was the "Jewish Abe Lincoln" and he was out to protect black players. When the humanitarian approach failed, he tried power. He said that the Trotters would not play in the arena of an owner who signed a black player.

But the time had come. Walter Brown and Red Auerbach were in Boston and Ned Irish and Joe Lapchick in New York for the 1950–51 season. Brown had drafted Chuck Cooper from Duquesne University. When Saperstein threatened to boycott the Boston Garden, Walter Brown told him he didn't have to withdraw because any team of his would never be allowed to play there. Irish and Lapchick went one better and signed Nat "Sweetwater" Clifton right off the Trotters' roster. The door had finally been opened.

The integration of professional baseball made the entry of Cooper and Clifton into the NBA far less dramatic. They didn't face most of the public abuse hurled at Jackie Robinson. Clifton certainly didn't see himself as a racial frontiersman. He played good solid basketball even though the race bar delayed his entry into the league until after his prime years. Joining the Knicks at age twenty-eight, Clifton averaged ten points a game over the next eight years.

However, Clifton was somewhat tentative in his first year and was getting pushed around a lot under the boards. Lapchick called him over on a train ride back from Indianapolis and told Clifton to push back. Nat didn't reply. "Can you fight?" Lapchick asked. "Coach, I'm terrible," Clifton answered. Lapchick could not understand. He had seen Nat play for the Trotters and had told Lou Effrat of the *Times* "Clifton owns the most beautiful hands and arms in basketball. They extend almost to his knees and make him a 6 foot 9 inch athlete. Besides, Sweetwater is an excellent hand-off man and outstanding underneath the boards, on defense as well as offense."

He reminded Clifton of these attributes that day on the train and said, "Terrible or not, I never saw a basketball fight where a guy really got hurt. So you go in swinging if you have to." Clifton opened up and explained that he was trying to make a good impression since the color bar had just fallen. Lapchick was sympathetic after all the years of seeing what white crowds, refs, and writers did to the Rens when they got into fights. But he told Clifton that the times had changed and that he could act freely. Nat improved that year but was still not up to his potential.

In his second year Clifton was hit hard by Boston Celtic Bob Harris after he pulled down a rebound in an exhibition game. They exchanged words and Clifton started back down the court. Harris chased him and they squared off. The Boston bench got up almost as a unit when Nat pulled his arm back. The punch floored Harris. Clifton turned toward the onrushing Celtics. When they saw Harris's fate they stopped dead in their tracks. Lapchick laughed, "You could smell the rubber burning on their shoes as they screeched to a halt."

Lapchick was ecstatic to see the fired-up Clifton who then went on to become one of the better rebounding and most respected forwards in the league. "I thought you told me you were a terrible fighter," he reminded Clifton. Clifton replied, "Coach, what I meant was—I'm terrible when I get mad."

Clifton actually got his professional start with the Rens. During the war he had served in Italy with Sonny Woods, another Ren. He joined the Trotters for two years while he played first base for the Wilkes Barre affiliate of the Cleveland Indians. He hit .321 there in 1950 before deciding it was to be all basketball for him in 1951.

Clifton developed an easy relationship with Lapchick. The coach was never big on enforcing rules with grown men and usually did so only after he was forced into it. One Sunday Clifton missed the curfew in the Knicks' training camp in Bear Mountain, New York. Lapchick happened to meet him at the door where Clifton explained that he had gone to nearby Highland Falls for a haircut. Lapchick laughed at his creativity.

Clifton was often teased by the New York press for his large facial features. Lapchick announced one day, "You know, you've made the all-ugly all-star team." Clifton countered, "Then I reckon we're still together because you must have been named coach."

That fondness between Clifton and Lapchick never bred a close personal relationship; Lapchick believed that there must be some professional distance between coach and player. There would be time for that later and he would become close to Carl Braun, Dick McGuire, Harry Gallatin, Vince Boryla and others who eventually joined the coaching fraternity.

Joe Lapchick didn't discuss the "nigger–lover" calls with the team or anyone else. It would be almost two decades before he knew that I had overheard some of those calls. Likewise, he didn't discuss the charge that he was anti-Semitic, which was apparently leveled by a Jewish ballplayer whom he had cut from the Knicks prior to signing Clifton.

This was even more ridiculous than the anti-black charge. He had Jewish teammates on the Celtics, many of his St. John's players were Jewish, his best man at his wedding was Jewish and two of his children had Jewish spouses. He knew more Yiddish than any other language. He discussed this with me in his last year. There was nothing he could do but continue to live by the moral code he had adopted so many years before. However, that didn't assuage the pain of thinking that someone—anyone—could believe he was something less than what he believed himself to be.

While he buried these things inside himself, Lapchick could not hide the anguish of coaching in professional basketball. In an article he wrote for *Collier's* in December 1954, titled "Each Game I Die," he wrote:

Within the first month of the season my weight drops from 195 to 178 pounds. I can no longer eat a normal meal and, unable to get a normal night's sleep, I have to rely on sedatives. My cigarette consumption goes up from one pack a day to two, and during a game I may have two or more cigarettes burning on the bench at the same time. One night, in fact, Bud Palmer sat on one of those hot butts. I have walked off the court unable to keep from crying.

He collapsed several times during his tenure with the Knicks. His health deteriorated badly in the later years as the pressures increased. At one point, the team had lost four straight before a game at Madison Square Garden with the Boston Celtics. Three of his regulars were out with injuries. After hours of tossing in bed the night before, he finally fell asleep only to wake up in a nightmare. His body was soaking wet and he was shaking. He had dreamt that the Knicks did not score a point! The Knicks won that day, but the nightmare never went away. Along with many other varieties of nightmares, it kept Joe Lapchick tossing and turning each night before and after a game. Each game was a doubleheader—the one on the court and the lonely replay in bed.

It was all part of his style. Leonard Koppett once wrote, "He was always a pro at heart. And to him being a pro meant putting out all the time as hard as you can. Many men in sports know this, feel it, and act upon it. Lapchick has the additional asset of being able to convey it. When things went bad for the Knicks, players weren't ashamed to be identified as Knicks, they felt ashamed to face Lapchick."

Things were not great for Lapchick or the Knicks in his last two and a half years. While always in the playoffs, they had not reached the finals since 1953. Lapchick was increasingly second-guessed by Ned Irish, the Knicks' boss. Irish was perhaps basketball's most successful entrepreneur, but he was not an affectionate man. Lapchick never criticized Irish publicly and was loyal to the man Roger Kahn later described as "the perfect mortgage forecloser."

By the beginning of the 1955–56 season, it seemed as though Ned Irish was ready to foreclose Lapchick as coach of the Knicks. Irish didn't fire him outright, but set up the situation so that Lapchick had no choice but to resign. Leonard Koppett wrote on January 30, 1956, that "Irish undercut Lapchick's authority by knocking Knick players, second-guessing the coach and interfering in decisions that should be strictly a coach's province. He did these things openly—sometimes in print, sometimes in the presence of players. He made it unmistakable that he no longer had confidence in Lapchick's judgment, thereby destroying the club's morale, shaking Joe's confidence in himself and finally tying Joe's hands . . . and his players were the first to realize it."

It was a far cry from the day Lapchick signed with the Knicks in March 1947 to become the highest-paid coach in basketball history. Citing "poor health and too many sleepless nights," Lapchick announced his resignation in January 1956.

It was surely the open rift with the Garden management that caused the final break. A glaring sign of this was the fact that Walter Brown and the Boston Celtics gave Lapchick a public send-off in the Knicks' last game in Boston, while the Garden management refused to even allow a local New York committee to stage a Joe Lapchick Night at Madison Square Garden. Leonard Koppett called the decision "a display of pettiness and blindness."

The New York press immediately took up the Lapchick case. Red Smith of the *New York Herald Tribune* wrote:

> What the Giants have been to professional football in New York, Joe Lapchick has been to basketball, both college and professional . . . nobody in any game has lent greater dignity to the American sports scene.

Leonard Koppett noted in the *New York Post* that "Joe Lapchick has one important failing as a coach—he's a nice guy . . . and soon Irish may find a song from 'Damn Yankees' haunting his thoughts. A man doesn't know what he has until he loses it." Warren Pack of the *New York Journal American* said, "We, the sports writers, will miss him at the Garden for he was always ready to give out with the truth, even when it affected him." Jimmy Cannon of the *Post* reported:

You're Joe Lapchick who plays every game twice . . . you're
haggard and jumpy . . . you've sickened with defeat in other years.
You've taken the game to hospitals with you . . . you're part of the
mythology of basketball . . . you and Irish have grown slowly apart.
Few people like the guy. You do. You defend him. You tell people
he's a good guy. This is a professional matter between an owner
and his coach. The boss wins them all. Owners don't resign because
they don't get along with the coach. The coach and the manager
take the fall. The owner stays.

Arthur Daly of *The New York Times* concluded that:

No coach in memory went through the agonizing torments of
Lapchick during a game. . . . He talks of going into public relations.
He should. Being a man of vast charm, amiability, graciousness
and winsomeness, he would do well in that field. If he returns to
basketball, it will kill him. Despite his all-encompassing love for
sport the big fellow should be too smart to toy with suicide. . . .
The world of sports will be poorer without big Joe. But he may be
a much happier man elsewhere.

Joe Lapchick didn't take Arthur Daly's advice because he
couldn't accept defeat. He had to return to coaching. He had to
recapture the rhythm of winning. But he had a perspective on
coaching:

There are no geniuses in coaching. The players always make the
coach, and we must never forget that. Sure, we make a contribution
to direct them to the type of game we want them to play. But the
coach isn't more important than the talent and commitment of his
players. A coach is never greater than his team.

Whatever the combination of talent and coaching, Lapchick's
St. John's teams won again for ten more years upon his return.
His intensity didn't change. "The game still tore me up inside,
but I only go through it twenty-five times a season instead of the
seventy-two I had with the pros, where you either win or get
out."
Still worried, Arthur Daly wrote about the game between St.

John's and national champion Ohio State in the 1961 Holiday
Festival:

> The tall and lean Lapchick looked like a man striving to achieve a
> mental breakdown. He was worse than he had ever been during his
> palmiest and balmiest days with the Knicks. He kept edging ahead
> in his chair until he pitched forward onto one knee at courtside. He
> would leap to his feet, screaming, exhorting and pleading. He'd let
> go withering blasts at the referees. He'd pound hands to temple
> when things went wrong. He'd untrigger himself by trips to the
> water cooler at the far end of the bench. Before the first half was
> over he had taken 24 such trips. Then count was lost.

There was to be a lot more winning and a lot more pain. The
triumphant ending at Madison Square Garden in 1965 topped the
cruel news of his mandatory retirement, just as his comeback at
St. John's restored his pride after he had left the Knicks.

Perhaps what Joe Lapchick said about cutting a player in the
Collier's story told me more about how he felt about being let go
himself than anything else: "When a kid fails you can't dismiss it
by saying, 'Well, he just went home.' He didn't just go home. In
many cases he's a hero in his hometown. Before he left they had
a dinner for him and gave him a watch. There were write-ups in
the paper. How is he going to feel when he goes back? How am I
going to feel?"

He couldn't allow himself to fail, although Ned Irish in the
mid-Fifties and St. John's a decade later made the ultimate cuts.
If they understood this deeply sensitive man, they didn't show it.
But Lapchick tried to ease their embarrassment at hurting a
popular public figure. He never publicly criticized either decision.
He decided first to prove them wrong and second to take them
off the hook. He later said of Ned Irish, "He was a tough man,
but he took basketball out of the dance halls. He gave it the
respectability it deserves. No one ever did more for the game."
As for St. John's, he never stopped being a fan.

Once he had achieved that last conquest at the NIT in 1965, he
said, "I shall settle for the todays because all your tomorrows
soon become yesterdays and then who gives a damn." It was an

ironic statement for a man who had experienced so many yester-days: the Celtics . . . the Rens . . . St. John's . . . the Knicks. For him they would last for the rest of his life. As he aged his yesterdays did become his tomorrows. The game and life all seemed to stand still. He could only passively watch basketball on television instead of on the sidelines; he could only passively watch the news about deteriorating race relations without the forum he once had to make his own quiet but meaningful changes through his sport. Whatever changes were to come, he knew that he would not take part in creating them. But Joe Lapchick helped build the stage so that those changes could someday begin. Sport's flickering torch would have to be picked up by others.

Part Five
**Race and Sport in America
in the 1990s**

Chapter 15

The True Believer and Beyond

Sport has become the broadest common cultural denominator in almost all societies. Men and women, blacks and whites, reactionaries and revolutionaries, Soviets and Americans, barefoot village people from the mountains of Kenya and sophisticated urbanites from New Delhi seem to "think sports." In most newspapers, the proportion of newsprint devoted to sports is usually as large or larger than that devoted to international events, domestic politics, economics, art, education, or religion. American television, especially on weekends, is saturated with sports events; there are several cable channels devoted to showing sports twenty-four hours a day.

Rabbis, priests, ministers, and politicians use sports metaphors to make their moral or political points. Values taught in sport will make their flocks better Jews, Catholics, Protestants, or Americans. Therefore, clergymen don't mind that Saturdays and Sundays are essentially the property of the NFL or the NBA. Religious services have become warm-ups for the bigger game to follow at the stadium. Religion and sport are on a continuum, teaching moral virtue to all who participate.

With so many Americans either playing themselves or watching others play, an enormous sports subculture has arisen. Many people in the subculture have come to accept a series of age-old verities about sport. I called such people "true believers." Here is their credo:

Sport can influence almost everything for the better. Sport contacts with other nations build friendships, peace, and understanding. Sport is a major social equalizer in America, leading blacks out of the ghetto through increased educational opportunity, changing attitudes of white teammates and opponents, and increasing employment opportunities for black athletes at the end of their sports careers. Women can assert themselves on athletic fields in ways that will break down "feminine" stereotypes and, the logic goes, prepare them to enter executive positions.

Sport goes beyond this; it can be an inspiration for everyone. It builds character, motivates individuals, generates teamwork, and teaches discipline through structured and contained competition. Values learned in sport are assets in all phases of life. Good athletes become good citizens and succeed as a consequence of their own dedication and hard work. Those athletes who make the pros have unlimited opportunities when their playing careers end. But, pro or not, everyone benefits from competition; schools, communities, and the nation come together to root for their team.

Certainly there are exceptions to such generalizations, but those who have joined the sports subculture see them as only that—as aberrations. This is because they tend to view society itself as healthy and on the right path. In fact, the draw of sport is so powerful that even many of those who are strong critics of other aspects of society view sport in the same positive light as the true believers.

I began my life as a true believer, but the life experiences I described in earlier chapters turned me into a true cynic about such sport verities. In 1980, with more than a decade of experience in the area of race, politics, and sport, I welcomed the request of my publisher to take a substantial look at racism in sports as part of *Broken Promises*. Looking more closely at sport and the problems associated with it made me want to do something actively to begin to help shape a different vision for sport, so I took a job as director of Northeastern University's Center for the Study of Sport in Society. After seven years as director, I have shed my cynical edge about sport. While hardly perfect, sport has made major improvements while society seems to have embarked on a self-destructive course.

The Center's mission is to increase awareness of sport and its relation to society, to develop programs which identify problems, offer solutions and promote the benefits of sport. When the Center's doors were opened in 1984 it seemed as though our public statements focused mainly on the many problems in sport. Seven years later, we now note that 74 percent of the public believes college sport is out of control while 86 percent of college presidents say university athletic programs get in the way of the educational mission of the university. I have no doubt that the work of the Center has helped shape that tone. But I believe that the pendulum may have now swung too far and that we may be overly critical of sport.

Sport in American Society

As we enter the 1990s society seems to have gone at least slightly mad. We need some perspective on the problems in sport:

—while we should continue to be upset about parents screaming at their children on youth sport playing fields while ignoring them in the classroom, we should be more concerned that many parents can't afford to go to their children's games because they are out holding two to three jobs just to survive.

—while we should continue to be concerned that some high school coaches oppose increased academic standards for athletes because they believe their players will drop our of school if they become ineligible instead of trying to raise their grades, we should be more concerned that many schools can't field full teams because kids are joining gangs, contributing to a drop-out rate of nearly 30 percent in cities all over the nation.

—while we should be anxious about the increasing number of games marred by violence, we should be far more concerned that an estimated 185,000 young people pack a gun each day when they go to high school.

—while we should be shocked that nine teenagers died between 1983 and 1990 because expensive athletic shoes had become such a status symbol that kids killed other kids to get them, we should remember that there were more than 100,000 homicides and 500,000 robberies in that same period.

—while we should continue to take note of how few athletes in revenue sports graduate in four years, we should not forget that only 14 percent of all entering freshmen graduate in four years.

—while we must do everything possible to end the use of performance-enhancing drugs in sports like football and track and field, we should be much more concerned about the fact that studies show that 40 percent of all steroids consumed in America are consumed by children under the age of sixteen who are not athletes but whose self-esteem is apparently so low that they literally are risking their futures to look better.

—while we should be tormented by the fact that there are stories about racism in sports, we should be tormented more by the fact that there were one hundred and seventy-five incidents of overt racism and another sixty-nine incidents of anti-Semitism reported on our college campuses in 1989.

—while we should be disheartened by how few blacks are hired in the front offices of our pro leagues and in college athletic departments, we should be more critical that only 1.56 percent of America's college faculties are black.

As these examples make clear, sport is hardly the source of society's problems; it merely reflects them. In fact, in some cases sports might be the only chance to keep kids in school and off drugs, teach values, instill discipline and foster brotherhood and sisterhood. However, it must be a newly reshaped sports system. I believe that the Center and another organization it founded, the National Consortium for Academics and Sport, have made an enormous difference. Both were created to help shape that new sports system and I look forward to a future when sport meets all the high expectations that society has placed on it. But we have a long way to go to get there.

Sport and the Student-Athlete

Everyone knows that professional sport is a business like any other, although most sports values are expected to apply. But a true believer would have different expectations for colleges, high schools, and youth leagues: dedication and loyalty to the team, hard work, honesty, discipline, character building, and a commitment to winning through excellence and not through destruction of the opposition. Our coaches are expected to be teachers of these virtues and nurturers of their athletes, both on and off the court.

The truth can be very different. The slogan "Winning isn't everything, it's the only thing" is a reality at too many schools. Under incredible pressures to win often enough to fill stadiums and to be attractive to television, winning at all costs is the philosophy of too many coaches. Some alumni and boosters pay coaches, players, and families of players. Too many athletes are tempted to disregard academics and dream of incomes far beyond their reach. Faculties have traditionally shrugged their shoulders while college presidents have tried to stay above the battlefield. Sanctions for violations were rare and selective. Ultimately, it paid to cheat. It was a system gone mad and finally brought us to the point that in 1990 National Collegiate Athletic Association (NCAA) Executive Director Dick Schultz had to call for extensive reform to turn college sports inside out in order to regain the public confidence. Between the NCAA Presidents Commission, the Knight Commission, the leadership of Conference Commissioners, and Dick Schultz himself, we have reached the stage where we may have the best chance for reform in recent decades. The changes legislated by the NCAA at its 1991 Convention are discussed in the conclusion. They are very encouraging to those seeking reform.

Money in College Sport

We must remember how we reached the point where the need to win at all costs seemed to be the prevailing philosophy. Why did it happen? A large part of the answer, of course, is money.

Athletic budgets have soared to finance dominant teams that will fill arenas and obtain lucrative television contracts. The NCAA's $1 billion, seven-year contract with CBS to televise their basketball (and other) championships was the culmination of this feeding frenzy.

More than thirty college teams earned more from 1990 bowl games than it cost to run an entire athletic program in 1975. There are now athletic budgets exceeding $15 million all over the country and these figures exclude lucrative booster donations. According to the College Football Association's *Financial Survey,* it cost an average of $10,738,000 to operate an athletic program in 1988–89, representing a 35 percent increase from 1985–86. Escalating costs were a target of NCAA legislation at the 1991 Convention.

Scandals in College Sport

Before 1980 we rarely read stories about abuses or exploitation of athletes. The extent of the athletic scandals revealed in 1980 made previous claims of such abuses by sports critics like Jack Scott and Harry Edwards in the late 1960s seem insignificant.

When the Center for the Study of Sport in Society opened in 1984, the prevailing wisdom was that we had to strike fast with new reform programs because the public's (and the media's) interest in such programs would be short-lived. However, every year since 1984 has witnessed an increasing number of athletic department scandals.

History should have told us something. In 1980 seven conferences incorporated the top sixty football programs in the country. Before the 1980 scandal broke, forty-two of the sixty had received public disciplinary action. That's 72 percent. Basketball was even worse. Between 1952 and 1980, only two schools (Chicago Loyola in 1963 and Marquette in 1967) that had won NCAA championships had not been subject to some form of public disciplinary action at one time or another because of their basketball programs.

So the scandal in 1980 was nothing new. Perhaps the only difference was that the stakes were higher, so colleges were taking more chances. And it was the glamour schools, not simply schools-on-the-make, that were caught. These included the University of Southern California (USC), Oregon State, Arizona State, and the University of California at Los Angeles (UCLA). At USC, nineteen football players enrolled in a speech course they didn't attend. USC had to forfeit an NCAA track title because it was revealed that Billy Mullins, its 1978 sprint star, was accepted on credits allegedly accumulated simultaneously from four widely separated junior colleges. Arizona State forfeited five football wins in 1979 after it was divulged that players were getting credits for extension courses they didn't take. (Earlier, coach Frank Kush reportedly said, "My job is to win football games. I've got to put people in the stadium, make money for the university, keep the alumni happy, and give the school a winning reputation.") Oregon State dropped its only win in an eleven-game season because it used an ineligible player. The FBI alleged that New Mexico's basketball coach arranged to forge a star player's transcript to get him into school. According to a university report, the Portland State basketball coach was accused of both paying players and taking kickbacks. He claimed he took money for the players but not for himself.

An internal investigation at the University of San Francisco, which was partially precipitated by the Quintin Dailey case (in which Dailey was accused of sexual abuse), revealed lucrative payoffs and special treatment for athletes, and led the university to temporarily drop its basketball program.

But the decade of the 1980s made the revelations of 1980 look small-time. According to the *Chronicle of Higher Education,* between 1980 and 1989 nearly half of the NCAA Division IA (schools with major football programs) were either censured, sanctioned, or put on probation at least once. More than one hundred schools were cited during the decade. One school was punished four times while several others were penalized two to three times.

A United States Government Accounting Office (GAO) report, issued in 1989, showed that 70 percent of Division I basketball schools and 51 percent of Division IA football schools graduated between zero and 40 percent of their basketball and football players, respectively. According to the NCAA, 33 percent of basketball players and 37 percent of football players graduate.

From my point of view, this is the greatest problem in college sport today. I am concerned about compliance violations, drugs and other problems. But our academic institutions are in the business of educating those who come to them. When that does not happen, we are failing in the educational mission of our universities.

More often than not, the black athlete is the ultimate victim of all these problems and is most likely to end up without an education (as we will see in Chapter 16). However, many white athletes are also seriously shortchanged in the process. Both are sucked into the cheating that has become so common it seems right. According to Allen Sack, who conducted a 1989 survey of 1,182 current and former NFL players, one-third reported receiving illegal payments while in college and more than half saw nothing wrong with the practice. Who can fully blame the athlete for taking what must simply appear to be his piece of the pie?

Are players on scholarship "student-athletes"? Most student-athletes do far better academically than non-athletes. However, the data from the GAO report clearly demonstrates that many student-athletes in the revenue sports of football and basketball are really athletes first and students second.

The Role of the Presidents

The NCAA is today handing out the biggest sanctions to schools which have lost "institutional control" of their athletic programs. The role or lack thereof of the president or chancellor is, thus, crucial. That is why I was especially shocked, when I was doing research for *Broken Promises,* by the cavalier attitude of William E. (Bud) Davis, president of the University of New Mexico. Davis told *Newsweek,* "Our recruits were recruited to be athletes, not students. There was never an expectation that they'd get their ass out of bed at eight o'clock to go to class and turn in their assignments."

The 1980s witnessed many college presidents lose their jobs, at least in part because of problems in their athletic departments. Bill Atchley was forced out at Clemson in 1986 after clashing with Bill McLellan, then Clemson's athletic director, over re-forms Atchley wanted adopted. Atchley noted that "unfortu-nately we don't have an academic page as exciting as the sports page." Clemson's current president, Max Lennon, has so far survived after he took control and fired Danny Ford, Clemson's very popular and highly successful football coach. Death threats and protests followed the firing.

David Roselle, then president at the University of Kentucky, fired basketball coach Eddie Sutton and athletic director Cliff Hagan in order to gain control of the athletic program during an NCAA investigation at Kentucky. Voted "Sportsman of the Year" by Kentucky sportswriters, Roselle's resolve probably saved the school from suspension. He was hailed nationally as a president who was determined to move a reform agenda. How-ever, later reports indicated that Roselle became discouraged by slow progress, and resigned to take the presidency at the Univer-sity of Delaware in 1990 after only two and a half years at Kentucky.

Joab Thomas was president at the University of Alabama when the school hired Bill Curry as football coach in 1987. Curry was not from Alabama, had a losing record at Georgia Tech and had a reputation for integrity. The first two were the ones that counted with Alabama alumni. Thomas also hired Steve Sloan, head football coach at Duke—another program known more for integ-rity than winning—as athletic director. The criticism of Thomas was unrelenting and he finally resigned under pressure in 1989. Sloan quickly followed and Curry left for the University of Kentucky, despite his winning record.

Marshall Criser reportedly quit as president at the University of Florida in 1990 in part because of the chaos in the athletic department which led to the firing of the head coaches in both football and basketball. John Schwada was the first presidential casualty of the 1980s when he quit his post at Arizona State in 1980 after exposure of the fact that players received credits for junior college classes they never took.

The Jan Kemp affair at the University of Georgia, revealing academic abuses of athletes, ultimately forced Georgia President Fred Davidson to resign in 1986. His statement that Georgia's

Developmental Studies Program was really fine because Georgia's athletes could become postal workers instead of sanitation workers made him a target of pressure.

William Lavery left as Virginia Tech's president in 1987 when simultaneous scandals in Tech's basketball and football programs broke into the news. North Carolina State's chancellor, Bruce Poulton resigned in 1989 and was followed by Jim Valvano, his athletic director and basketball coach. The publication of Peter Golenbach's *Personal Fouls,* which alleged numerous violations and abuses, was a very hot topic during the 1989–90 basketball season. The portrayal of Poulton in the book was very negative and he was forced to step down.

The fact that two hundred thirty-three presidents attended the 1991 NCAA Convention to lead the charge for reform reflected the heightened awareness of presidents. They worked closely with athletic department and conference officials, which should mean that legislated reforms will work at the institutional level.

While it appeared routine for winning coaches implicated in scandals to get other head coaching jobs (more than twenty of the top programs in the 1989–90 year were led by coaches who had off-the-field or court problems at other schools), college presidents were not so fortunate. As of this writing, former presidents Thomas, Lavery and Poulton were on faculties; Davidson was head of the National Science Center Foundation in Georgia, and Schwada had retired. The good news is that Atchley and Roselle, who acted on principle, are presidents at the University of the Pacific and the University of Delaware.

Pressures on Coaches

Under tremendous pressure to produce, some coaches opt for the simple answer: do everything possible to get star athletes for their team. This applies to recruiting and to keeping the athletes eligible to play.

The extremely high turnover rate for Division I basketball coaches indicates the extent of the pressure. A *Washington Post* survey showed that between 1970 and 1980, forty-nine schools had at least three basketball coaches. The sampling came from one hundred ten major schools in the eleven most powerful basketball conferences, plus fifteen other institutions with major athletic programs. More revealing was the fact that only 10 percent of the coaches at Division I basketball schools in 1970 were at the same schools in 1980. UCLA, the most glamorous school of all, had four coaches in ten years. Between 1980 and 1990, the turnover rate for basketball coaches reached 24 percent annually.

The Problems Start Early: Youth Sport and High School Sport

We cannot simply blame coaches, athletic directors or presidents for such problems in sport. The chain of problems in sport starts early. Parents push their children in the Little League and Pop Warner League. The pressure starts there. The position specialization starts there. The end of most athletic careers starts there. Parents don't want each child to play in each game. They want *their* child to play the whole game. When Little League and Pop Warner football instituted a rule that every child had to play, 1,800 teams withdrew from the league. Stories appeared about fathers assaulting coaches because their sons weren't getting enough playing time.

Families move near schools with better athletic programs. In the early Eighties, I was shocked to discover that parents in Georgia and Texas were arranging for their children to repeat the eighth grade to increase their chances for college scholarships five years later by giving them one more year to mature. I have since learned that is common practice in many states.

Many athletes have told me about loving parents who went to all their games from youth sport through high school. Sadly, many of those same parents rarely went to parent-teacher conferences about academic performance. Those same parents rarely failed to give advice to their children about how to play the game, but only talked about school work if the children were at risk of losing their eligibility. The subtle message starts early: "Sports are more important to mom and dad than school; if I'm good at sports perhaps I don't need to be good in school." The cycle of the dumb jock has begun right there in the living room.

We have become familiar with headlines about scandals in sport. Headline stories in 1989–90 exposed the fixing of transcripts, illegal recruiting, fixing of games, and more generally the persistence of racism in sport. Stories highlighted arrests of athletes for stealing and sexual offenses, as well as for their use of recreational drugs and steroids. The difference between these stories and previous ones was that these were all stories about high school sport.

The pressures have gotten worse in high school. They were already intense enough, but now we have a nationally televised high school game-of-the-week in basketball and football. All-star classics and all-star summer camps seem to be popping up everywhere. Amateur Athletic Union (AAU) high school basketball is creating even more havoc.

Many teenagers already have gone through a recruiting process—to get to high school. Coaches even help a prospect's family relocate nearer to the school. High school teachers reportedly pass illiterate players to keep them eligible. The seemingly easy ride to the top has begun. In 1983, less than 100 of 16,000 high school districts required a "C" average to participate in sport. The fact that between 25 and 30 percent of high school senior football and basketball players reportedly leave school functionally illiterate has prompted six states and hundreds of local school districts to adopt "no pass/no play" standards. Wherever they have been adopted, athletes have met the call and increased their grades. We have always challenged them athletically. We must pose the same challenge academically. However, there are still forty-four states without a minimum "C" requirement. This means that a student-athlete can play for four years with less than a "C" average—perhaps without receiving a "C" in a single course.

College Recruiters and the High School Athlete

For those whose sports dreams are still alive in the twelfth grade, the easy life can continue unabated. Some college coaches offer players a variety of inducements to come to their school. Payoffs have included jobs, housing, cars, clothing, meals, transportation, and direct cash handouts. By now most fans have read of the famous $1,000 payment to a high school recruit's father that fell out of an Emery Air express package. That eventually led to heavy penalties at the University of Kentucky. Most fans know that Southern Methodist University (SMU) was paying $7,500 or more to selected football players. For that and other indiscretions, football was suspended at SMU.

But according to many, those payments were small-time. Just one story will illustrate the point. I was first told about this case by a man brought in as athletic director to clean up an athletic department that suffered from a terrible reputation. In the middle of his reform tenure at this school, he learned that his basketball coach had offered $25,000 to a standout forward from Los Angeles. The coach was appalled because that figure didn't even put him in the running. The director, realizing that he was living in the belly of the beast he was supposed to change, quit.

In the meantime, the player's mother reportedly received $60,000 in cash after her son signed a letter of intent with an untainted school in the South, a school known for winning with integrity. The player enrolled that fall at yet another school, but no one could legally ask the mother for the cash back. (No one ever said he received any money from the school he played for.) I had this story confirmed by many sources, but no one wrote about it until the publication of *Raw Recruits* by Alex Wolff and Armen Keteyian.

Taking Responsibility

Between the athletes and the coaches are the boosters and alumni. Together, the latter now contribute a significant portion of the athletic budget and almost all of the illegal money; they have a great deal of control when presidents surrender the reins. Through 1990, over half of the actions taken by the NCAA Committee on Infractions have been against booster-related offenses.

Many administrators have appeared to condone or at least ignore departures from the rules. After all, a winning team enhances the school's prestige even if it is at the educational expense of the same student-athletes responsible for that prestige. A winner brings in television money, exposure and gate receipts. At private institutions, winning teams can be a drawing card for new students, and thus more revenues. But with the increasing number of presidents who have lost their jobs, presidents are reempowering the NCAA Presidents Commission and more are taking control on their own campuses.

Then, of course, there is the faculty. Many have suggested, even expected, that faculty obtain more critical acadamic control as if they were super ombudsmen of athletic practices. However, the historical reality is that they tend to be either fans themselves or consider themselves above sports, and thereby absolved of any special academic responsibility for athletes. As the new decade began, there were encouraging signs of increased potential for faculty involvement, including the creation of a permanent committee addressing problems in athletics within the American Association of University Professors.

Even though there are several encouraging signs from other areas, the key role will no doubt be played by the NCAA, led by Executive Director Dick Schultz. This point was emphasized by the results legislated at their 1991 convention.

If a school wants to be on television, compete for national championships and have big-time athletic programs, it must belong to the NCAA. That fact, of course, can be used for the good or otherwise. George Sage, the highly respected sports scholar, wrote (prior to Dick Schultz taking over from Walter Byers in 1988) that the NCAA is a "business organization that is part of the entertainment industry whose product is competitive intercollegiate sports events." He argued that it is a cartel with a monopoly on the production and sale of this commodity and the wages of the sports labor force. The "wages" for student-athletes are their scholarships, which have a significant dollar value. (However, if the student-athletes don't receive an education and graduate, then they have given away their talents for free.)

The NCAA is its own police force and penalizes those who

violate NCAA rules and regulations. However, many believe that its investigation unit is underfinanced and relies too much on rumor and innuendo, sometimes from rival schools that may have a self-interest in a specific case. Newspapers uncover as many scandals as the unit.

The NCAA regulates everything regarding athletes. The "transfer rule" of one-year mandatory ineligibility restricts mobility if a player changes schools; the "five-year rule" allows colleges to "redshirt" players, that is, to allow them to sit out a year and defer eligibility; and the "freshmen eligibility rule," which allows freshmen to play varsity sports right away, reduces costs. In a time when "cost containment" in athletics is a major concern, all of these rules keep costs down. But whether they are in the best interest of the student-athlete is open to serious question. Several are being reviewed now by reform-minded groups; one additional rule that should be considered is a guaranteed fifth year of scholarship after an athlete's eligibility has expired. If only 14 percent of all entering freshmen graduate in four years, athletes, with their extra time-demands, cannot be expected to do better.

The NCAA has come a long way in a short time since the tenure of former director Walter Byers. However, the NCAA is the sum of its parts. While it can pass rules and will sometimes catch and prosecute violators, it is ultimately up to the individual institutions to maintain their own integrity. The institutions are not going to make things right unless they have the will to create and maintain clean, ethical programs. While Dick Schultz and the current leadership at the NCAA have set the tone, the morality must start at home.

But where does that leave us? Prescriptions for change to decades-old, complex problems cannot be simplistic. To be truly successful, changes must emanate from all sectors of the campus, bringing together forces frequently thought of as antagonists: governing boards, presidents and athletic directors, coaches and faculty, students and student-athletes. Institutions of higher education must work more closely in the community with high schools to better prepare high school student-athletes for college.

We must see what we have in common—love of sport—and stop emphasizing the differences.

In a book I coauthored with John Slaughter, former chair of the NCAA Presidents Commission, called *The Rules of the Game: Ethics in College Sport,* numerous proposals for reform are described in great detail. I also offer several substantial reform proposals in the conclusion of this book.

Chapter 16

A Long Way to Go

If Bob Douglas were to return today, he might easily believe it was the 1920s instead of the 1990s. The Klan is publicly on the march; David Duke, one of its leaders, was a serious candidate for U.S. Senator in 1990. Hate crimes against blacks increased 149 percent between 1987 and 1989. The income gap between blacks and whites has widened. The Reagan administration either swept away or emasculated most of the social programs designed to aid the poor. A Louis Harris Poll showed that blacks in overwhelming numbers believe their conditions worsened in the 1980s, while whites believe that the state of black America vastly improved. Blacks felt that they were worse off in areas such as education, housing, and justice, and that American institutions such as the police, Congress, and the President do more to keep them down than to help them. Whites, of course, held exactly the opposite viewpoint.

Most frightening were the attitudes of America's youth in 1990. The Center for the Study of Sport in Society and the Reebok Foundation commissioned the Northeastern University/Reebok Foundation Study on Youth Attitudes on Racism, conducted by Louis Harris. The results were shocking:

- 57 percent reported having seen or heard a racial act with violent overtones either very often (21 percent) or once in a while (36 percent).

- one in three said that they would openly join in a confrontation against another racial or religious group if they agreed with those who stirred it up.

- another 17 percent, while they would not join, would feel that the victims deserved what they got.

- one of four said that they had been the victim of such an incident, including nearly half of all black high school students.

According to Harris, the nation's leading pollster, these numbers were much higher than previously thought. "America faces a critical situation," he reported. "Our findings show that racial and religious harassment and violence are now commonplace among our young people rather than the exception. Far from being concentrated in any one area, confrontations occur in every region of the country and in all types of communities."

Racism in High School Sport

The 1980s started with more of the same for blacks in sport. Whites assumed that racial barriers in sport were long gone while blacks knew they were, to a large degree, still there. Then Al Campanis and Jimmy "The Greek" Snyder made us take another look with their racist remarks on network television in 1987 and 1988. That look definitely led to some positive signs as the decade of the 1990s opened. However, we should not have needed those chance statements to wake us up. All we needed to do was to take a look around.

They still talk about Darryl Williams in racially charged Boston. A fifteen-year-old from Roxbury, Boston's Harlem, he caught a pass that gave his visiting Jamaica Plain High School a 6–0 halftime lead over Charlestown High. It was his first varsity start. September 1979 seemed like a good time for Darryl. He probably had visions of being on his way to the NFL. As Jamaica Plain gathered in a huddle before the second half, a sniper made sure his dreams were finished. Darryl's career was over, but at least his life was saved. His presence in the game at Charlestown and his fate that day were probably the products of the 1974 court-ordered busing that had placed Boston on national television as a center of racial hatred and violence.

It took Darryl Williams eleven years to return to that field, accompanied by *Boston Globe* reporter Dan Shaughnessy. Williams told Shaughnessy what he thought the three convicted snipers were doing: "What were they doing? Besides getting ready to make my life a living hell . . . I think they were trying to kill somebody black, not wound somebody black, not make somebody black paralyzed; their intention was to kill somebody black."

The 1980s started with a cross being burned during the halftime festivities of a football game between black and white high schools in Durham, North Carolina. The 1980s ended with claims that two high school teams in Mississippi's Private School Association forfeited football games against the Columbus Heritage Academy team because it included a reserve running back named Scott Fuller who happened to be black. Fuller was the first black player in the North Central Athletic Association Conference. The other schools denied that this was the reason they had forfeited. However, the charges seemed to be substantiated when Heritage's girls basketball team had to withdraw from an early season basketball tournament in Dekalb, Mississippi, when other teams made it known that they were ready to cancel the entire tournament because Heritage included Amy Walker, a black freshman, on its team.

Glenn Collins, a former professional football player who had attended Mississippi State, was not allowed to enter a high school broadcast booth to cover a game for WJXN radio in Jackson, Mississippi, at all-white East Holmes Academy. Lee Adams, a WJXN official, said he was told not to bring Collins because blacks are not welcome. The school denied the statement.

Charges of racism dominated the 1989 football season at Conway High School in Conway, South Carolina. The protests began when coach Chuck Jordan replaced quarterback Carlos Hunt, who is black and led the team to a winning record in 1988, with Mickey Wilson, who is white. The Reverend H. H. Singleton, head of the Conway NAACP and a middle school teacher, called for a boycott, and thirty black players quit the team. The Conway School Board fired Singleton for his role in the protest, claiming he disrupted the learning process at the school.

The issue of private sports clubs and country clubs was much in the news in 1990 after the Shoal Creek controversy with the Professional Golfers Association. However, the immediate and widespread response in 1990 stood in sharp contrast to what happened a few years earlier in Louisiana when two black members of a Catholic high school golf team were not allowed to participate in a twelve-team tournament because it was being played on a segregated private course. Their school went ahead and competed without them. The commissioner of the Louisiana High School Athletic Association said, "Unfortunately, every school and every area doesn't have a municipal golf course. Some schools wouldn't have a team if they didn't use the private clubs. This is true even in tennis and sometimes swimming. So we don't knock the local clubs that cooperate with the high schools." The principal of the school, a Catholic nun, added, "It's not that big an issue, and there's no reason to keep badgering us about it."

Integration of College Sport

By 1970, black athletes had power on the playing field. Their numbers were increasing at all levels in basketball, football, baseball, boxing, and track and field. As the mood of the country shifted slightly toward giving blacks more educational opportunities, coaches with an eye toward the scoreboard took advantage of "open admissions" policies. White coaches, administrators, boosters, and players had to adjust. If they had been racist before, they would have to tone it down.

It only took one afternoon to convert legendary Alabama coach Bear Bryant. Southern Cal blasted Alabama in Birmingham by a score of 42–21. Sam Cunningham, a black fullback, slammed

Alabama for three touchdowns. Bryant reportedly walked off the turf muttering, "He just did more for integration in the South in sixty minutes than Martin Luther King did in twenty years." That night he began making plans to bring blacks to Alabama. Adolph Rupp, the historic Kentucky coach, saw the light a few years earlier in 1966 when Texas Western, with five black starters, shocked favored (and all-white) Kentucky in the NCAA finals.

The University of Texas at El Paso (UTEP), as Texas Western is now known, had learned the lesson even earlier when it reportedly became the first school in Texas to admit a black athlete. The only problem was they forgot to turn down the racist rhetoric. Jim Bouden, then assistant athletic director, painted a picture of racism at UTEP so deep that Jack Olsen devoted one part of his landmark series in *Sports Illustrated* on the black athlete to it.

Blacks across the country thought that Texas Western's victory over all-white Kentucky for the national championship had enabled them to take one more step forward. Blacks celebrated and cheered, but once again they were betrayed; the five black starters never graduated. UTEP's racism surfaced again and again. Bouden told Olsen, referring to his boss, athletic director George McCarthy: "This is the first institution in Texas—right here—that had a colored athlete. George McCarthy's done more for 'em than this damn guy Harry Edwards. . . . George McCarthy's done more for the nigger race than Harry Edwards'll do if he lives to be a hundred."

Yet, even in the 1960s there were plenty of white coaches trying to deal honestly and fairly with blacks. Dick Hays, who had been the University of Kansas coach, told Olsen after he left Kansas:

Sure we broke down some of the physical segregation. . . . We did all the formal things, but the times called for more than that. What I wanted to do was reach the minds and hearts of my white players so that they would become determined not to permit the Negro to be anything less than a complete human being. What I had hoped was to use the basketball to turn out a bunch of white college graduates who would walk that extra mile for some Negro because of the experiences they had as members of an integrated basketball team. I don't think I produced even one such white man.

Hays actually quit his job when he was pressured not to play four blacks at once. This was a man of principle and commitment. Yet his case points out one of the real problems that persists today. Hays told Olsen that his only "integrated player" was Maurice King. Hays meant it as a compliment. But this is how he explained it: "There must have been something exceptional about him [King] because he got along so well with the others. The rest of the Negroes spent their time off the court with other Negroes." King was willing to hang around with whites and they let him. But that is precisely the problem. White coaches, no matter how well meaning they are, naturally view events from a white perspective.

When Rudy Washington was hired to coach at Drake University in the spring of 1990, he became only the fortieth black coach at a major college (excluding the historically black colleges). Many believed that Rudy's vocal leadership in forming the Black Coaches Association in the wake of Al Campanis's remarks delayed his getting a head coaching job.

How are white coaches going to develop the sensitivity to understand black players? The older coaches probably didn't play with blacks. They didn't have a Bob Douglas to teach them. Some major schools have black assistants, who should help with the problem. However, their primary purpose is to help recruit more blacks. There is some hope that the younger white coaches, who have played with blacks, will be more sensitive to their needs, but this has yet to be proven.

Black Student-Athletes: High School vs. College

One of the most hallowed assumptions about race and sport is that athletic contact between blacks and whites will favorably change racial perceptions. It has now become clear to me that for this change to take place, you need a committed coach to guide his players' social relations. The Northeastern University/Reebok

Foundation Study on Youth Attitudes on Racism mentioned above showed that a 70–27 percent majority of high school students reported that they had become friends with someone from a different racial or ethnic group through playing sports. Among blacks, a 77–19 percent majority reported this result; the comparable majority was 68–29 among whites and 79–17 among Hispanics. That was encouraging news, indeed.

However, predominantly white campuses, like corporate boardrooms, naturally reflect the value system of the dominant white culture. They are not equal meeting grounds for white students and blacks, whether from urban or rural America.

With American public opinion of college sport already at a seemingly all-time low, the wide-ranging debate and protest against the NCAA's Proposition 42, which would have made athletes who did not achieve certain academic standards unable to receive a scholarship, made the issue of race among the central ethical issues in college sport in the 1990s. The fact that black athletes are the objects of low academic expectations (only 31 percent of the black athletes in the 1989 NCAA study on college athletes, known as the AIR Study, said that their coaches encouraged good grades), that they are not receiving the education promised by colleges (graduation rates for black athletes are significantly less than for whites), and that they have few black coaches or faculty members to model themselves after on campus is drawing attention.

In fact, while only 7 percent of all students at predominantly white colleges are black, 56 percent of all basketball players and 37 percent of all football players at these colleges are black. Many enter with the academic odds already stacked against them. All colleges and universities have some form of "special admittance" program in which a certain percentage of students who do not meet the normal admission standards of the school are allowed in anyway. According to the NCAA, about 3 percent of all students enter as special admissions while more than 20 percent of football and basketball players enter under this program. Since there are so many football and basketball players who are black, one might assume that a very large percentage of special admits playing in these sports are black.

The 1989 NCAA study presented a wealth of data. That black athletes feel racially isolated on college campuses, are overrepresented in football and basketball, have high expectations of pro careers, and are uninvolved in other extracurricular activities did not surprise most close to college sport.

However, the results of the NCAA study stood in stark contrast to the results presented in *The Women's Sports Foundation Report: Minorities in Sports: The Effect of Varsity Participation on the Social, Educational, and Career Mobility of Minority Students*. Published in 1989, it was the first major study of minorities playing high school sports. It clearly established that in comparison to black non-athletes, black high school athletes feel better about themselves, are more involved in extracurricular activities other than sport, are more involved in the broader community, aspire to be community leaders and have better grade point averages and standardized test scores. Almost all those results contradict the view that most of white society has about the black athlete.

The Northeastern University/Reebok Foundation Study on Youth Attitudes on Racism asked high school student-athletes a number of questions about the benefits of sport. Earlier in this chapter I noted that one clear benefit was friendship across racial lines. Other questions drew out the following benefits for all athletes:

- a 61–36 percent majority felt that playing sports helped them "in becoming a better student." Blacks (79–17) and football and basketball players (68–31) felt this even more than other student-athletes.

- by 56–41 percent, a majority believed that playing on teams helped them "avoid drugs." Again, blacks (74–25) and football and basketball players (67–32) benefited most.

- a 53–43 percent majority believed sports competition helped them "in becoming better citizens." This was especially true among blacks (67–28), Hispanics (60–34) and football and basketball players (62–36).

- a 52–45 percent majority of varsity athletes believed that their sports activity helped them in "staying in school." Again, the groups this helped most were blacks (72–24), football and basketball players (61–36), and Hispanics (58–39).

According to Louis Harris, it is apparent that most varsity athletes believe that their playing on teams has helped them on balance to become better students, better citizens and to avoid drugs: "It is especially significant to note that the value of playing sports in all these areas was significantly higher for African-American student-athletes in particular and for football and basketball players in general. It merits considerable attention by colleges and universities where the experience of African-American student-athletes as well as their football and basketball players is significantly different and appears much more negative."

The primary question which now must be asked is what happens to the black athlete between high school and college that seems to totally change how he perceives himself. Among other things, he leaves a high school that is either overwhelmingly black or at least partially integrated; if he is from an urban area, he leaves behind a core of black teachers and coaches; if he lives on campus or goes to school away from home, he leaves behind whatever positive support network existed in the community in which he was raised and leaves behind possible black role models who are not exclusively athletes.

He arrives in college to discover that the proportion of black students on the predominantly white campuses is only 7 percent; that only 1.56 percent of the faculty positions at colleges and universities are held by blacks; and that the athletic department hires just slightly more blacks than the faculty and actually hires fewer blacks than are employed in professional sport.

A great deal of emphasis has been placed on racial discrimination in professional sport, especially the hiring practices of professional franchises. However, a look at the numbers of positions which could be available in our colleges and universities shows us that there are far more problems as well as far more possibilities there than in the pros.

Bill Russell described the feeling of being in a white world many years ago in *Second Wind:* "You are a Negro. A living, smarting, hurting, smelling, greasy substance that covers you. A morass to fight from." While the militancy and struggle of the Sixties and Seventies have reduced the negative self-perceptions of most young blacks, the stereotypes still exist for many whites, stereotypes and all the taboos that go with them.

White and black athletes can meet on campus carrying a great deal of racial baggage. Their prejudices won't automatically evaporate with the sweat as they play together on a team. The key to racial harmony on a team is the attitude and leadership of the coach. He (or she) must be committed to equality and clearly demonstrate this to the team. In 1980, I was very skeptical about the potential for this; by 1990, I was counting on it to lead us away from the race hate that was spreading through society.

However, I know that this will not be easy. The history of young athletes, and students in general, makes it an uphill task. Chances are that competition at the high school level bred some animosity; usually white teams play against black teams, reflecting urban residential housing patterns. There is virtually no playground competition between blacks and whites as few dare to leave their neighborhood.

On a college team, blacks and whites are competing for playing time, while in the society at large, black and white workers compete for jobs, public housing, even welfare. A primary difference is that whites are apt to accept blacks on the team since they will help the team win more games and perhaps get them more exposure. It is easy for white athletes, no matter what their racial attitudes might be, to accept blacks on their teams for two other reasons. First, they need not have any social contact with black teammates. Sports that blacks dominate are not sports like golf, tennis, and swimming where socializing is almost a prerequisite of competing. Players need not mingle after basketball, baseball, or football. More importantly, black male players need not mingle with white women after those games. Housing on campus, and social discrimination through fraternities and sororities, further isolates the black athletes.

Whether in high school or college, the black student-athlete faces special problems as an athlete, as a student, and as a member of the campus community.

Genetics and Theories of Racial Superiority in Sport

Most of white society believed we were on the road to progress until Al Campanis and Jimmy "The Greek" Snyder made us challenge our perceptions. Their statements on national television that blacks and whites are physically and mentally different were repugnant to much of the country and led to widespread self-examination. Like many whites who accept black dominance in sport, Campanis believed that blacks had less intellectual capacity. It makes things seem simple to people like Campanis: blacks sure can play, but they can't organize or manage affairs or lead whites.

Such people wouldn't see much to contradict this view if they looked to society at large. In 1990, white men and women were twice as likely to hold executive, administrative and managerial positions as black men. At the same time, blacks were twice as likely to hold positions of manual labor as whites. Decades of viewing this pattern could easily reinforce the Campanis viewpoint: whites are intelligent and blacks are powerful physically.

I find it more than strange that we never explained white sports dominance in the 1930s with reference to white physical characteristics. You sometimes hear a joke told that the world's shortest book would be the book of Jewish sports heroes. It is surprising for many to discover that Jewish players dominated basketball in the 1920s and 1930s. Did writers talk about their size? Not at all. They discussed mentality, even if it reinforced a different kind of ethnic stereotype about Jewish people.

Ed Sullivan, then a sports columnist for the *New York Daily News,* wrote a column in 1933 under the headline "Jews are Star Players":

> Holman, Jewish star of the Celtics, is a marvelous player. He has always reminded me of Benny Leonard. Both are of the same alertness and general make-up. Jewish players seem to take natu-

rally to the game. Perhaps this is because the Jew is a natural gambler and will take chances. Perhaps it is because he devotes himself more closely to a problem than others will. Whatever the reason, the fact remains that some of the greatest stars of today are Jewish players.

Holman is a case in point. Chick Passon, who leads the scorers of the American Basketball League with 143 points in fourteen games, is Jewish. He plays on the Philadelphia team. Dave Banks, another sharpshooter, and Benny Borgeman of the Fort Wayne club, who comes from Paterson, N.J., are Jewish youngsters and crackerjacks.

Whatever the reason, the fact remains that some of the greatest stars of today are Jewish players.

Shortly after Sullivan wrote that column, all-black teams began to beat all-white teams. The Rens defeated the Celtics in basketball. According to John Holway, author of *Voices from the Great Black Baseball Leagues,* teams from the Negro baseball leagues beat white major league teams in over 60 percent of their 445 games. Joe Louis became acceptable after he beat Max Schmeling; Jesse Owens became an acceptable black star after he won big for America in the Berlin Olympics in 1936.

Suddenly genetic theories appeared. The Germans claimed Owens and other black Americans were successful because of their peculiar bone structure. An English report charged that blacks had undergone leg operations to increase their speed. The American Olympic Committee was attacked for bringing "black auxiliaries" to the games. The late Avery Brundage, long-time International Olympic Committee president, stated later that "one could see, particularly with Jesse Owens, how the Negroes could excel in athletics. Their muscle structure lends itself to this sort of competition." The University of Southern California's track coach, Dean Cromwell, wrote in *Championship Technique in Track and Field,* "The Negro excels in the events he does because he is closer to the primitive than the white man. It was not that long ago that his ability to spring and jump was a life and death matter to him." That book was published in 1941.

The South Africans openly deprecated the achievements of the blacks. In 1968, their white Olympic chief, Frank Braun, said,

"Some sports the African is not suited for. In swimming, the water closes in on their pores so they cannot get rid of carbon dioxide and they tire quickly." Swimming seems to be a special obsession for whites. Al Campanis added to his misery when Ted Koppel offered him the opportunity to soften his statement about blacks not having the "necessities" to lead. Campanis responded with a physical explanation that asserted that blacks are not good swimmers because of a lack of buoyancy.

Things became more serious when blacks were not only playing but dominating sports in the 1970s. Martin Kane's article "Black Is Best" for *Sports Illustrated* in 1971 brought nods of agreement from whites and outrage from blacks. Blacks had more tendon and less muscle, giving blacks an advantage in "double-jointedness and general looseness of joints," Kane claimed. Also, blacks "have superior capacity to relax under pressure." Like Braun and later Campanis, Kane said, "perhaps because of a physical inheritance, no black has ever been a swimming champion."

Of course, the theories have had to change from time to time. Blacks weren't supposed to be able to run long distances. We had a genetic explanation for that too until Africans came to dominate the long-distance races; shortly thereafter American track coaches developed an interest in Africa. Now we have a black medalist in swimming in the Olympics, so the swimming theory may be challenged.

Whites have conceded the physical superiority of blacks because it fits the image: whites still have the brains. Theorists like Arthur Jensen emerged to "prove" that whites have inherently higher IQs than blacks. "All the racial upheaval of the 1960s had taught *Sports Illustrated* was that it's okay to be racist as long as you try to sound like a doctor," Bill Russell countered. His theory of blacks' success: "I worked at basketball up to eight hours a day for twenty years—straining, learning, sweating, and studying." Many whites were all too ready to ignore things like hard work and determination or the social, economic, and political factors involved in the success of black athletes.

Kareem Abdul-Jabbar summarized this well in a *Sports Illustrated* story about him:

Yes, I was just like the rest of those black athletes you've read about, the ones that put all their waking energies into learning the moves. That might be a sad commentary on America in general, but that's the way it's going to be until black people can flow without prejudice into any occupation they can master. For now it's still pretty much music and sports for us.

After fifty years of trying to prove the genetic superiority of blacks as athletes, science has proved little. Culture, class and environment still tell us the most. Instead of developing theories about why black Americans excel in sports, perhaps more time will now be spent on the achievement of black Americans in human rights, medicine, law, science, the arts and education who overcame the attitudes and institutions of whites to excel in fields where brains dictate the champions.

Coaches: A View in Black and White

The coach becomes the black student-athlete's main contact, and the court becomes the only home where he is comfortable. But there are some black athletes who feel that their white coaches discriminate against them and that their academic advisers give them different counseling. This may reflect either the racism the athlete experiences from them or a general distrust of whites. Even well-intentioned acts can be interpreted by blacks as being racially motivated. The same phenomenon, of course, can work the other way.

Over the years, there have been black student-athletes who have made similar complaints: subtle racism evidenced in different treatment during recruitment; poor academic advice; harsh discipline; positional segregation on the playing field and social segregation off it; blame for ills for which they are not responsible. Then there are the complaints of overt racism: racial abuse; blacks being benched in games more quickly than whites; marginal whites being kept on the bench while only blacks who play are retained; extra money for the white players; summer jobs for whites and good jobs for their wives.

To say that most or even many white coaches are racist is a great exaggeration. But most white coaches were raised with white values in a white culture. The norm for them is what is important for a white society. As recently as 1989 there were coaches and athletic directors who were still accepting memberships in all-white country clubs as perks for their jobs and not seeing this as a contradiction. The whistle was not blown until Wade Houston was hired as the University of Tennessee's basketball coach and apparently was not going to be offered a membership in the all-white Cherokee Country Club; Houston is black. University President Lamar Alexander forced an end to all such "privileges." Recently the Memphis State athletic director, his assistant and the football coach belonged to country clubs with no black members. Their memberships were paid for with school funds while basketball coach Larry Finch, who is black, declined membership, saying, "Any club that doesn't want me, or my kids or players, I don't want to be any part of."

Stereotypes of the Black Athlete

If the white coach accepts stereotypical images of what black society is and what kind of men it produces (and I believe that many do, just as surveys show many white Americans do), he may believe that blacks are less motivated, less disciplined, less intelligent, and more physically gifted. He may think that all blacks are raised in a culture bombarded by drugs, violence, and sexuality, and that they are more comfortable with other blacks. He might believe those characteristics to be a product of society, or he might simply believe that they are the way God chose to make things. He might recognize himself as a racist, one who dislikes blacks because of the negative traits he believes they possess. More than likely, however, he views himself as a coach trying to help. In either case, he acts on these images and his black players are victimized.

Motivation and Discipline

Even a coach who is well intentioned might believe blacks to be less motivated and less disciplined than whites and lean heavily on them in practice and in games. (Indeed, 62 percent of all whites believe blacks are less hard-working.) He may push them physically, inspire them by any means possible. He may make the black athlete who complains of injury learn to push himself harder, to endure more and more pain.

A racist coach who believes that blacks are unmotivated and undisciplined translates these words into "lazy" and "insubordinate." He may be acting out his hate and want to punish black players for their being black, so he might yank blacks off the court after a bad play, not bring them on road trips, or play only a few at any given time. He must show blacks who is boss. John Thompson, among the nation's most successful college basketball coaches, told *Sports Illustrated* why he wants his predominantly black teams to be known as disciplined:

> Undisciplined, that means nigger. They're all big and fast and can leap like kangaroos and eat watermelon in the locker room, but they can't play as a team and they choke under pressure. It's the idea that a black man doesn't have the intelligence or the character to practice self-control. In basketball it's been a self-fulfilling prophecy. White men run the game. A white coach recruits a good black player. He knows the kid's got talent, but he also knows that because he's black he's undisciplined. So he doesn't try to give the player any discipline. He puts him in the free-lance, one-on-one, hot dog role, and turns to the little white guard for discipline. Other black kids see this and they think this is how they are expected to play, and so the image is perpetuated.

Intelligence and Studies

The well-intentioned coach who thinks that blacks are less intelligent (53 percent of all whites believe blacks are less intelligent) may feel he is "protecting" them by suggesting that they first attend a junior college or take less demanding courses to reduce the pressure as they adjust to life in their new society. He may discuss the "adjustments" with the players' professors and get them tutors. As a coach, he naturally looks to professional athletics for role models for black athletes. How many black doctors, lawyers, accountants, or psychoanalysts is he apt to know? It is not surprising that many black athletes major in physical education or athletic administration.

On the other hand, the less well-intentioned coach is increasingly suggesting junior colleges to blacks because they can mature athletically there and the coach can watch their skills develop while they pile up enough easy credits to help them slide through their junior and senior years. Harry Edwards calls the junior college phenomenon "the new slave trade." The racist coach doesn't worry about black professional role models like doctors or lawyers because he probably couldn't conceive of a black role model in the first place. Black athletes are thus steered into courses in physical education and athletic administration because coaches think they may have a better line on grading in those departments.

It's not just coaches—55 percent of black football and basketball players surveyed in the NCAA's AIR Study felt that it was harder for them to get professors to consider them as serious students compared to their white teammates.

All coaches have a high stake in keeping athletes eligible. After that eligibility runs out, the well-intentioned coach might, if he has the time (which is not likely), try to help the athlete to graduate. But for the racist, the black athlete becomes invisible. Tutors suddenly disappear, professors suddenly rediscover how to demand more in class, and the student realizes there are no more activity courses to take.

In one of the most important scandals of the decade, Memphis State, a 1985 NCAA Final Four participant, fell into disgrace. There were many allegations about the improprieties of the school and its coach, Dana Kirk. One that could not be disputed was the fact that twelve years had gone by without Memphis State graduating a single black basketball player. Like several other urban institutions, Memphis State built a winning program with the talents of fine black athletes. The fact that none had graduated brought back memories of Texas Western's NCAA championship team which failed to graduate a single starter, all of whom were black. But this went on at Memphis State for more than a decade.

The NAACP sued the school. Publicity finally led to the dismissal of Kirk. Indications are that Larry Finch, who replaced Kirk, has run a clean program. When there is a will, there is usually a way to overcome problems. Perhaps the fact that Finch is black has resulted in a different approach to black players.

I do not mean to single out Memphis State. In most studies or journalistic reports I read and on some of the campuses I visit, the pattern is similar: the academic profile of black football and basketball players and their treatment as students is different from whites, and their graduation rate is lower.

Positional Segregation in College

The issue of positional segregation in college is becoming less of a factor. For years, whites played the "thinking positions." The controlling position in baseball is the pitcher; in football, it is the quarterback. Everyone loves the smooth, ball-handling guard in basketball. These are the glamour positions that fans and the press focus on. These have largely been white positions.

College baseball still poses the greatest problem at all positions, as fewer and fewer blacks play college baseball. Only 6 of the 176 players in the 1990 College World Series were black—down from only 8 in 1989. Only 7.2 percent of all college baseball players in Division I were black in 1988.

However, in a major shift in the 1988 and 1989 seasons, large numbers of black quarterbacks were leading their football teams. Between 1960 and 1986, only seven black quarterbacks were among the top ten candidates for the Heisman Trophy and none finished higher than fourth. In 1987, 1988 and 1989, names like Don McPherson (Syracuse), Rodney Peete (USC), Darien Hagan (Colorado), Reggie Slack (Auburn), Tony Rice (Notre Dame), Stevie Thompson (Oklahoma) and Major Harris (West Virginia) all finished among the top ten vote getters. In 1989, Andre Ware (Houston) became the first black quarterback to win the award.

The point guard in basketball is now manned by as many blacks as whites. Sherman Douglas (Syracuse), Pooh Richardson (UCLA), Dana Barros (Boston College), Charles Smith (Georgetown), Gary Payton (Oregon State), Rumeal Robinson (Michigan) and Kenny Anderson (Georgia Tech) were among the many recent star black point guards. Hopefully, this bodes well for an end to positional segregation in college sport in the near future. (Positional segregation in pro sport will be discussed in depth in Chapter 17.)

Playing Time and Quotas in College

Do college coaches impose quotas so that some whites start? The evidence seems clear that some do, but black dominance in college basketball seems to be changing this also. With 56 percent of Division I players being black, positional segregation would be difficult. Do coaches get pressured to play whites? Lou Carnesseca of St. John's told me he would quit before buckling under to such pressure. He admits that his colleagues do receive such pressure, although it seems to be diminishing.

There are more than a few people in the press and in the coaching business who believe that much of the early negative attention focused on the University of Nevada–Las Vegas's Jerry Tarkanian was due to the fact that he developed teams dominated by blacks at a time when this wasn't well accepted. Bill Walton, the best white player of the 1970s, defended Tarkanian when he said, "I can't be quiet when I see what the NCAA is doing to hurt Jerry Tarkanian only because he has a reputation for giving a second chance to many black athletes other coaches have branded as troublemakers."

Georgetown's John Thompson told *Sports Illustrated* that after he started five black freshmen in 1973, a white woman called, oblivious to Thompson's color or size (6 feet 10 inches tall, 300 pounds). She was angry about a photo in the newspaper showing Georgetown blacks towering over a white teammate. She demanded that Coach Thompson stop "abnormal niggers bullying white students." "I told her things were worse than she thought," he went on, "And I was going to send her two tickets to our next game so she could come see for herself, that what she would see would make her blood run cold. I was very sorry that lady couldn't use those tickets. They were for seats right behind where I sit on the bench. I wanted her to get a look at the most abnormal nigger of them all."

Black Athletes Speaking Out

The coach is the authority. Athletes have rarely spoken out. This creates problems for all coaches who come up against an outspoken player. When the player is black and not a superstar, he will often be let go. Only the superstars like Bill Russell, Kareem Abdul-Jabbar, and Muhammad Ali can securely remain because no one can afford to let them go.

I have already discussed the outcry from the press and fans when Russell first spoke up. When Abdul-Jabbar (Lew Alcindor) was at UCLA he said the press "twisted my words and made me look stupid." Once, after he had talked at length about race, Malcolm X, and the future of America, a reporter wrote that he was eccentric and surly and should be sent back to New York.

When he chose not to join the U.S. Olympic team in turbulent 1968, Abdul-Jabbar was called a "traitor" and an "uppity nigger." He explained why he chose to work in New York instead of going to the Olympics:

> I was talking to little black kids who are going to suffer because they don't have any examples to model themselves on. I tried to give them some kind of example. They dig basketball, so they dig me. They can relate to me and if I tell them something, they listen. I look at it this way: if I can change ten would-be junkies into useful citizens, turn them on to school and to useful lives, maybe get them started on how to run a crane for $4 an hour, that's the most important thing I can do right now. . . . Each of those ten turns on another ten . . . pretty soon you can see an end to some of the black suffering that goes on today. That, in my opinion, is where it's at. By comparison, an Olympic gold medal is a joke.

Muhammad Ali, who had refused to go into the army, knew you had to be at the top to speak out if you were black. He said, "You are only free if you are number one. Otherwise you are a slave." It's ironic that Bob Arum, the lawyer who helped Ali win his freedom before the Supreme Court in 1971, said at the time, "This case proves that our justice system works—if you have the money and influence to go all the way." In the best interpretation, one can assume that Arum was being cynical, since most blacks have neither the money nor the influence to make the system work. (Within a decade Arum was promoting boxing events in South Africa. Many agreed that these matches were part and parcel of the apartheid system, helping to maintain the economic and political enslavement of more than twenty million black South Africans; Arum insisted he was helping South African blacks.)

In the summer of 1978 I traveled to Kutscher's Country Club in Monticello, New York, to attend the NBA Maurice Stokes All-Star Game. I spoke to the players about signing a pledge that they would not compete in South Africa until apartheid in sports was eradicated. Twenty-two of the twenty-five players were black. It was very unlikely that any of them would have been asked to go to South Africa to play. They were all established pros, but they all said, "No." Explanations varied, but there was a common theme: to speak out on politics could spell the end of their athletic careers. If this was true in the pros, surely college athletes today who want to be pros, especially black college athletes, will not speak out unless pushed to an extreme.

Can black athletes speak out today without fear of retribution? Tommy Harper's case is instructive. His contract was not renewed by the Boston Red Sox in December of 1985. The Red Sox said he was let go because he was not doing a good job as special assistant to the general manager. Harper, however, charged that he was fired because he spoke out against racist practices by the Red Sox. Earlier in 1985 he had told the *Boston Globe* that the Sox allowed white players to receive passes to the whites-only Elks Club in Winter Haven, Florida, where they held spring training. (The Sox later stopped the tradition.) Harper sued and the Equal Employment Opportunity Commission ruled that the firing was a retaliatory action against Harper because he spoke out against discrimination. It took him a while to get back into baseball. As of this writing, he is a coach for the Montreal Expos.

There are positive examples as well. It did not go unnoticed that a group of black athletes at Auburn asked the president of the university to get a Confederate flag removed from a dormitory; it was removed. In 1987, the Pittsburgh basketball team wore ribbons as a protest against their school's investments in

South Africa. In 1990, black athletes at the University of Texas at Austin led a protest against racism on campus. They had even been encouraged by members of the athletic department. Whether or not this will become a trend is hard to see, but the positive and widespread media coverage of their actions stood in dramatic contrast to early reactions to Russell, Ali and Abdul-Jabbar.

Interracial Dating

Interracial dating on campus is still a volatile issue although it surely is far more common in 1990 than it was in 1970 or even 1980. Howie Evans, then a black assistant coach at Fordham and a columnist for the *Amsterdam News,* told me of the time when he used to work at a black community center in New York. Recruiters from predominantly white southern schools were coming there to recruit black women for their schools. Those coaches seemed to think that they understood the powerful sexual drives of black men, so they went out to get them some "safe" women friends from the North. A racist white coach will do anything to prevent interracial sex. This is hardly unique to coaches in our society. An administrator at the University of Texas at El Paso, for example, reportedly used to tell his black players to go across the border to Mexico to satisfy their needs.

When I talk to black athletes after a lecture, I try to ask them about this. It doesn't matter where I am—Los Angeles, Denver, New York, Nashville, or Norfolk—almost everyone says there is pressure, now usually very subtle, not to date white women. It doesn't matter how big the star, what era he played in, or whether he was amateur or pro.

The black athletes also tell me that the assumption on campus is that they want white women more than black women. Not that blacks say they do, but that whites believe they do. If a white student wants to sleep with a coed, that's part of college life in our times. If a black student wants to do the same, that's the primal animal working out his natural instincts.

Jack Johnson lived with a white woman and was tried under the Mann Act. That was a long time ago. Yet Elgin Baylor was told not to bring a white coed to a dance at Seattle University and he agreed. That was the 1950s and Elgin was as good a player as there was. Junior Coffey was told not to date a white woman at the University of Washington. He refused and never started for his team again. That was the early 1960s and he had been the nation's third-leading rusher at the time. Lew Alcindor stopped dating a white woman at UCLA because both he and the woman were feeling the pressure. That was the late 1960s, and he was arguably the most dominant basketball player of his time. Cleon Jones of the New York Mets was arrested by Florida police who alleged they found him sleeping naked in a van with a white woman. Much publicity followed, but when charges were finally dropped, it was hardly mentioned. The Mets fined Jones $2,000 and forced him to make a public apology at a news conference in the presence of his wife for soiling the image of the All-American game. That was 1975; Cleon Jones once hit .340 and led the Mets to the world championship.

A white coed charged that she was molested by three black football players at the University of Arkansas. Was she crying rape? The three students said it was a "playful act." Apparently a roomful of students were present and affirmed that not much had happened. But that "not much" still involved not one but three black men and a white woman. That was 1978 and football coach Lou Holtz suspended all three from the Orange Bowl, the game toward which they had worked all season.

Superstar David Thompson of the Denver Nuggets married a white woman. He said both sets of parents were reluctant to accept the interracial marriage. Injured in 1979–80, Thompson's career went sour. Rumors of the reasons for his demise spread. In Denver at the start of the 1980–81 season, I asked a white cab driver what happened to the Nuggets the year before. Without hesitation he replied, "David Thompson wore himself out screwing that white bitch!" I asked him if he knew Mrs. Thompson or had read anything about her. He sensed where the question came from and got mad: "I don't read about no nigger-loving whores." He refused to take my money for the fare. David Thompson had twice been College Player of the Year, had led North Carolina State to the national championship, had averaged 25.2 points per game in his four previous NBA seasons, and had made Denver owner Carl Scheer's life considerably more comfortable by help- ing to fill the arena with fans. Yet Scheer, for whatever reason, asked David Thompson to pay back part of his 1979–80 salary and publicly take the blame for the poor Denver season. Thomp- son took the blame, but only loaned the Nuggets $200,000 for two years. Thompson was finally traded to Seattle after the 1981–82 season. He later admitted to having a drug problem, which may have affected his playing.

But one had to wonder if Thompson would have been treated that way if he had played for the Nuggets in the 1990s, when they became the first pro team owned by blacks—Peter Bynoe and Bertram Lee. Would Lee, Bynoe and Bernie Bickerstaff, the NBA's fourth black general manager, start with a different set of assumptions about Thompson?

How does racial rejection affect black men? Kareem Abdul- Jabbar talked abut how he felt after being rejected by a white girl at a dance in New York while he was in high school. Having known him since he was an eighth-grader, I can say that at every stage of development Kareem was mature, intelligent, and ra- tional. But on that night he and his friend hit the streets to do damage. They walked toward Fifth Avenue, where they intended to smash store windows, but by the time they got there they had walked off their rage. Kareem wondered how many were unable to release that rage caused by the granite wall of racial rejection; how many killed or beat up some white person without knowing why they did it? He told *Sports Illustrated*:

> That blind rage at Whitey is part of the black condition; all black men reach it; some pass through to a higher plateau of understand- ing, but some never get out of the rage period and their lives are blighted for it. I understand them, and I don't turn from them. I once felt the same way myself.

I remember the reaction of my white fellow graduate students when they read this. They thought it was one of the scariest things they had ever read. They fantasized that such a rage might be turned on them.

The case involving Quintin Dailey in his last year at the University of San Francisco has been the most controversial and most closely scrutinized of all. The case posed issues relevant to all the questions raised about black athletes in this book. Unfortunately, it offered few answers.

Dailey was accused of raping a white nursing student. The woman who said she was Dailey's victim seemed to have convinced the public that Dailey was guilty, although Dailey produced several people who cast doubt on her story. His failure to pass a polygraph test turned the scales against him. The press began to ask if he would get away with attempted rape because he was a superstar. Faced with a jail sentence but proclaiming his innocence, Quintin Dailey chose to plead guilty to a reduced charge of aggravated assault. As part of the plea, he was placed on probation for three years. The Chicago Bulls knew when they drafted him that Dailey would not go to jail.

The Bulls were heavily criticized for picking Dailey in the first place. But the fires were intensified when he spoke at a Bulls press conference. "Nobody heard my side of the story when it happened," Dailey said. "I really don't want to get into it now. I have forgotten about the episode. When you've got other, greater things ahead of you, I can put it behind me. Right now, it's forgotten." The national press was furious at what it interpreted as such blatantly callous and unrepenting remarks. Women's groups in a number of cities set up picket lines at many Bulls games. In San Antonio, a fan dressed up as a nurse and let two others do a mock reenactment of what was supposed to have happened in San Francisco. It all finally caught up to Dailey. In mid-December 1982, he asked for a leave of absence from the Bulls due to extreme emotional stress. By the spring of 1983, he was reportedly in a drug-rehabilitation clinic.

Even before the public pressure started, Dailey's agent, Bob Woolf, said that what the press had done was "just like a lynching." Was the overwhelming reaction due to the fact that Dailey was alleged to have tried to force sex on a white woman? Was his guilt so clear that all that followed was justified? Everyone who knew Dailey, whether or not they supported him in this particular case, said he was an outstanding young man who had never been in trouble before. If he really was innocent, why should he have made repentant remarks at the press conference? Even if he was guilty, why was he singled out for such an unrelenting torrent of criticism? Other athletes have been charged with similar or worse sexual offenses and have paid much smaller prices. I honestly do not know the answers, but I keep coming back to the same question: Would the reaction have been the same if the woman had been black?

From 1988 through 1990, there were thirty newspaper accounts of athletes who were charged with some form of sexual assault on women. Twenty-one of the thirty were white athletes, yet the only cover story done by *Sports Illustrated* on this issue was about black athletes charged with these offenses while playing at Oklahoma and Colorado.

In 1990 stories appeared in print and on television implying that athletes are more inclined toward sexual assault than non-athletes. *The New York Times,* which broke the story, cited fifteen cases in the past year; that data was provided to the *Times* by the Center for the Study of Sport in Society. At the time, I argued with the writer that, while it was tragic for all the victims, fifteen cases in a country where there were more than 100,000 sexual assaults reported in the same period was, as we social scientists like to say, statistically insignificant. Did the story, which was reprinted all over the country, gain credibility because white Americans generally accept the stereotype that blacks have a greater sexual drive than whites? Or, if they were sensitive enough to know that rape is not a sexual act but a crime of violence, did they accept it because it fit yet another stereotype, that blacks are more prone to violence? I must note that not one story I saw pointed out that twelve of the fifteen athletes were white; the reader was left to make his own assumptions. That rarely happens when the story is about the problems of black athletes; we usually get pictures and text to nail home the race of the player.

Black Stereotypes in the Media

The virtually all-white sports media also covers sport from a perspective that has not been the most sensitive. A 1989 series in the *Washington Post* looked at the balance of power on network television. The story noted that "While black ex-jock analysts are commonplace, neither NBC nor ABC has a black play-by-play announcer; CBS has two. While blacks are found in entry-level production positions, they do not move up the ladder. Of an estimated 60 producers and directors working at ABC, NBC and CBS, only one is black." ESPN had 4 of 38 combined, by far the best.

This results, in part, in a completely different way in which the play of black and white athletes is described. The *Boston Globe*'s Derek Jackson analyzed seven NFL playoff games and five NCAA basketball games during 1988–89. Seventy-seven percent of the adjectives used to describe white football players referred to their brains while 65 percent of the adjectives used for blacks referred to brawn. In basketball, 63 percent of white descriptors alluded to brains while 77 percent of the descriptors for blacks pointed to brawn. In both sports, more than 80 percent of the references to dumb plays were about black athletes. Jackson painted a frightening picture for the black athlete: "By their intransigence of the last two years, the nation's broadcasters clearly are not interested in rearranging their thought patterns. Until they do, no one will give a second thought to how black players leave the game with a verbal résumé more worthy of a mugger than a coach."

The Options for Black Athletes Choosing a College

Well-intentioned or racist, the effects of the actions of white coaches on black athletes are not dissimilar. Study after study has shown the devastating consequences to the psyche of the person. As long as the act is perceived as being racially motivated—even if it is a well-intentioned act—the end result is the same.

So what should the black athlete do? Should he attend a historically black college? After all, black colleges have turned out great pro athletes for years. But black college athletic programs started to decline when the white schools began to integrate. They don't have million-dollar booster clubs to compete with white schools to get star black athletes. Big white schools also offer the lure of bowl games, television coverage, and a "good education."

Grambling's Eddie Robinson, who is the winningest coach in the history of college football and has sent more players to the NFL than any coach in history, explained the situation to the *Boston Globe*: "It would be real hard for me to tell a boy, living in a shotgun house with five sleeping in one room, to turn down a new house, a car, a better job for his daddy. I know it's wrong, but it's hard for a man to walk in another man's shoes."

The Southwestern Athletic Conference, which included Grambling, Jackson State, and Southern, used to provide thirty-five to forty players a year to the NFL in the early 1970s. Six were chosen in 1981. A total of only 18 of the 332 selected were from historically black colleges. The figures got worse throughout the 1980s.

Historically black schools were up in arms in 1990 as the NCAA moved to adopt a rule that only the top 30 basketball conferences (out of 35) would get an automatic bid to the financially lucrative NCAA tournament. North Carolina A&T University President Edward Fort charged that "The NCAA men's basketball committee has failed to uphold its responsibility of equity. These new rules would eliminate a large number of black schools from competing in the automatic berth competition." That would certainly further reduce their chances of recruiting top players.

Late in 1990, NBA Players Association Director Charles Grantham told the Congressional Black Caucus that the black athlete who wants to turn pro has little realistic choice: "Exposure on TV means the scouts will see you and, if they like you, a higher position in the draft. That means more money, much more money."

Could Eddie Robinson coach at Michigan or in the NFL? "I would at least like the opportunity to turn down a job," he noted. "Every white coach in the country with my tenure has had that opportunity." Eddie Robinson is black; he became a coach before white institutions were ready for him.

Playing for a black coach at a predominantly white institution is another option for the black student-athlete. Many of today's black players (and their parents) would like to attend schools with black coaches. For basketball players, that amounts to forty schools, as of this writing. The NCAA has more than 800 member schools, with approximately thirteen players per team. Therefore, of the 10,400 slots for basketball players, approximately 520 slots fall under black basketball coaches (up from 200 in 1984). The slots are far fewer in college football (where there were only two black head coaches in the 1990 season) and do not exist in college baseball (where there was not one black manager). In fact, of the 1,165 head coaching positions at the 278 Division I, IA and IAA programs (excluding the historically black schools) in the college sports blacks compete in most (men's and women's basketball, football, track and field and baseball) only 47 (or 4 percent) were held by black Americans in the 1990–91 school year. There are no other sports in which the figures even approximate one percent. According to the Black Coaches Association (BCA), less than 200 (5 percent) of the more than 4,000 assistant coaches in these sports were held by blacks in 1990–91.

Slightly more than one percent of college athletic directors are black (3 of 278), while less than one percent of the college positions of assistant and associate athletic director, business and ticket manager, sports information director, and trainer were held by blacks.

Statements that there simply aren't enough jobs available for blacks in coaching or the athletic departments are belied by the numbers. There are 800 NCAA members in all divisions, with an average of 15.5 teams per school. That amounts to 12,400 teams. NCAA teams have an average of 2 assistants per team. The National Association of Intercollegiate Athletics (NAIA) has 503 members with an average of 7.66 teams per school and 1.5 assistants per team. There are 550 National Junior College Athletic Association (NJCAA) schools, with an average of 6.52 teams per school and one assistant coach per team. A conservative estimate is that there are an average of ten non-coaching positions per school in athletic departments at all levels.

Excluding NJCAA athletic department employees, that means

there are approximately 68,888 college sports-related jobs. When so very few are held by black Americans, there should be little wonder that black student-athletes feel isolated on campus. Pressure needs to be placed here to change these percentages. The coaches are available—there are 2,500 members of the BCA. If there is to be a more promising future for the black student-athlete, then more black coaches and assistants will have to be hired.

How do present-day black coaches fare? When Tulsa hired Nolan Richardson in 1980, he became the fourteenth black head basketball coach at a major college. Tulsa President J. Paschal Twyman told *Sports Illustrated,* "There was a race factor, to be sure. Tulsa's population is about 11 percent black but we did our homework. We asked around the community and felt out our booster club. We'd been losing for five years, attendance was down, the program was at the bottom, and it was having an impact on our budget. We knew we were breaking some ice here, but we decided to fly with it. We needed to win badly."

Richardson brought four members of his undefeated national junior college championship team to Tulsa and they won the NIT championship. In 1985 he was hired by Arkansas and became the Southwest Conference's first black head basketball coach. When his first two teams lost thirty games, the *Arkansas Democrat* ran a headline: "Richardson is History." When he led the team to the Final Four in 1990 the headline in the same paper was: "A Marriage Made in Heaven." People were saying that his presence, and especially his success, was leading to improved race relations in northern Arkansas.

Georgetown, sitting in its own white enclave in mostly black Washington, had won 296 and lost 302 games between 1947 and 1972. Georgetown needed to win and it needed to relate more to its environment, a black environment. The Georgetown president, the Reverend Timothy S. Healy, S.J., told *Sports Illustrated:*

There is something about Washington, D.C., that has always reminded me of a cuckoo's nest. The local people make the nest. The cuckoos—the federal people and all their hangers-on—move into the nest. They fly in and out, but their main interests are elsewhere. They don't really care a lot about what they do in, or to, the nest. I think Georgetown has been, to an extent, one of the cuckoos. After the 1968 riots it became obvious that the university's position [being predominantly white and isolated from the black community] wasn't very smart or defensible—socially, intellectually, morally, or empirically. We began making some changes, some statements to the local community that we were going to try to be at least more responsible and useful. I think it's fair to say that hiring John Thompson was one of those statements.

Thompson has won a lot of games and will win many more. In becoming the first black coach to win the national championship in 1984, Thompson made many people angry. This was especially true of some media figures. They said he was arrogant and abrasive, and kept his team insulated from the public. They said his team was overly aggressive. The attack was prolonged and lasted throughout the entire NCAA tournament. You could rarely read about Georgetown, on its way to dominate the tournament, without negative personal comments in the article. It was vicious.

But one had to wonder if we were not hearing the same old tune. After all, Thompson was breaking all the molds shaped by a stereotyping public. First, he was a big winner with a lot of black recruits coming to the no-longer-lily-white campus. Second, these black players were not a freewheeling, footloose team but one of the most disciplined teams in the country. Even more importantly, at a time of great negative publicity concerning the academic abuse of college athletes, Thompson's players had one of the highest graduation rates in America. Was there some jealousy involved in the attacks? Didn't these same scribes used to call aggressive white teams "hustling teams"? White coaches like John Wooden were called fatherly figures when they kept the press at arm's length from their teams.

The attacks continued as Thompson was openly blamed for not winning the gold medal in the 1988 Seoul Olympics. In the 1990 Goodwill Games, some of the same writers were relenting, saying that the U.S. team, led by Mike Krzyzewski, lost because reality had caught up with American basketball: foreigners were getting to be fine players also. They stated that, in retrospect, the criticism leveled at John Thompson's coaching was excessive.

Even if you accept the fact that Thompson's style was a tough one for the public to grapple with, this still doesn't explain the degree of the attacks against him. The racial issue seemed, once again, to be a factor. While I applaud the writers who wrote balanced pieces on John Thompson and Georgetown, the others clearly showed us how far we have to go.

For now, most black athletes will have to play for white coaches and many may have the problems mentioned. Academically, the black athlete may enter college at a disadvantage, one artificially maintained because he might be steered into easier courses. He is less likely to get a degree. Athletically, he will have to be the best because otherwise he won't stay long. With prevailing stereotypes, some coaches will make assumptions about him they would never make about whites. Socially, he will be in an alien world, segregated in student housing, off-campus housing, on road trips, and in bed. Increasingly he will be forced to withdraw into the safer athletic subculture, becoming insulated from both black and white non-athletes.

The odds are surely not in favor of the black student-athlete. If, after enduring all these problems he doesn't get a degree, then why does he subject himself to all of this in the first place? The answer is simple. He assumes that sports is his way out of poverty. How prevalent is this belief? The NCAA AIR study on the black college athlete showed that in 1989, approximately 45 percent of black basketball and football players at predominantly white schools think they will make the pros. Less than one percent will. The Northeastern University/Reebok Foundation study conducted in 1990 showed that 43 percent of black high school student-athletes think they can make the pros as well.

Sport has been promoted as the hope of black people. But too often those are empty hopes, blighted hopes. Go into Harlem or Watts and you see the results—black kids going for the hoop, going for the gold. Many cold nights I used to come home late from the United Nations and hear a ball bounce against the pavement in a schoolyard as a couple of kids tried to see the basket that was dimly lighted by a streetlamp forty feet away.

Those kids believed. Work hard here and you will control. While they may be controlling that missed shot, if they are forgetting their studies, they will slip farther and farther toward the bottomless pit of functional illiteracy.

Those kids were becoming involved in a cycle that trades away their education for the promise of a stardom that is very unlikely to ever be real. A black high school student has a better chance of becoming a doctor or attorney than he has of becoming a professional athlete. But those civic role models are not as visible as black athletes. So for them the model looks like this: play, play, play. If you are good, play until you are eighteen. If you are very good, keep going until you are twenty-two. If you're great, play until you are thirty. Unfortunately, too many schools "pass" students, including ballplayers, to the next level without regard to academic achievement. For ballplayers it is just that much easier. They have been conditioned that academic work is not necessary; just work on your body. The promise of the pros is the shared dream, no matter how unrealistic.

The Story of Fred Buttler

I was asked by United Press to write a five-part series on racism in sports after Al Campanis made his infamous remarks in 1987. I decided to write one part on Fred Buttler. Fred Buttler is but one tragic example of a man who didn't make it in the pros and paid the price for not being properly educated. Buttler is a classic case of how the educational system can abuse athletes, especially black athletes.

Fred possessed enormous physical promise when he attended Warren Lane Elementary in Inglewood, California. Coaches at Warren watched as he beat older children in every sport he took up. Everyone began telling him he would someday play in the NFL. However, his mother Edna saw that he could not do his schoolwork. She asked that he be held back in the third grade to improve his reading skills. She questioned school officials when they promoted him to Monroe Junior High School after the sixth grade. She was told not to be so concerned, that he was progressing at a normal pace.

He was an immediate football star at Monroe, but he still could not read. He and four other black athletes, who were called the "Hersheys" by the nearly all-white student body, sat in disbelief as they were told they were "just too bright to be in the eighth grade" and were therefore being skipped into Morningside High after the seventh grade. Mrs. Buttler complained to the Monroe administration that it was not fair to send an illiterate to high school. She was patronizingly told, "It's the best for Fred."

Edna Buttler watched in dismay as her son accumulated a three-year C+ average at Morningside while never opening a book. There was no need to do so; all the teachers made "special arrangements" for the star football player. At times he handed in blank exams; they were returned with all the right answers. At other times he was given oral exams. Most of the time he didn't have to take any exams. There was no point—he could not read them.

Fred Buttler said later that the teachers always made him feel good and gave him confidence that he would make the pros: "No matter how much trouble I had understanding things in class, I always figured I would make a good living playing ball for the pros. . . . Football was going to make me famous. And I knew I wasn't just dreaming because everyone told me I was good." When he graduated from Morningside, he had a second-grade reading level—about the same level he had when his mother had requested that he be left back in the third grade nine years before. Despite the fact that he couldn't read the playbook, he received a football scholarship from El Camino Junior College.

Carl Mersola is now a professor of physical education and contemporary health. He was a quarterback and receivers coach and advisor at El Camino when Fred went there. He stated frankly that "You didn't have to read or write to be in junior college. Fred survived by taking 12 units of vocational courses and physical education classes. He took a few academic classes but I don't know how he got through them. Fred could barely write his own name. He couldn't write his address."

Fred helped lead El Camino to two outstanding seasons as a

cornerback. He assumed that after two more years of college he would end up with a pro football contract. Mersola suggests that while Fred was good, "no one thought he was good enough to make the pros." But no one told Fred.

Mersola did tell the Cal State-LA recruiters that he couldn't read or write. He told them "there was no way Buttler could graduate, that he wouldn't even graduate from El Camino." Cal State still wanted him. Fred decided to attend Cal State-LA. Mersola told me that he spent many hours filling out Fred's complicated admissions and grant-in-aid forms.

Fred was promised remedial reading help at Cal State but he never received it. "I think some of the coaches were probably happy I couldn't read," he recalled, "because that meant I wouldn't waste time on schoolwork since that way I could concentrate on playing for them." The dream continued during his first one and a half years at Cal State.

He maintained a C+ average as a physical education major and played well. But as his eligibility ran out at the end of the fall semester, so did the great interest and the support from the faculty. Suddenly the C+ former football star was a failing student and was flunked out of Cal State within months.

Dr. Al Marino was associate chair of the Physical Education Department and associate athletic director at Cal State-LA. Marino, who spent a great deal of time with Buttler, did remember, and the memories were not without pain: "Fred Buttler had no business in higher education. He knew he could not read or write. He can't be totally absolved of blame . . . at some point he must have taken inventory of his own skills. Fred Buttler was not stupid. He made the decision to apply to college; he had to understand that he would have to be a student, that he would have to read and write."

But we know that Fred Buttler had been told since elementary school that going to school was simply his ticket to the pros. No one ever delivered programs to develop his academic skills, even when Edna Buttler demanded them.

However, Buttler was hardly Marino's target. "There were many guilty people, but the largest culprit was the system and the program into which he was admitted. . . . Cal State-LA deemed him acceptable. After that it's an educator's job to educate him—essentially to educate an illiterate. It was like he was going into battle without any weapons. Fred Buttler did not have the skills to survive at a university.''

With all the outrage now directed at the scandal of college athletes not graduating, blame is usually affixed to the coach or athletic department. Marino would have none of this. While he wouldn't give the person's name, there was no doubt who he meant: "If you're looking for guilt, you must look to the department chair who is responsible for *all* of the students enrolled in Phys Ed classes. Academic integrity at that time was not of the highest order. The athletic director, in this case, was not at fault.''

In the end, Fred Buttler had no degree, no offers to play pro football and no skills to use for gainful employment. And he still could not read. That was 1976. He became a factory worker and lived with his mother.

Further tragedy entered Fred's life when he was involved in the death of his father. Fred was put in jail after a gun went off at home and his father was killed. He was not allowed to attend the funeral. However, he was soon released and the charges were dropped after the police determined that it had been an accidental shooting. Fred was not able to visit his father's grave, since he could neither read a map nor the street signs to find it.

Perhaps, if Buttler had demanded a quality education in return for his outstanding athletic contributions, his story might have had a happier ending. But that would be asking a great deal from a process that started in elementary school. At the age of nine or ten kids shouldn't have to make such decisions. And, in this case, Fred's mother had tried to intervene on his behalf. But the educational system was in full gear, stripping this young man of his future.

Neither Fred Buttler nor his mother could be located a decade after the Cal State-LA experience. No one at Warren Lane Elementary, Monroe Junior High or Morningside High could provide any information about Fred. Mersola and Marino did not know where he was. It was as if he never stepped foot on the face of the earth. Dr. Marino is no longer at Cal State-LA. The "hypocrisy of athletics in higher education" influenced his decision to leave the academy. He now works for a securities firm.

Tom "Satch" Sanders, the former Boston Celtic great now working for the NBA, sounded an ominous warning: "I remember when a high draft pick was cut from the Celtics one year, and he sat in front of his locker with his head down crying out 'What am I going to do now?' The young man did not have a college degree, and without basketball felt completely lost. I was to see this scene repeated many times during my career as a player and coach. Those of us who made it can count dozens of others who weren't prepared for the big fall. They are the tragedies. Buttler's story is not unique."

Buttler is only one tragic example of a young man who didn't make it in the pros and paid the price for failing to receive a proper education. When we hear stories like his it makes us shudder but we gain comfort thinking it is an isolated case. The same was true when we learned about Kevin Ross playing for Creighton University, an outstanding Jesuit school. After his four years of college eligibility ran out he attended Marva Collins's Westside Preparatory School in Chicago, beginning in the fifth grade. We heard about Kevin's tragedy every time a new academic scandal came up. Then Dexter Manley, the great Washington Redskins star, testified in the Senate that he went through four years at Oklahoma State as an illiterate and had to learn to read and write on his own while playing pro ball. The tremendous lack of self-confidence this produced had to have contributed to Manley's cocaine problem.

Still we want to think of Buttler or Ross or Manley as the ones who fell through the cracks. But if 25 to 30 percent of high school football players are reportedly functionally illiterate, then there are thousands of Fred Buttlers, Kevin Rosses, and Dexter Manleys out there waiting to happen. That price is a great one for so many of our young student-athletes who somewhere in their careers become simply athletes.

A look at the numbers opens our eyes. In 1989–90, according to the National Federation of State High School Associations (NFSHA), 517,271 kids played high school basketball. Less than

4,000 played for Division I colleges. In other words, less than 1 in 130 who played in high school ever play at a Division I college. According to the NCAA, 56 percent, or approximately 2,240 Division I college basketball players, were black.

About fifty players will join the NBA each year. Thirty-eight (75 percent) will be black. In other words, the odds against black college senior ballplayers making the NBA are 15 to 1. Since NFSHA does not break down their statistics by race and sport, we can only state the odds against any high school basketball player making the NBA, which are approximately 10,345 to 1. If we assume that the percentage of high school basketball players who are black is the same as it is for colleges (the overall percentage of black athletes playing all sports in high school and college is about the same), then there would be approximately 289,672 black high school basketball players. If 38 of them make the pros, then the chances of a black high school basketball player making the pros are approximately 1 in 7,622. No Las Vegas house would call that a good bet. Yet so many black youths continue to place it with the highest stakes of all, their own futures.

The same figures apply to football. According to NFSHA, there were 947,755 students playing high school football in 1989–90; some 22,000 play at a Division I college. Therefore, 1 in 43 high school players will play at a Division I college. If 37 percent are black, then there are some 8,140 black college football players in Division I. In a good year, 150 rookies might make an NFL roster; 90 will be black. Therefore, the odds of a senior black college player making the NFL are 23 to 1. If we assume that the same percentage of blacks play football in high school as in college, then there are approximately 350,699 black high school football players. The odds against making the NFL are 3,897 to 1 for black high school players.

Combining football and basketball, the overall odds of a high school player (black or white) making the pros are approximately 7,325 to 1. It should be noted that the expansion of professional leagues combined with fewer students playing high school sport has reduced those odds from 12,000 to 1 when I first computed

Odds Against Making the Pros

	All High School Players	Number Making Pros Each Year	Odds Against
Football	947,755	150	6,318 to 1
Basketball	517,271	50	10,345 to 1
Combined	1,465,026	200	7,325 to 1

	*Black High School Players	Blacks Making Pros Each Year	Odds Against
Football	350,699	90	3,897 to 1
Basketball	289,672	38	7,622 to 1
Combined	640,371	128	5,003 to 1

	All College	Number Making Pros	Odds Against
Football	5,500	150	37 to 1
Basketball	1,000	50	20 to 1
Combined	6,500	200	33 to 1

	Black College Seniors	Blacks Making Pros Each Year	Odds Against
Football	2,035	90	23 to 1
Basketball	560	38	15 to 1
Combined	2,595	128	20 to 1

*Figures for black high school athletes are estimates based on assumption that proportions of black and white athletes in high school and college are equal and are derived from college statistics.

them for *Broken Promises,* in 1983. However, the odds are still astronomical.

Harry Edwards is now known as an advisor to major league baseball and the San Francisco 49ers as well as a University of California–Berkeley professor of sociology. He has tried to help the black athlete deal with the system intelligently, teaching what he sees as the reality of blacks playing sport in white America. His vision is mostly tragic.

Edwards calls the black athlete today's modern-day gladiator, brought to college to perform. Based on his extensive research over more than two decades, Harry Edwards concludes that:

- 25 to 30 percent of the black high school athletes are functionally illiterate.

- 20 to 25 percent in junior colleges are illiterate.

- 15 to 20 percent at four-year colleges are illiterate.

- 65 to 75 percent of black athletes who are awarded athletic scholarships may never graduate.

- an estimated 75 percent of those who do graduate obtain either physical education degrees or have majors generally held in low repute.

- approximately three million black youths over twelve place a high priority on a sports career.

- less than 10 percent of all athletic scholarships go to blacks, less than their proportion in the population. Those scholarships are concentrated in football, basketball, baseball, and track. The first two generate revenues for colleges to pay for all other college sports combined. In other words, the black athlete, in addition to everything else, helps raise the money to carry the white sports like fencing, swimming, tennis, golf, and lacrosse.

Arthur Ashe, Kareem Abdul-Jabbar, and others have been exhorting young blacks to study to become lawyers and doctors, to develop their minds. Julius Erving (Dr. J), Isiah Thomas and Michael Jordan all went back to school to get their degrees, setting an outstanding example for young children about the importance these millionaires placed on education.

While young blacks may hear Ashe and Abdul-Jabbar tell them to study, they see the money that hundreds of black athletes make from sports. Black athletes can now earn as much for a single game as a high school teacher makes in a year. Such figures are no aid in attracting young blacks to the books. The picture seemed dimmer than ever for the 1990–91 academic year. According to the *Almanac of the Chronicle of Higher Education,* undergraduate black enrollment for men showed a decade-long decline from 464,000 in 1980–81 to 443,000 in 1990–91. (There was an increase in enrollment for black women from 643,000 to 687,000).

For all too many, that means back to the hoop or diamond. The myth about sports being an escape from poverty is perpetuated.

In 1968 Jack Olsen wrote in *Sports Illustrated*, "At most, sports had led a few thousand Negroes into a better life while substituting a meaningless dream for hundreds and thousands of other Negroes. It has helped perpetuate an oppressive system." When I wrote *Broken Promises* in 1983, I said, "The only difference today is that more blacks are chasing that meaningless dream. And as each one falls, America's cheap labor pool swells. After the fall, the assembly line looks good." I now believe we have turned the educational corner and a light is burning, even if somewhat dimly. I write this with both a deep concern and a sense of profound optimism. That concern stems from the fact that while we have the constitutional right to freedom of expression in America, it has become meaningless for a large part of a generation of our children who are functionally illiterate. While sport in America can do so many good things, too many of our athletes are falling into that pool of illiterates.

The optimism comes from the fact that athletes have produced wherever we have asked more of them academically. The problem is that we rarely ask. Educators finally realize that we cannot afford to allow student-athletes to be used to try to build athletic powers when they do not receive a real opportunity to complete an education that prepares them for life.

The typical student-athlete, contrary to the public's image, performs as well or better academically than other students at both the college and high school levels. Based on data compiled from the first NCAA Division I Academic Reporting Forms, student-athletes who enrolled as freshmen in 1980–81 posted a median graduation rate of 66.6 percent compared to 59 percent for all students. A Department of Education study of 58,000 high school sophomores and seniors documented that high school athletes outperform non-athletes academically. Eighty-eight percent of varsity athletes had better than a 2.0 (C) grade point average while 30 percent of all students had below a C average.

However, the figures can be misleading, as was shown earlier. The vast majority of the educational problems of athletes exist in men's football and basketball, the revenue sports. The worst victim is still the black athlete.

It seems as though we have always viewed athletes as "dumb jocks." That stigma was even more frequently attached to black athletes. As an athlete you aren't expected to be as smart as other students because you have the strong body while others have the big brain. Non-athletes joke about your intelligence. Even athletes joke among themselves. A bad grade becomes a funny joke in an attempt to mask the pain. However, public recognition of the problem has led to a movement for higher academic standards by the colleges and, increasingly, by high schools.

The 1991 NCAA Convention presented the most hopeful developments at that level in my lifetime. Executive Director Dick Schultz personally took the debate to a new level while the Presidents Commission reasserted itself. In 1983, under the leadership of the Presidents Commission, the NCAA developed Proposition 48. Widespread controversy followed, based on the fear that athletes, especially black athletes, could not meet the new standards. Although reluctant at first, I now support Proposition 48, which was passed by the NCAA to create new eligibility standards for incoming freshmen. However, I also agree with the concern of educators and civil rights leaders who believe that scores on standardized tests may be culturally and racially biased and are not effective measures of the academic potential of all students.

Proposition 48 was developed in response to decreasing graduation rates in the revenue sports and the increasing illiteracy rates of high school athletes. Under Proposition 48, an incoming college freshman, in order to be eligible to play a sport in the freshman year at any NCAA Div. I or IA program, had to (1) maintain a "C" high school average in 11 core curriculum courses, and (2) score above a 700 on the combined verbal and math sections of the Scholastic Aptitude Test or a 15 on the American College Test.

The new standards only referred to the athlete's academic record in high school. While the core curriculum and grade point standards won widespread approval, the requirement for minimum scores on standardized tests angered black educators and civil rights leaders. Many educators agreed that standardized achievement tests are culturally and racially biased. Black leaders charged that Proposition 48 would limit black athletes' opportunities to obtain college athletic scholarships.

An NCAA study undertaken prior to implementation seemed to bear out that fear. The study showed that 6 out of 7 black players in men's basketball and 3 out of 4 black players in men's football at the nation's largest schools would have been ineligible as freshmen. At the same time, 1 out of 3 white players in men's basketball and 1 out of 2 white players in men's football would have been ineligible.

However, when implemented in the fall of 1986, Proposition 48 actually sidelined far fewer athletes. According to NCAA figures, only 10.3 percent of football players and 11.35 percent of basketball players overall had to sit out in 1989–90. While the earlier NCAA study predicted that more than 80 percent of black athletes would have been ineligible, 16 percent were actually ineligible in 1989–90. In previous years, the results were even better.

While Proposition 48 continues to have a disproportionately heavier impact on blacks (approximately 65 percent of all Proposition 48 admissions between 1986–87 and 1989–90), the percentage of all black athletes who fail to meet Proposition 48 requirements is about one-fifth the number predicted in the NCAA study. The predictions of academic disaster proved false; the athletes have overwhelmingly met the new standards.

The debate about Proposition 48 seemed to explode when it was modified at the 1989 NCAA Convention by the adoption of Proposition 42. The new proposition, taken together with the standards established by Proposition 48, would now mean that someone who did not qualify could not receive an athletic scholarship in the first year. Previously, under Proposition 48, the athlete could have received the scholarship but could not have played in the first year.

Considering that the overwhelming number of Proposition 48 students were black, the new rule created a tremendous controversy. Temple basketball coach John Chaney called it "racist." In protest of Proposition 42, John Thompson walked off the court in Georgetown's first game after the NCAA convention. His stature seemed to contribute to the debate's actually being aired. Many coaches maintained that Proposition 42 would deny the student the chance to get an education if he could not receive a scholarship. They would not have the chance to prove themselves academically. Proponents such as Arthur Ashe said it would put increased pressure on high school players to study harder.

Based on the available data, I strongly supported the opponents. The number of Proposition 48 ineligible students cited above indicates that the threat of loss of eligibility was already effectively putting pressure on high school student-athletes. Furthermore, of those relatively few who failed to meet the standards in 1986–87 and 1987–88, 79 percent were in good academic standing in 1988–89. That was on par with their fellow students who had originally met the Proposition 48 standards. Academic advisors said that they were able to pay more attention to the Proposition 48 students since they were identified as being "at risk."

A more impressive fact emerged when that NCAA study mentioned earlier was analyzed. Of the 69 percent of all black male athletes who would not have met Proposition 48 standards, 54 percent graduated. This stands in dramatic contrast to the 31 percent of all black male athletes in that class who graduated. In other words, the black students who came in at risk graduated at a much higher rate than regular student-athletes. Many were given that extra emphasis on academics in their first year.

Delegates at the 1990 NCAA Convention effectively eliminated the problems with Proposition 42 by allowing Proposition 48–ineligible students to receive institutional aid based on need. This resolution came from the Presidents Commission.

Ideally, I favor a policy in which all freshmen student-athletes in the revenue sports would be ineligible to participate in competition. They would be allowed to practice with their teammates. This would allow them the opportunity to adjust to college life without the demands of their sport to impede their progress. If the student-athletes make good academic progress toward graduation, they could earn a fourth year of eligibility. Such legislation would eliminate the need for Proposition 48 and be fair to everyone.

Higher academic standards for high school athletes have been a distant goal in most parts of the nation. As recently as 1983, less than 100 of the 16,000 school districts in the United States had a minimum "C" average for participation in extracurricular activities. Texas is now just one of a growing number of states where at least a "C" average is required. The others are California, Hawaii, Mississippi, New Mexico and West Virginia. Innumerable local districts have acted where states have not.

By 1990, the results of "no-pass, no-play" were evident: (1) grades will improve with increased academic standards; (2) those who participate in extracurricular activities do much better academically than those who do not; (3) coaches will rally to assist their players academically if standards are put in place. The predictions of academic disaster for athletes who were asked to do more proved false. The players produced and improved their performance just like they do on the field or court. It should not have surprised us as much as it did. The myth of the dumb jock was being buried. But the grave is still fresh.

I wrote earlier about Fred Buttler. Now I must share with you an inspiring story. In Dade County, Florida, Clint Albury took over as coach of Killian High School early in the 1980s. He discovered his team's grade point average was 1.3. Horrified, he instituted a mandatory study hall. Although there were no state eligibility standards, Albury brought in honor students to tutor his athletes. In a specialized study hall, they taught math and English three days a week, science and history the other two.

The team's seniors graduated with a grade point average which had been raised to 2.45. No one failed a course. All had met Proposition 48 standards. At the end of the season, 23 of the 27 senior players signed scholarship offers with colleges and universities. That was believed to be the highest number of signed players in Dade County history, and testimony to Albury. Perhaps a bigger testimony was the fact that of the 57 seniors who played for Albury while he was coach, 40 had either graduated or were on track to graduate from college in the 1990–91 year.

But the most startling case was that of Paul Moore. He was the type of player that many would say could never be eligible under a 2.0 system. He would, according to the argument, be victimized by society's good intentions. Moore was reading on a first- or second-grade level three years ago. Albury, who is a black and a psychologist, made no assumptions about Moore's intelligence. He had Moore tested and discovered a learning disability. Then Coach Albury got him into a program for learning disabled students. He graduated with an eleventh-grade reading level, earned a 2.3 grade point average in core courses and exceeded 700 on his SATs. Redshirted as a freshman, he was playing regularly in his junior year in 1990 for highly ranked Florida State. He had a 2.6 grade point average and was on track for graduation in 1991. Albury's own "no-pass, no-play" rule proved effective. He had faith that his players could do the academic work.

In an ideal sense, educators say there is much to learn from sport. It teaches the virtues of self-discipline, hard work, group problem-solving, competitive spirit, and pride in accomplishment. It provides many lessons about limits and capabilities, about dealing with failure and adversity, about teamwork and cooperation. These are all lessons that can be translated into being a good student, member of the community or corporate citizen. But the athletes must understand that they are transferable into other areas of their lives.

The overall message to the players has to be that the school will provide special attention to its student-athletes to assure their academic preparation; however, in exchange for this, it will be expected that student-athletes will fulfill the same academic requirements as all students.

Then we won't have to wonder what will happen when the cheering stops. We will have athletes whose full human potential has been developed to prepare them for life after sport.

Chapter 17

Greater Promises

In 1987, Al Campanis said blacks simply don't have the "necessities" to lead in sports. In 1988, Jimmy "The Greek" Snyder informed us that blacks were created differently than whites. In 1989, Roger Stanton wrote that white football players' IQs would be higher than blacks 100 percent of the time. In 1990, Hall Thompson told us that blacks weren't members of the country club at the Shoal Creek golf course because "that's not done in Birmingham."

Highly publicized statements by these men forced American sports fans to reexamine their belief that sport was the great racial equalizer in our society. While the integration of professional baseball (17 percent black), basketball (75 percent black), and football (60 percent black) has been remarkable and there is no other sector of the American economy where blacks have a greater role, we now realize that sports was never a level playing field where equality prevailed.

But the black athlete who makes the pros seems like he is finally on nearly equal footing with white athletes. He is there because of his talent. The world appears golden to him—and to most observers. That today's pro athlete is wealthy is beyond dispute. No one could dare to dream of the average salaries of the pros. A new NBA or NFL rookie enters the league certain that he will not face the discrimination he may have known in high school or college. Perhaps a coaching career looms ahead, or a front-office job will follow after he finishes playing. In any event, if he is exceptional, he will be remembered in the minds of fans and the media.

In the 1940s, owners realized that there was an enormous black market that had been untapped prior to the arrival of Jackie Robinson at Ebbets Field in 1947. The integration of baseball, basketball, and football went much farther than anyone could have imagined at that time. Movement was slow at first as the waters were tested. The NBA and NFL were integrated in 1950. Ten years after the barriers fell in Brooklyn, Major League Baseball had only eighteen black players. The NFL was only 14 percent black and the NBA only 7 percent black. However, the complexion of America's three major sports was very different four decades later. And blacks have broken into other sports and have become dominant in boxing and track and field.

Tennis, Golf, and Hockey

Althea Gibson astonished the tennis world when she beat Darlene Hard for the 1957 Wimbledon crown. Arthur Ashe won the U.S. Open in 1968 when he overwhelmed Tom Okker. Leslie Allen captured headlines in 1980 when she became the first black woman since Gibson to win a major tennis tournament. 1983 brought forth two African-born tennis stars for the first time. As we enter the 1990s, Zina Garrison looks like she may be near the very top of women's tennis and Lori McNeil also shows flashes of brilliance. Blacks have been represented at the top levels of tennis for all four of our integrated sports decades. However, fewer than two stars per decade is hardly dominance. As recently as 1988 there were Congressional hearings on discrimination in United States Tennis Association junior programs.

Pete Brown became the first black man to win a Professional Golf Association (PGA) event when he won the 1964 Waco Turner Open. Charlie Sifford, the first black on the PGA tour, had won the Long Beach Open in 1957 and the Alameda Open in 1960, but the PGA made both events "unofficial." However, Brown was an official winner at last in 1964, when public pressure made it impossible to deny black golfers any longer. Lee Elder achieved moderate success in the 1970s and early 1980s. Calvin Peete and Jim Thorpe were the only blacks on the PGA tour in 1990. Victories for black golfers, like black tennis players, have not been common in the last three decades.

Ironically, golf presented the most newsworthy story about racism in sport in 1990. The PGA had scheduled its championship at the Shoal Creek Country Club in Birmingham, Alabama. The media, much more conscious about race in the post-Campanis era of sport, discovered that Shoal Creek did not accept blacks as members. The story, which was given widespread coverage, unraveled one of sports' best kept but widely known secrets. It turned out that 17 of the 39 PGA Tour events for 1990 were scheduled for all-white clubs.

Civil rights organizations announced that they would picket Shoal Creek after its founder, Hall Thompson, told the press that "The country club is our home and we pick and choose who we want." Thompson emphasized that there were no black members because "that's not done in Birmingham." It was tragically ironic that Richard Arrington, a black man, could be mayor of Birmingham but couldn't join the country club.

The PGA, while claiming to oppose discrimination, also said that "The PGA of America recognizes that private clubs have a legal right to determine their own membership . . . should the law change, the PGA of course would take into account the legal compliance of the club's membership policy in making future PGA Championship site selections." Said another way, the PGA would continue to hold events at such clubs as long as it was legal.

That changed quickly when IBM, Toyota, and Anheuser-Busch, the sponsors of the PGA Championship television coverage, pulled out. Delta Airlines, the official airline of the tour, pulled back. More than $2 million in advertising revenue was withdrawn and the PGA began to act.

The PGA was suddenly forced to contemplate a future in which corporations would not be able to participate in its tacit complicity in segregation, legal or not. It announced there would be no more sites chosen which restrict minorities, including women, starting in 1995. Jim Awtrey, executive director of the PGA, added, "We are already holding conversations with the sites already selected for 1991 through 1994 and are reviewing the new policy announced today with them. We believe this is a positive step for golf." But according to an Associated Press report, none of the next four PGA Championship sites for 1991 (Crooked Stick in Carmel, Indiana), 1992 (Bellerive in St. Louis), 1993 (Aronomink in Newton Square, Pennsylvania) and 1994 (Oak Tree in Edmond, Oklahoma) had any black members. Three days later all four clubs agreed to integrate. The home course of the Masters in Augusta, Georgia, announced its first black member, as did Shoal Creek itself.

The media all across the country lifted the membership veils of country clubs and discovered the situation for blacks was not any different in New Rochelle, New York, than it was in Birmingham, Alabama. But the threats of corporate withdrawals and moral outrage had no doubt changed forever the ability of country clubs to remain totally hidden from public view. Like Al Campanis and Jimmy "The Greek" Snyder, Hall Thompson inadvertently set off a chain reaction that would possibly diminish the effects of racism in sport. In golf, that had been a very long time coming.

There were never any illusions about the rise of blacks in the National Hockey League when Willie O. Ree joined the Boston Bruins to become the NHL's first black player in the late 1950s. Hockey was neither an American playground nor a country club sport. Hockey rose out of the Canadian junior league in a nation where there were few blacks. Such underexposure to the game has resulted in the fact that in 1990 Graeme Townshend became only the thirteenth black player in NHL history. His stay with the Boston Bruins in 1990 was a brief one, yet he quickly had to face what Willie O. Ree faced throughout his much earlier career. A fight erupted on the ice in which fans didn't see much unusual action. Townshend made contact with the Rangers' left wing, Kris King. He heard a racial slur and exploded, going after King. This was the same Graeme Townshend who was called "nigger" by his college coach at Rensselaer Polytechnic Institute. Asked why it goes on, Townshend said, "We'll never get rid of it . . . I expect it. It's an on-ice thing. I don't hear it off the ice." With only thirteen black players in the history of professional hockey, there aren't many role models for young blacks to emulate.

The Big Three Sports

But no other sports were like the big three, where barriers fell quickly. In 1966, Emmett Ashford became a major league umpire after a twenty-two-year career. In April 1966, Red Auerbach named Bill Russell as the first black coach in any of sport's big leagues. (John McLendon had been hired to coach the Cleveland Pipers in the American Basketball Association in 1961, but the ABA was not considered on a par with the NBA in 1961.)

The civil rights movement, the acknowledgment of black athletic talent, and the owners' vision of a black market have indeed opened the doors in the last forty years. No matter how conservative America becomes, it is difficult to imagine a decrease in black participation in baseball, football, and basketball. However, increasing racism could easily further delay black emergence in other sports.

Blacks have access to basketball courts and parks that can be used as baseball diamonds and football fields. However, they have little or no access to golf, tennis, swimming, and ice-skating facilities. For the most part, these facilities are in the suburbs and are expensive to join. Also, the socializing that exists almost as part of these sports will further inhibit the acceptance of blacks. Social relationships in country club sports are part of the package. We didn't really need Shoal Creek to discover that.

If blacks do use role models to determine what athletic direction they might choose, the choices are surely broader in the big three sports. Black youth will be motivated by the breadth of the examples they see. Seven star tennis players in four decades and even fewer golfers do not compare with the 75 percent black NBA.

So the question becomes how good the options are for the black athlete in baseball, football, and basketball. Is he treated equally in each sport? Is he viewed as the equal of his white counterparts by coaches, the front office, and the fans? Is he paid the same? Are the stereotypes applied to him earlier in his career still assumed by whites? Does he face quotas? Is he limited to playing certain positions because of stacking? Must he perform better than whites in order to stay on the team? Does his fame endure after his playing career? Will he become a coach in the pros or join the front office of his team? Will he be out on the street when his sports career is terminated?

Salaries and Endorsements

For the black superstars, life is secure. Their salaries are equal to white stars. Black superstars have come a long way since 1966 when Frank Robinson, the Most Valuable Player (MVP) in the American League, was offered only two speaking engagements and one television commercial. (By comparison, Carl Yastrzemski, the 1967 winner, estimated that his extra income resulting from the MVP award was $150,000 to $200,000 in endorsements and speaking engagements.) The multimillion-dollar contracts for Michael Jordan placed him in the top ten endorsement earners in 1990. Bo Jackson seemed sure to crack it. Yet while a poll showed that eight of the ten most popular athletes in America were black, only Michael Jordan was among the top ten in endorsements.

It is more difficult to tell if salary equality and endorsement income comparisons apply across the board since teams do not reveal the salaries of all their players and companies rarely announce the value of endorsement packages. Information to compare salaries between blacks and whites has been very difficult to get. In the early 1980s, whatever information that was obtained showed whites outearning blacks consistently in the NFL. In a 1983 National Football League Players Association (NFLPA) study conducted by former pro star David Meggyesy, it made no difference whether you played offense or defense, started or sat on the bench. White offensive players earned an average of $4,970 more than black offensive players. The biggest difference was on defense, where whites took home $11,100 more than blacks ($97,100 compared to $86,000).

Meggyesy's preliminary study was delivered to the NFLPA with the following cover memo in May 1983:

Consistent with this historical pattern of racial discrimination, a similar pattern exists today regarding players' salaries. Simply put, in the NFL, black professional football players earn less than their white counterparts. Numerous theories have been presented as to why racial discrimination exists in the NFL. These theories are beside the point; the real issue is that racial discrimination does exist, and that it must be eliminated.

It has been easier to obtain data in recent years for the NFL and Major League Baseball. According to a *USA Today* survey of NFL salaries in 1988, black salaries in the NFL topped whites for the first time. The article provided a breakdown of salaries for players by race and by position. The league average for all players was $249,791. The average black player's salary was $253,916 compared to $236,516 for whites. This data represents a dramatic turnaround. Possible explanations include the higher proportion of veteran black players and lower numbers of younger, marginal blacks on teams. The survey did not break down the data, however, and thus it is difficult to interpret.

According to the survey, the only significant salary difference between white and black players was at quarterback. The overall average salary for quarterbacks was $434,939. Blacks at that position averaged $717,875 while whites averaged $421,466. The $200,000 plus difference was largely accounted for by the elite status of all three blacks at this position—Randall Cunningham, Doug Williams, and Warren Moon. In addition, there were many marginal white quarterbacks (second and third stringers) bringing down the average for whites.

Still there is a perception among some black players that whites continue to be paid more for comparable talent. In October 1989, Joey Browner, the Pro Bowl safety for the Minnesota Vikings, charged Viking Executive Vice President Mike Lynn with being a racist because he pays more to white players. His sentiments were echoed by other Pro Bowlers: wide receiver Anthony Carter and tight end Steve Jordan. Jordan claimed that "White players have signed more readily and with more ease." Lynn denied the charges and said the problem was money and not color.

In Major League Baseball, the salary results for 1989 were similar to those in 1988. Excluding pitchers, white players on average make more money than blacks, Latins and Hispanic-Americans. The average salary for whites was $590,593; blacks were next with $566,756. Latin players averaged $491,803 while Hispanic-Americans made an average of $413,114, nearly $180,000 less than their white colleagues. The position of pitcher was the only one in which salaries did not vary much according to race. All four groups of veterans averaged about $800,000.

The 1990 season seemed to show that average black salaries are brought up by the stars. In spite of the fact that blacks represent only 17 percent of all baseball players, 43 black players earned more than $700,000 in 1990 compared to a total of 59 whites earning the same amount. That is disproportionate by any standard.

Salary scales are being redefined with the 1990 collective bargaining agreement. The $3 million club of players grew to 23 players by December of 1990; another 86 had contracts worth $2 million. When all sports are looked at, there are 168 players making $1 million and 52 making $2 million or more a year according to the 1990 *Sport* "100 Survey." In baseball, three of the top ten earners were black; five of the top ten in the NFL and nine out of ten in the NBA were black. At the top, there certainly was equity in proportion to numbers in the respective leagues. Therein, of course, lies the unrealistic dream of so many young athletes who think they can attain the same status.

Stereotypes in Pro Sport

There are still situations in which black pros, even when they are superstars, are viewed differently than whites. Some blacks are accused by white teammates, management, the press and fans of being lazy.

Reggie Jackson opened up in a *Sports Illustrated* cover story, hitting on so many of the white stereotypes of the black athlete.

Average Salary by Position by Race*

Position	White	Black	Latin	Hispanic
Catcher	$475,567	$73,000	$592,000	$155,000
1st Base	$731,636	$734,366	$885,000	$1,034,000
2nd Base	$502,471	$635,000	$453,688	$207,500
3rd Base	$615,660	$393,500	$345,000	$412,500
Shortstop	$581,656	$752,500	$490,133	—
Outfield	$636,569	$812,171	$185,000	$669,689
Total Average	$590,593	$566,756	$491,803	$413,114

*Excludes pitchers.

He talked about how if a black isn't smiling, he is viewed as a "militant." He explained how a white player discovered to be taking drugs is portrayed as a single case while a black athlete caught seems to tarnish all black athletes.

The media was constantly on Jim Rice in his last few years in Boston. Oil Can Boyd, whose career picked up again when he joined the Montreal Expos, always faced the rumors that he was exaggerating injuries. While Boyd was viewed as a flake, Rice was seen as surly and a "militant." Both had accused the Red Sox of being racist.

Houston's star pitcher, J. R. Richard, may be the worst victim yet of the "lazy" tag. He was in the midst of his best season in 1980 with a 10–4 record, 119 strikeouts and a league-leading 1.80 earned run average (ERA). He had struck out more than 600 batters in his previous two seasons. He had not missed a turn in the starting rotation in five years, and his highest ERA in those five years was 3.11. He had won 20, 18, 18, and 18 in his last four full seasons. There were few if any better pitchers in baseball.

On June 17, Richard complained of "deadness" in his arm and sat out until June 28, when he was knocked out by Cincinnati after only 3½ innings. The media attack began. Reporters alleged that Richard was a loafer and speculated that he might be into drugs. But he pitched better on July 3 (six innings, three hits, two runs) and in the All-Star game, which he started (two innings, one hit, three strikeouts). Then he lasted only three innings against Atlanta on July 14. The media attack intensified even as

Richard went on the disabled list. Hospital tests discovered a clot, but doctors said he could pitch under supervision. Then during his first workout, he had a stroke and nearly died.

The critics were silenced. Enos Cabell, the Astros third baseman, told *Sports Illustrated* that the criticism would not have come down if Richard had been white: "We always knew we had to be better. There is a difference." Carolyn Richard, J.R.'s wife, added, "Black and big, a big star. . . . Other guys had problems on the Astros. Ken Forsch [a white pitcher] was out a whole half of a season . . . I've never seen a player dragged through the mud like this. It's something we'll never forget. Never."

Charlie Sanders of the Detroit Lions was chosen at tight end on the NFL's "Team of the Seventies." He had been selected for the Pro Bowl seven times and caught 336 passes in ten years. He hurt his knee on a preseason play in 1986 but continued to play on the advice of team physicians. On game day, doctors had to wire his knee, shoot it with electrical charges, and heavily wrap his leg. The pain was enormous, but he played. The media printed stories saying that coaches thought Sanders was a hypochondriac. In November 1977, he went to see a specialist in Toronto who performed an arthroscopy and discovered that the bone "was completely rotted out."

Sanders asked Ira Berkow of *The New York Times*, "Why wasn't I given an arthroscopy earlier, or why did people refuse to believe I was in such pain? I don't know." He discovered that Lions' physicians had withheld medical information from him. One of the Lions' physicians told Berkow, "Sometimes it's not good to tell a patient everything . . . you wind up scaring the patient needlessly." Unlike the Astros, the Lions have not apologized. In fact, they appealed a workmen's compensation award to Sanders of $32,500 cash plus $156 per week for the injury; the case was later settled out of court and Sanders was hired as a part-time community relations worker for the Lions.

These are the cases of black superstars. Coaches complain even more often about marginal pros who are black. But if a marginal black pro grumbles, he can be let go.

Drugs in Black and White

Considerable publicity has been given to athletes taking drugs in pro sports. Early in the 1980s some NBA executives estimated that 40 to 75 percent of the players used cocaine and 10 percent used freebase, a form of cocaine. More than a few people assumed it was a black problem.

Simon Gourdine, the former NBA deputy commissioner, wondered whether the furor caused by the drug revelations was racially motivated. He told *The New York Times,* "If someone chose to, they could have concluded that 100 percent of the black players were involved with drugs. Anytime there are social problems like drugs or alcohol, the perception is that it's a black player involved. That concerns me."

In September 1983, the NBA and the NBA Players Association took a strong stand on drugs. Starting at the end of 1983, any player known to be distributing or using drugs would be banned from the NBA. However, if a player turned himself in for using, he would receive professional help. Knowing how difficult that was, players were allowed a second chance if they turned themselves in. A third occurrence meant that the player would be banned for life.

Considering how bad the problem in the NBA was, the policy has proved to be a model for other pro sports. However, it took the death of Len Bias and the banning of Michael Ray Richardson by the NBA to nail home the seriousness of the problem and to signal the turnaround.

The most frightening sports-related event of the late 1980s was undoubtedly the sudden, shocking death of Len Bias. In a three-day period, the twenty-two-year-old Bias became the top draft choice of the world champion Boston Celtics, signed a million-dollar shoe endorsement contract, and died from a cocaine-related heart attack. The sports world mourned this superstar, this role model turned negative example.

But Bias's death was not the only sports drug story of 1986. I had to wonder what lure cocaine offers that would make an athlete like Len Bias risk everything for that flash of instant pleasure, what power it possesses to have induced Don Rogers, the 1984 NFL Rookie of the Year, to ingest enough cocaine to kill himself eight days after the Bias tragedy.

The horror of Len Bias's death brought home the fact that drugs were not limited to pro athletes. Doctors' testimony that a single exposure to cocaine could kill someone as physically fit as Bias might have awakened young athletes as no other incident could have. It appeared clear that other college basketball players were using cocaine. Yet only a short time before the death of Bias, sports fans seemed shocked when fifty-seven of the top collegiate prospects for the NFL draft tested positive for drugs.

The NBA policy is working because the league and players association are working together. There is no question of racial discrimination any longer under the inspired leadership of Commissioner David Stern and NBA Players Association chief Charles Grantham. But if the NBA is turning it around, the NFL seems to have its hands tied because of the rancor of the NFLPA. Some believe that race is still a factor there.

Pete Rozelle suspended four players—all blacks—prior to the 1983 season for cocaine use. Yet no one believed that Pete Johnson, Ross Browner, E. J. Junior, and Greg Stremrick were the only users in the NFL. In 1986, seven New England Patriots were said to be "seriously" involved with drugs. This story was printed a day after the Patriots played in the Super Bowl. All seven players listed were black. Of the thirty players suspended in 1988 and 1989, twenty-six were black. There were quiet rumblings among the black players in the NFL that they were being singled out.

In January 1990, Washington, D.C., television station WJLA reported that three prominent white quarterbacks had tested positively for high levels of cocaine and that the findings were covered up. The station also charged that NFL clubs protected certain players—stars and whites—by warning them when "random" tests were scheduled. The NFL denied both allegations and a third charge that Dr. Forest Tennant, the person in charge of the NFL's drug testing program, mixed up samples and wrote players' names on the urine samples in violation of the anonymity policy. A prominent black player told the *Boston Globe,* "A lot of guys wondered why so many of the suspended players were black. A lot of guys don't feel it's a coincidence." Gene Upshaw, the head of the NFL Players Association, while agreeing that certain players believe the drug testing policy is racist, said he did not believe it: "I don't want anyone to leave with the impression that the NFL is a racist organization. I don't want to believe that and I don't. But this report doesn't surprise me." Tennant left his post later in 1990 although still adamantly denying the charges.

Just as whites in society believe that blacks use drugs more than whites, a significant segment of the public seems to perceive that black athletes use drugs more than white athletes. In reality, national surveys consistently show that a higher percentage of whites use drugs than do blacks. There is no statistical data to support a higher use of drugs by black athletes over whites.

Are There Quotas in Pro Sports?

A denial quickly follows every charge of a quota. The NBA management denied quotas existed when Bill Russell first exposed them in the 1960s. They were denied again in 1980 when the league took action against Ted Stepien, then the new owner in Cleveland, who proclaimed, "I think the Cavs have too many blacks, ten of eleven. You need a blend of white and black. I think that draws and I think that's a better team." He sent black star Campy Russell as a gift to the Knicks. He dumped black guard Foots Walker, who was third in the league in assists. He obtained undistinguished whites Mike Bratz and Roger Phegley in trades. He offered his budding superstar Mike Mitchell (black) to San Antonio for Mark Olberding (white). In only his second year, Mitchell had averaged 22.2 points per game, shot 52 percent, and led the team in blocked shots. Olberding averaged 10.5 points per game, his best in five seasons. But San Antonio reportedly nixed the deal because Olberding was their only white starter.

Officials inside the NBA office insist that personnel decisions are made on the basis of merit, not black or white. However,

Lenny Wilkens, who has had the longest tenure of any black coach in pro sports, said, "The unwritten rule is that there should be a minimum of three white players on each team." Larry Fleischer, the late counsel to the NBA Players Association, said simply, "There are a number of players in the NBA who are on teams not because of their ability but because they are white."

Is there a system in the 75 percent black NBA to regulate the number of whites per team? In 1982–83, the preseason team rosters revealed some interesting evidence. Fourteen of the twenty-three teams listed at least three whites on the roster. The nine exceptions included Atlanta, San Francisco, Houston, New York, Philadelphia, and Washington, all of which have large black populations, ranging from 18 to 26 percent in their metropolitan areas.

The decade passed on with even more striking numbers. By 1990–91, twenty-one of twenty-seven teams listed having three or more whites on their preseason rosters. Was the racial balance an accident? The exceptions were Atlanta, Detroit, Washington, Los Angeles, Portland and Houston. All except Portland had metropolitan area populations ranging from 18 to 24 percent black.

As will be seen in this chapter, the NBA has such an outstanding record regarding race equity that it could be given the benefit of the doubt in the area of quotas. In 1990, NBA explanations that personnel decisions are made purely on the basis of talent are credible.

Are black baseball players still evenly distributed through a quota system? In 1983, twenty-two of the twenty-six teams in the majors had a percentage of blacks within one percent of the average in all baseball. In 1990, only eighteen of the twenty-six teams fell within this range. This seemed to represent evidence contradicting the charge of using quotas. There have never been serious charges of quotas in the NFL.

In 1983 it seemed like more than a coincidence that more than 75 percent of basketball and baseball teams conformed to the overall racial percentages in the population. It seemed hard to believe that the distribution of blacks and whites could be so if it occurred by chance. Like other factors, this now appears to be changing for the better.

Levels of Performance of Blacks and Whites

Quotas aside, it seems apparent that blacks must perform better than whites to remain in the NBA. Front-office people deny this, but candid white sports personalities do not. Al McGuire noted, "If a white and black player are equal, I think the white player would get the edge in time played and pictures in the program." Former Knick superstar Dave DeBusschere said simply, "The white guy has a better opportunity." The numbers portray the issue clearly; all figures that follow come from the *1990–91 Official NBA Register*.

To be sure, there are genuine white stars like Larry Bird, Chris Mullin, Kevin McHale, John Stockton, Mark Price, Jack Sikma and Tom Chambers. But a look at who the NBA teams carry is revealing. Only the Celtics, Hornets and Suns had a team points per game (ppg) average for their white players of more than 10 ppg. Twelve teams had thirty-six white players with a collective average below 6 ppg. Collectively, the career average of the twenty-nine whites on the Clippers, Timberwolves, Bulls, Nets, Magic, Kings, Spurs, Supersonics and Bullets was below 4.8 ppg.

The mean career scoring average for whites in the league was 7.3 ppg while for blacks it was 10.1 ppg. Of the 277 blacks listed, 145 (52 percent) had averages greater than 10 ppg. Of the 84 whites, only 17 (20 percent) had career averages greater than 10 ppg. As Enos Cabell said about baseball, "There is a difference."

Blacks dominate the top of the league as well. In 1989–90, eight of the top ten scorers were black, as were eight of the top ten players in field-goal percentage and nine of the top ten in rebounds. If you look at the top five scorers on all the NBA teams, 113 out of 135 (84 percent) were black.

The question of who is best aroused a brief but ugly racial controversy after the Boston Celtics knocked the Detroit Pistons out of the playoffs in May of 1987. Detroit's Dennis Rodman, in the heat of the moment, said that Boston's Larry Bird was "way overrated. Why does he get so much publicity? Because he's white. You never hear about a black player being the greatest." Piston star Isiah Thomas agreed with Rodman and the fires were lit. Boston fans, especially white Boston fans, were enraged.

Rodman and Thomas could not have chosen a worse target. Larry Bird did so many things well on the court and was clearly one of the best players in the NBA at that time. Both apologized, Thomas in a press conference arranged by the NBA and Rodman in a more quiet way.

But Rodman's and Thomas's spontaneous responses may have been set up by the widely held belief that whites get more attention from many basketball writers and fans than their numbers in the league would dictate. It was an era in which John Koncak signed a contract with Atlanta that made him the nineteenth highest paid player in the NBA. At the time of the signing, he was not a regular starter and had a career scoring average under 7 ppg. In 1989–90, Koncak made more money than either of his star black teammates Moses Malone and Dominique Wilkins. They had a collective average of 22.8 ppg and 8.2 rebounds each per game. Koncak averaged only 3.7 ppg and 4.1 rebounds per game.

In spite of the fact that blacks in the league outnumber whites by almost three to one, white players with five years of experience in the NBA and who averaged under 6 ppg actually outnumber blacks in the same category thirteen to nine. Black veterans averaging more than 10 ppg outnumber whites in the same category eighty-one to thirteen.

Rodman was way off base with Bird, but his frustration may have reflected other things. As more blacks come into the league, some owners seem to have disregarded performance, retaining marginal white ballplayers in order to maintain a white presence on their teams. Black athletes have claimed that this was the case for many years. Going strictly by the numbers, it still appears true today.

Historically, statistics show that blacks in baseball have to perform even better than those in basketball via-à-vis their white teammates. That finally seems to be changing.

Only 5 percent of blacks had career batting averages below

.221, compared to 12 percent of whites. While 28 percent of whites hit below a career average .241, only 17 percent of blacks hit below that average. On the other end of the spectrum, 25 percent of blacks had lifetime averages above .281, compared to only 13 percent of whites. There is still a significant difference.

However, the differences in performance are diminishing when compared to statistics based on data compiled seven years earlier from *1983 Who's Who in Baseball*. It was not the slight improvement of whites that narrowed the gap. This covergence was due to the dramatic decline in the league-wide performance of blacks. In 1983, 58 percent of the black players had career averages above .270, while only 26 percent of the white players had such career averages. In 1990, the percentage of blacks with better than a .270 average had dropped a stunning 21 percent (from 58 to 37 percent) as the white percentage grew slightly to 27 percent. In 1983, only 9 percent of blacks had career averages below .240 compared to 17 percent in 1990; in 1983, less than 1 percent of blacks had career averages below .220 compared to 5 percent in 1990; only 3.7 percent had averages above .300 in 1990 while 5.5 percent hit for that average in 1983. The erosion has been a gradual one since 1983 as monitored in the annual *Who's Who*.

The story for pitchers is the same, representing a similar decline in black performance. In 1983, 18 percent of blacks had career winning records above .600. That dropped to 14 percent by 1990 (for whites it was 10 percent in 1983 and 9 percent in 1990). The huge change came in the percentage of pitchers winning more than half of their games. In 1990, only 36 percent of black pitchers had a career winning record (in 1983, 53 percent had winning records) versus 44 percent of white pitchers (also a large drop from 56 percent in 1983). Moreover, 42 percent of black pitchers won less than 40 percent of the time while only 13 percent of whites fell below this marginal figure. In 1983, only 12 percent of black pitchers and 16 percent of white pitchers fell below this mark.

There were similar trends in pitchers' career earned run averages (ERA). In 1983, almost three times as many whites as blacks (31 percent versus 11.7 percent) had ERAs greater than 4.01. By 1990, 42 percent of the ERAs of black pitchers had risen above

4.01 (versus 11.7 percent in 1983). The percentage of whites in this category did not vary much (31 percent in 1983 versus 34 in 1990). In 1990, 58 percent of whites had more respectable ERAs, between 3.01 and 4.00, compared to only 36 percent of blacks. Whereas black pitchers had consistently lower ERAs in 1983, whites held that distinction in 1990. In 1983, I wrote that blacks "are better, and they have to be, for it is next to impossible for black pitchers to play Major League Baseball unless they are excellent black pitchers." While blacks still make up less than 5 percent of big league pitching staffs, those who make it are no longer only dominant players.

This poses the question: Is the diminishing interest in Major League Baseball in the black community already resulting in fewer superstar and star players that those collective statistics of both hitters and pitchers would drop so precipitously and so fast?

In spite of an overall decline in the statistical performance of blacks throughout baseball, blacks dominate the elite categories in baseball just as they do in basketball. This is especially remarkable considering that less than one out of five players in baseball is black. For the 1990 season, looking at both the National and American Leagues, half or more of the top ten players in the following categories were black: batting average, home runs, slugging percentage, runs, total bases and stolen bases. For both leagues combined, eight of the twenty leaders in runs batted in were black, as were nine out of twenty in on-base percentage.

The popularity of baseball in Hispanic-American communities and in Latin America has resulted in increased recruitment of Latin American and Hispanic-American ballplayers. Two percent of the players in 1990 were Hispanic-Americans and nearly eleven percent were born in Latin America. They were also leaders, especially in the American League, where at least one Latin or Hispanic player was in the top ten in batting average (two), home runs, runs batted in, runs, slugging and on-base percentage (two), stolen bases (three), and total bases. The rapid rise of players from these communities appears to resemble the way it was in the early days for black players. The lessons of the decline of blacks for others should be studied closely.

Thus, unlike basketball, baseball's chances of becoming "whiter" are excellent. According to a 1978 study by James Curtis and John Loy, the percentage of black Americans in baseball rose from 10 percent in 1960 to 16 percent in 1968 to 27 percent in 1975. This increase was followed by a decline; only 19 percent of the players were black Americans in 1983, falling to 16.6 percent in 1990.

Who Will Pay to See a Game: The Issue of Black and White Fans

Will white fans watch black teams? Why do so few blacks attend pro sports events? The debate about white fans soared in the early 1980s as attendance in baseball, football, and hockey soared while it declined in basketball. It was said that race was a primary factor in the NBA because there were too many black players.

A fan at a football game can hardly tell who is black and who is white under all the gear. In baseball, the players are so spread out on the field that a racist fan would not feel overwhelmed by large numbers of blacks. But in basketball there is no way to hide black bodies glistening with sweat. Ten could be concentrated in a 100-square-foot area and that apparently seemed too much for some fans.

A random sample survey of Philadelphia fans during the 1980–81 season confirmed this. Philadelphia had the best record in the NBA and featured Julius Erving, the league's most exciting player. The survey was taken by the Philadelphia *Daily News* because the 76ers were bringing in only 55 percent of their capacity and ranked only ninth in total attendance. Fifty-seven percent of the 955 respondents agreed that "a white audience won't pay to watch black athletes." Julius Erving agreed: "I would like to say that race is not involved, but that would be naive."

The Boston Celtics have always had white superstars. Then (and now) it was Larry Bird. The Celtics sold out 95 percent of their seats, compared to 55 percent in Philadelphia. The teams were fierce rivals and had nearly identical records. Yet, the

Celtics were almost always sold out and the 76ers had only a half-full house. The Celtics made Larry Bird the highest-paid player in the NBA and Kevin McHale the fourth highest-paid player prior to the 1983–84 season. Bird was close to the best, if not the best, but as outstanding as McHale was, he was not the NBA's fourth-best player in that season.

All that has changed under the leadership of NBA Commissioner David Stern. With the problems of drugs diminished, Stern marketed the league and its increased number of black players, coaches and general managers. The NBA, which has the highest percentage of blacks in all three categories and the only black owners in the 1990–91 season, is experiencing record attendance and revenues. The standard of play and the community involvement of the league has been raised and the fans turn out. Surely there are lessons for baseball and football—and society as a whole. White fans will turn out for a quality team that is marketed well.

The most frequently asked question about fans today is what has happened to the black fans. There has been a steady decline in numbers over an extended period of time. According to a 1989 study by the Simmons Market Research Bureau, only 6.1 percent of all adults who attend Major League Baseball games and 7.9 percent of adults attending NFL games are black. Those games are played in urban areas where the black populations are well above the national average. Only the NBA, with 12.3 percent black adult attendance, reflects the percentage of blacks in the national population.

As bad as those figures were, they may be an overestimate. A team of journalists from the Philadelphia *Daily News* monitored ten NFL, NBA and Major League Baseball games across the country in 1989. In almost every instance, the percentage of blacks attending the games was substantially below the Simmons figures. The average for baseball games was 0.8 to 2.1 percent; for football about 2 percent; for basketball about 10 percent. The *Daily News* also polled all twenty-six major league baseball teams for the racial breakdown of their crowds. The eight teams that responded were based in cities with black populations of between

13.9 and 24.9 percent of their total population, yet none exceeded an average of more than 4 percent of ticket sales to blacks.

To be sure, there are economic reasons involved. The median family income for blacks was $18,098 in 1989 compared to $32,274 for whites. The Census Bureau estimates that 33 percent of blacks live below the poverty level. Taking a family of four to a game is a $100 investment for an NBA or NFL game and slightly less for baseball.

But there are other, equally crucial factors involved. As will be seen in succeeding sections of this chapter, there are fewer and fewer black players in baseball. Many in the black community resent how few blacks are hired in the front offices of Major League Baseball and the NFL. They say there is no reason to support such a system.

Yet another factor that keeps black fans away is the location of the arenas and stadiums. Since 1975, eight NFL and three NBA teams built new stadiums in the suburbs. Sacramento and Charlotte, both new NBA franchises, built their arenas away from the downtown area. The Reverend Jim Holley, an Operation PUSH official, accused the Detroit Pistons of playing "plantation basketball . . . with black people performing for the amusement of upscale whites." The charge came after the Pistons moved to Auburn Hills—forty miles from Detroit. Piston officials told the *Daily News* that such charges were "unfair and inaccurate." However, no matter what the intention of franchise owners, moves of arenas to suburban communities in a national climate where race-hate crimes are on the rise will surely discourage many black fans from going to the game.

Blacks Playing Baseball

Major league baseball has the smallest percentage of blacks of the three major sports. (All figures are taken from the *1990 Who's Who in Baseball*.) Only 16.6 percent of major league players are black Americans. It was 19 percent when *Broken Promises* was written in 1983. This represents a dramatic decline from the 1960s when nearly 25 percent of all players were black Americans.

Youth baseball, once a common sight, has become a rarity in urban communities. As was seen in the preceding chapter, college baseball is slowly replacing the minor leagues as a talent pool and there are only a few blacks playing college baseball. Pro scouts reportedly do not go to urban areas to look at baseball teams, so talented black teenagers there may never be discovered.

The problem is likely to get worse as baseball games shift from networks to cable television as their primary carrier. Harry Edwards told the *Daily News* that "The black working class and underclass which produces most of the players aren't going to pay for cable . . . fewer and fewer black kids are going to get to watch baseball. And that's going to mean the role models won't be there for them . . . fewer and fewer of them will play baseball."

Some of the reasons for blacks losing interest in baseball were given earlier. Former Commissioner Bowie Kuhn said that blacks viewed ballparks as "a white man's place to be." The number of minor league teams has decreased rapidly in the 1970s and 1980s as college baseball has taken up more of their role. In 1970, blacks used to make up 30 to 40 percent of the players in the minor leagues; the minors were only 15 percent black in the 1980s. This reflected several things. First, since many blacks who sign contracts are more talented than whites, they move up to the majors faster. Second, some blacks—but not many—were going to college on scholarships. A third, less tangible factor may reflect racial tensions in big cities. Most scouts are white and may be reluctant to go see blacks play in the inner cities.

But the colleges do not represent a new hope for seeing more blacks playing baseball. As was pointed out earlier, there is a parallel decline in the number of black baseball players going to college. Since the proportion of college players selected in the baseball draft has continued to rise, the prospects for blacks going to the majors have become even dimmer.

Ken Hudson is a vice-president for the Boston Celtics and was the first black referee in the NBA. He summed it up for the Philadelphia *Daily News:* "Baseball has become, for lack of a better word, a white game. The interest in the game among blacks just isn't what it used to be. It has died off, from top to bottom. Blacks aren't playing it. They see people like Michael Jordan . . .

football players coming out of college and making nice salaries. Then they look at baseball, where unless you're the exception rather than the rule, you've got to go to the minor leagues.''

Positional Segregation in the NFL and Major League Baseball

Are blacks also outperforming whites in professional football? It is harder to tell since football as played in the NFL is almost totally segregated by position.

I was living in Denver when the Broncos drafted Marlin Briscoe from the University of Omaha in the late 1960s. He was drafted as a defensive back in spite of the fact that he was a star quarterback in college. Injuries subsequently compelled the Broncos to play him at quarterback. He passed for three touchdowns in his first game; the following week he was on the bench watching the woeful Broncos fall behind 14–0. The coach sent him in and they won 21–14, but still he didn't play in the next game. When the regular quarterback was injured, Briscoe started and passed for four touchdowns, winning the game. That was their last victory, but in two of the final three losses Briscoe passed for more than 200 yards. In his five starts he had done this four times. At the end of the season, Briscoe was released and never played quarterback again. That was my first introduction to the word "stacking," or segregation by position.

Is it true now in the NFL? The statistics in the twenty-eight NFL 1990 team media guides are overwhelming. On offense, 93 percent of the quarterbacks were white (versus 99 percent in 1983); 87 percent of the centers, 76 percent of the offensive guards, and 71 percent of the tackles were white. (97, 77 and 68 percent were the respective percentages in 1983). Sociologist Jonathon Brower did a survey of coaches and asked them how they would characterize the three positions dominated by whites. They used the following words: intelligence, leadership, emotional control, decision-making, and technique.

The fact that Doug Williams led the Washington Redskins to a Super Bowl victory, coupled with the tremendous recent success of other star black quarterbacks like Warren Moon and Randall Cunningham and the emergence of others like Don McPherson, Rodney Peete, Gil Renfroe and Vince Evans in 1990, showed that there could be rapid progress in eliminating positional segregation at the club level. The wealth of great black college quarterbacks should also hasten this.

Williams told of both the peaks and valleys of his career as a black quarterback in his book, *Quarterback: Shattering the NFL Myth:* "When the USFL folded in 1986, a lot of the league's quarterbacks were picked up. . . . Not one [team] offered to give me a tryout, much less a contract." Eventually the Redskins picked him up as a back-up to Jay Schroeder. In their Super Bowl season, many Redskins told Williams that he should be the starter. Williams wrote, "I didn't want to get caught up in a racial issue again. . . . I had been fighting being a black quarterback all my life, and to make this a black issue would have been detrimental to the team. I think I could have split the team, so I didn't want to think that way."

Of course, Coach Joe Gibbs did start him. In approaching the championship game, Williams tried to put himself in the place of "any other warm-blooded, black America. I wanted to be proud of Doug Williams playing in the Super Bowl. I tried to put myself in the place of another black American. If Randall Cunningham or Warren Moon had been playing, I would have been proud."

A note of caution to temper this optimism is sounded by the story of Rodney Peete. Prior to the 1989 draft, Peete was rated by most scouting combines as among the top three quarterbacks available. Charges of racism flared when he was picked on the sixth round and was the ninth quarterback chosen. Mike Wilbon of the *Washington Post* wrote that "The fact that eight other quarterbacks were chosen before Peete says one thing to me about NFL people and what they're looking for in a quarterback. If he's white and can stand up straight, he's a better prospect than a black quarterback with various and obvious talents." Chosen by the Detroit Lions, Peete started some games as a rookie in 1989 and won the starting job in 1990 with Andre Ware behind him. The story recalled an earlier era when Warren Moon, who was the NFL's highest paid player in 1989, was not even chosen in the draft and had to prove himself in Canada. There are, however, several positions dominated by blacks. In 1990, 88 percent of the running backs (88 percent in 1983) and 85 percent of the wide receivers were black (77 percent in 1983). The defensive position that shows the most meaningful statistical difference by race is cornerback. Ninety-six percent of the cornerbacks were black in 1990 (up from 92 percent in 1983). The words used by coaches for the positions of running back, wide receiver, and defensive back were: strength, quickness, and instinct. All three are black-dominated positions.

There were no black coaches in the NFL until Art Shell became the Raiders coach in 1989. If the white coaches hold traditional racial beliefs, then it is easy to imagine that player assignments could be made according to race.

The table on page 294 was compiled from veterans listed in the 1990 media guides and demonstrates the patterns.

I have worked closely with Keith Lee since 1984. Keith, who played as a defensive back in the NFL for six years, tried to be a stereotype-breaker by resisting the conversion from his natural slot as a quarterback to a defensive back. A stand-out quarterback at Gardena High School in Los Angeles, Keith was heavily recruited by PAC-10 and Western Athletic Conference schools. None, however, was willing to let him play quarterback, so Keith played two outstanding seasons in a junior college to prove he could do it. The same schools made the same offers again. Only Colorado State stepped up with a promise that he could play quarterback. He started for both years and was good enough to be drafted by Buffalo as a defensive back. But Keith had proved his point. He resented seeing the "self-selection by some black athletes who assessed their chances of success, saw the patterns of positional segregation, saw what happened to Marlin Briscoe, and [chose] to change positions. I knew I could play quarterback in college and I was not going to do anything less."

Keith Lee does not hesitate when asked who his greatest hero is: Joe Gilliam. Gilliam fought all the odds and insisted he could be an NFL quarterback. It wasn't easy. In 1974, Joe Gilliam was named as starting quarterback for the Pittsburgh Steelers. Despite leading them to a 4–0–1 record and first place in the AFC

Positions Played in the NFL by Race

Position	Whites by Percentage		Blacks by Percentage	
	1983	*1990*	*1983*	*1990*
Offense:				
Quarterback	99	93	1	7
Running back	12	12	88	88
Wide receiver	23	15	77	85
Center	97	87	3	13
Guard	77	76	23	24
Tight end	52	61	48	39
Tackle	68	71	32	29
Kicker	98	95	2	5
Defense:				
Cornerback	8	4	92	96
Safety	43	17	57	83
Linebacker	53	65	47	35
Defensive end	31	28	69	72
Defensive tackle	47	50	53	50

Central Division, Gilliam was benched allegedly because the Steelers were "weak offensively." The fact that their points-per-game average was better than 75 percent of the teams in the NFL and that they were in first place in the division seemed irrelevant. What appeared to be most relevant was that Joe Gilliam was black. He persisted and starred in the NFL.

In 1976, James Harris became the NFC's leading passer after never being given the opportunity to play quarterback for Buffalo. After helping to win twenty of the twenty-four games he started and being named Most Valuable Player in the Pro Bowl, James Harris was traded for future draft choices.

At one time, such examples taught black high school quarterbacks that they should try out for other positions. Later it taught the Keith Lees not to switch. But the roles played by Gilliam and Harris were not lost on Doug Williams as he approached the Super Bowl as the first black quarterback: "James Harris or Joe

Gilliam would have deserved to be the first. They opened the door for me, and if you don't want to call it a door, say it's a wall. They'll still be talking about black and white quarterbacks in 1998. Some things we can help change, but some things they won't change." The fact that the Redskins decided to go with younger quarterbacks one year after Williams's Super Bowl triumph and not one team was willing to pick up Doug Williams is another reason to temper the optimism on a trend toward black quarterbacks in the NFL.

Williams was obviously hurt and wrote in his book, "All I wanted was a chance to prove myself. If I didn't make the team in training camp, fine. Then they could cut me. But, as it turned out, they wouldn't even give me a shot." An astute observer, Williams believed "it was a combination of finances and avoiding controversy. Black quarterbacks are always going to be controversial in the NFL. . . . No question. Black quarterbacks do not get a chance to sit around and make money as backups in the NFL. . . . The backup quarterback position is for white players only. Blacks need not apply. I really thought the Redskins were above that. . . . I can say Doug Williams deserved a better farewell from the Redskins." While it is no longer impossible for a black to make it at quarterback in the NFL, the 93 percent white figure shows it is still unlikely.

Baseball has its own positional segregation. The pitcher and the catcher are central to every play of the game. Of the forty-nine catchers listed in the *1989 Who's Who in Baseball,* only one was black; seven were Latins or Hispanic. Only eleven (5 percent) of the 304 pitchers were black, down from 7 percent in 1983. Another twenty-three (7.5 percent) were Latin or Hispanic, the same as 1983. It is unfortunately not surprising that these pivotal "thinking positions" were held mostly by whites.

What was surprising was who was playing second base, shortstop, and third base. All three are also considered to be thinking positions. In 1989, blacks made up 21 percent of second basemen, 15 percent of shortstops, and 14 percent of third basemen (versus 21, 11, and 9 percent in 1983). Likewise, 18 percent of first basemen were black in 1989, and these increases put blacks nearly on par with their overall percentage in the league for all infield positions. This may indicate a significant shift away from positional segregation in baseball although, like the positive developments in football at quarterback, it is too soon to tell what the long-term effects might be.

However, outfielders, like first basemen, mainly react to other players; not as much skill and training are considered necessary to hold these positions. The percentage of blacks in the three outfield positions in 1989 increased slightly to 68 percent from 65 percent in 1983. Despite being outnumbered in the league by more than six to one, blacks have a numerical superiority over whites in the outfield (56 to 47).

Positional segregation got worse for many years. In 1960, there were 5.6 times as many black outfielders as pitchers; in 1970 there were 6.7 times as many; by 1980, the data showed 8.8 times as many black outfielders as pitchers. In 1990, the figure had dropped to 5.2 times as many. However, this was due to the reduction of the number of black outfielders and not due to an increase in the number of black pitchers. In fact, the total of black pitchers and catchers had declined slightly between the late 1960s and 1990. By 1990, disproportionate numbers of blacks and whites (relative to their respective representation in the total number of players) existed only in the roles of pitcher, catcher, and outfielder. According to *Who's Who in Baseball* for 1983 and 1989, the positional breakdown is as shown in the chart.

As the number of black players in the league has decreased, the number of Latins and Hispanics has increased. Thus the declining interest in baseball in the black community described earlier has coincided with an increase in interest in the Latin American and Hispanic communities. The greater interest has resulted in more players at lower levels and, consequently, more pros.

In 1978, Calvin Griffith, the owner of the Minnesota Twins, shocked the country when he spoke to a Lions Club in Waseca, Minnesota: "I'll tell you why we came to Minnesota in 1961. It was when I found out you had only 15,000 blacks here. Black people don't go to ball games, but they'll fill up a rassling ring and put up such a chant it'll scare you to death. . . . We came here because you've got good, hard-working white people here."

Positions Played in Major League Baseball by Race

	Whites by Percentage		Blacks by Percentage		Latins and Hispanics by Percentage	
Position	*1983*	*1989*	*1983*	*1989*	*1983*	*1989*
Pitcher	86	87	7	5	7	8
Catcher	93	84	0	2	7	14
1B	55	74	38	18	7	8
2B	65	55	21	21	14	24
3B	82	73	5	15	13	12
SS	73	44	11	14	16	42
Outfield	45	40	46	47	9	13
Overall	70	70	19	17	9	13

Many understood what Griffith was saying. Whites understood he wanted to make more money. Blacks understood he was a racist. Rod Carew was the star of the Twins at the time. He had been baseball's most consistent hitter for twelve seasons in a row, with a .333 lifetime average. Although Griffith later apologized and said the statements were taken out of context, Carew said, "I refuse to be a slave on his plantation and play for a bigot." He was traded to California. It is no small irony that following Jackie Robinson blacks were allowed to play professional sports largely to increase attendance. Now some clubs seem to be reducing the number of blacks because they fear that too many blacks will hurt attendance.

Halls of Fame

I remember the day my father was elected to the Basketball Hall of Fame. It was one of the happiest days of his life. There was no reason to doubt he would be selected, yet the fact of his election was nevertheless a proud moment, and my father went to the ceremony with joy.

When Bill Russell followed Bob Douglas as the second black

man elected to the Hall, he refused to go to the induction because of the racism in the sport. That was in 1974. Blacks were already dominating basketball and yet there were only two black men in the Hall of Fame. Abe Saperstein, the white owner of the Harlem Globetrotters, was admitted before Bob Douglas.

I assumed that the controversy created by Bill Russell would move more blacks into the Hall quickly. Between 1974 and 1990, sixty whites and eighteen blacks were chosen. That made a total of one hundred fifty-two whites and twenty blacks. The NBA was 75 percent black while the Basketball Hall of Fame was 88 percent white in 1990 (down from 94 percent in 1980).

The National Baseball Hall of Fame is in Cooperstown, New York. In 1962 Jackie Robinson was appropriately the first black inducted. His induction didn't exactly open the floodgates for blacks. By 1990, only twenty-five blacks had been chosen compared to one hundred eighty-one whites. Baseball is 17 percent black; the Baseball Hall of Fame is 12 percent black.

Emlen Tunnell, the great New York Giant defensive back, was the first black elected to the Pro Football Hall of Fame in 1967. Jim Brown was inducted in 1971. By 1990, Tunnell and Brown were joined by thirty other black inductees; there were one hundred twenty-three whites in the Hall. The NFL was 60 percent black while the Pro Football Hall of Fame was 79 percent white (down from 86 percent in 1980).

Jim Brown, who played in Russell's era and dominated football much like Russell did basketball, was always equally outspoken about race. In 1990, he threatened to have his name removed from the Pro Football Hall of Fame "because it is racist." He was upset that two NFL greats, John Mackey, the former Baltimore Colts tight end, and Lynn Swann, the former Pittsburgh Steelers wide receiver, had not been chosen despite being eligible since 1977 and 1987, respectively.

Brown's protest came after a decade in which 38 percent (20 of 53) of new football inductees were black, far better than baseball's Hall of Fame at 29 percent (11 of 37) or basketball's at 25 percent (13 of 38). While there has been improvement in all three halls of fame, it is surprising that basketball has shown the smallest improvement.

Black Head Coaches and Managers

Who knows sports better than the athletes who play them? It is natural to think that one could transmit the skills and knowledge accumulated over the course of many years of playing to young players. Many athletes have dreamed of this. Black athletes have also dreamed of it; they want to become managers and coaches.

When their careers are over they may, perhaps, approach the general manager for a job coaching or in the front office.

Baseball

That dream had barely begun when Jack Olsen interviewed Larry Doby in 1968 for *Sports Illustrated*. The number of blacks in the major leagues had only started to rise. Doby, of course, was the first black allowed into the American League. In 1968, he hoped to be the first black manager, and remarked, "Wouldn't it be a shame if baseball waited until the ball park is burned down before it stepped in and did the right thing." In 1968, there was only one black coach, Jim Gilliam of the Dodgers; there were no black managers and only a handful of blacks in the front offices. Many whites thought having blacks in such positions would be bad publicity. Others thought blacks weren't smart enough. Many didn't want blacks to be in charge of whites.

Doby also told Olsen that "Black athletes are cattle. They're raised, fed, sold, and killed. Baseball moved me toward the front of the bus, and it let me ride there as long as I could run. And then it told me to get off at the back door."

After the article appeared, Doby was suddenly hired as a coach by Cleveland. It must have hurt though when Frank Robinson was hired by Cleveland in late 1974 to manage the team for which Doby was coach. There had been a lot of talk about which black man would be chosen as the first black manager. Speculation had centered largely on Gilliam, Doby, and Hank Aaron. White writers wrote for years and at length about which blacks might be qualified to manage while white owners hired white manager after white manager.

Robinson managed Cleveland in 1975 and 1976, but was fired

in early 1977. Under his guidance, the Indians had achieved their best two-season record in ten years, yet he was let go early in the next year. Before he was canned, Robinson had a highly publicized argument with Gaylord Perry, his white pitching star. The next day a sign was hung at the ballpark: "Sickle Cell Anemia: White Man's Hope." Larry Doby was finally hired to manage the White Sox for the tail end of the 1978 season. It was hardly a real chance.

Henry Aaron seemed certain to be the next black named as manager in 1978 when the incumbent manager of the Atlanta Braves was fired during the season. After all, Aaron had just broken Babe Ruth's all-time home run record in spite of death threats, racial harassment, and the need for police protection. It seemed that some whites couldn't stand to see a black man break the greatest record of the greatest white baseball superstar of all time. But Aaron seemed the natural choice to become manager. In fact, he was traded to Milwaukee. He told Phil Musick, his biographer:

> The owners seem to have gotten together and decided that certain men—certain white men—should be hired and rehired no matter what kind of failures they've been . . . as soon as they're fired by one owner, they're hired by another.
>
> Baseball is no different than stagnant water. The Negro has progressed no further than the field. Until we crack that area, there is no real hope for black kids coming into sports. We're greats on the field for twenty years, then they're finished with us.

Late in 1980, Maury Wills, the former Dodger shortstop, was hired to manage the Seattle Mariners. Frank Robinson came back as manager when the San Francisco Giants hired him for the 1981 season. Thus 1981 marked the first time two black managers were working simultaneously in the game. Wills and Robinson were the only major-league managers with Hall of Fame credentials. *The New York Times* duly recorded it as a historic event, and just in time, for Wills was fired only twenty-four games into the season.

By April 1987, no one in power seemed to care very much

about the fact that there were no black managers or general managers around to celebrate the fortieth anniversary of Jackie Robinson breaking the color barrier in baseball. Nor did anyone seem to care that the number of black players was decreasing and that few blacks were paying to see the national pastime being played. Stories were being written and television shows being planned to celebrate the Robinson story and talk about how much sports had done for blacks in America.

Nightline, usually a hard-hitting news show, was ready to join in and had lined up several celebrities. Don Newcombe, who had played with Jackie Robinson, was scheduled to appear, representing the Dodgers. When he couldn't make it, Dodger Vice-President Al Campanis took his place. It seemed a perfect choice, since Campanis had been with the organization at the time Robinson played. Ted Koppel, the brilliant host of the show, asked Campanis to address the issue of why there had been so few black managers in baseball.

Campanis stunned Koppel and everyone watching when he stated that blacks may not have the "necessities" to lead ballclubs, that they may not be able to lead others. At that point, the celebration was over and the investigations began. Campanis was fired, but it was obvious that he was not the only baseball executive with that opinion; there were few blacks in top positions in the sport.

Dave Winfield, the great baseball slugger, commented in his book *A Player's Life,* "While Campanis' remarks were hardly representative of all management . . . he nevertheless showed how entrenched in old stereotypes a lot of baseball people are." When George Steinbrenner, then owner of the New York Yankees, was asked on *Face the Nation* if he was ready to pledge to hire minorities for the Yankees as soon as possible, he responded that the "chief accountant in my finance department happens to be a young black boy."

Peter Ueberroth, then commissioner of baseball, went into action when story after story reported baseball's sad record. In 1987, forty years after the barriers had fallen, there wasn't a single black manager or general manager; only seventeen out of eight hundred seventy-nine front office positions were held by black Americans.

Ueberroth hired Clifford Alexander, former Secretary of the Army, to seek out blacks and other minorities for the front offices. Alexander was supposed to concentrate on people who had not necessarily been baseball players. His biggest move, however, was to hire Harry Edwards, best known for his strong views on race and his progressive attitude toward changing sports. Edwards and Ueberroth seemed like an unusual match, but the hiring, while raising hopes for immediate change, also subdued the media's criticism. Ueberroth had bought time.

I was asked to be on the task force for Operation PUSH and the NAACP as they prepared to stoke up the fires. Harry Edwards and I were asked to speak at the PUSH Convention in Chicago. Edwards couldn't make it, but I remember feeling that all would be well with Harry at the helm. Therefore, I addressed my remarks to how bad the hiring practices were in college sport and how many more opportunities there were at that level. The crowd was surprised by the information and Jesse Jackson announced on the spot that PUSH would target the colleges. Everyone said the hiring of Harry Edwards had been a result of the pressure from the black community and that things would get better in a hurry in baseball.

Shortly after that, I spoke at the NAACP Convention in New York. A press conference was held to announce that the NAACP would be working closely with the NBA and the NFL to increase the hiring of minorities in those sports.

I was asked to speak at a closed-door luncheon with members of the NAACP board, Ben Hooks, the executive director of the NAACP, Howard Cosell, the legendary commentator, and a few former players from different sports. The other speaker was Peter Ueberroth. Howard Cosell introduced us and told Ueberroth that baseball should be working with the Center for the Study of Sport in Society. He responded by saying we should write to Harry Edwards, "who was handling all such matters." That gave me confidence that we would be working with baseball soon.

Ueberroth told the gathering about his record on racial hiring practices dating back to the Olympics. He proudly told them how he had hired Anita DeFrantz as a vice president for the Los Angeles Olympic Organizing Committee and that now she was "the most important black woman sports official in the world." My optimism for baseball took a jolt because I knew that De-Frantz, the only top black official at the LAOOC, was also the only top official that Ueberroth did not help get another major position after the Olympics.

With each managerial change in baseball that year, hopes were raised only to fall; no black was hired. Tension rose until Baltimore, which had started its 1988 season with one of the longest losing streaks in history, hired Frank Robinson. Robinson brought them out of the hole after a few more losses and did well enough to be rehired for 1989.

What followed seemed like a dream to those who had hoped for progress on the racial front. The Orioles did better all year than anyone had a right to expect. In mid-season, the Toronto Blue Jays hired the league's second black, Cito Gaston, as an "interim manager," making it clear he was there temporarily until they could find the right manager. However, public pressure forced the management to hire him when the Blue Jays won big for Gaston. The American League East went down to the wire, with the Gaston-led Blue Jays edging out the Robinson-led Orioles for the division crown. The start of the 1990 season marked the first time that two black managers ended one season and started the next at the helm of their teams.

Yes, there had been progress, but Frank Robinson was quick to point out the continuing hypocrisy in his book *Extra Innings,* written with Berry Stainback. His special targets were those men who were supposed to be leading the charge: Ueberroth, Edwards and Alexander. Robinson was active in founding the Baseball Network, an organization of former players who wanted to help former black players get jobs in baseball. Robinson charged that the Network was never provided help by the Commissioner or Harry Edwards. He said that he and Hank Aaron were not invited to a meeting that Edwards and Ueberroth had organized with black players and coaches at the All-Star game. "That was insulting, but worse was the fact that Edwards and Ueberroth offered no information on affirmative action progress at that meeting." While Harry Edwards said an attempt had been made to invite Robinson, *The New York Times* reported that Robinson was, in fact, not invited.

In 1989, not a single third base coach was black. Robinson wrote about what that meant for black managerial opportunities: "The third base coach is traditionally next in line to become manager if he wishes. The normal line of progression in baseball goes from bullpen coach to first base coach to third base coach, but blacks are almost never allowed in that line. They are not moved from the coaching box to third. For example, Manny Mota, a Hispanic black, has been the first base coach for the Dodgers for more than ten years." Robinson discussed the traditional reasons given for why blacks don't move up: "One of the biggest cop-outs ballclubs use when they refuse to hire a black as a major league manager is, 'You don't have the experience.' Robinson had accumulated several years experience managing in Puerto Rico when Gabe Paul, general manager of the Yankees, told him, "Frank, if you had just one year's minor league managing experience, I'd hire you to manage the Yankees."

The Yankees later hired Dick Howser and Lou Piniella, neither of whom had any managing experience. San Diego hired Jerry Coleman, their radio announcer, to manage them in 1980. Others who joined the fraternity without managing experience: Yogi Berra, Pete Rose, George Bamberger, Joe Torre, Jim Fregosi, Harvey Keune, Roger Craig, and Bobby Valentine. Robinson noted what they all had in common: "They are all white. The list goes on and on."

Another reason given for the lack of black managers is that former black players, used to big salaries, won't work in the minors for minor league salaries. Luis Tiant, a great star for the Red Sox and Yankees for nearly two decades after emigrating from Cuba, has wanted nothing more than to coach or manage in baseball. Now working with me at the Center as part of Project Teamwork, a project working with kids on improving race relations, Tiant maintains he has never been given a serious offer. Is the money important? When he isn't working for Teamwork, he is a volunteer pitching coach for Northeastern University. He wants to be part of the game he has given so much to for so long but believes that the color of his skin has kept him out.

George Scott is another example. He has been seeking a big league job since he retired in 1979 after a fine fourteen-year career. After managing for six years in the Mexican League and in winter leagues in Puerto Rico and Venezuela, he was reported to have asked the Red Sox for a minor league job. Scott said he would take a job for as little as $12,000 a year to prove himself. He is still waiting for the call.

In *A Player's Life* (1990), Dave Winfield addressed yet another problem, the notion that "Baseball's first enduring black manager or general manager must do no wrong, must be impeccable . . . instead of placing so much emphasis on the one perfect individual to carry the banner for all of us, we should work on putting qualified minorities into coaching and administration at all levels—and, by the way, into the Players Association office, which is now all white." (Both the NBA (1989) and NFL (1982) players associations have been led by black directors—Charles Grantham with the NBAPA and Gene Upshaw with the NFLPA.)

Opportunities for blacks as managers in the minor leagues and in college are even fewer than in the pros. Kansas State was the only Division I school with a black manager in 1983; in 1990, there was not one. However, a look at baseball's front office positions later in this chapter shows how far blacks have to go to break into the levels suggested by Winfield.

The NBA

Ever since Bill Russell took over the Boston Celtics in the 1966–67 season, the NBA has been far ahead of the other leagues. As the 1990–91 season started, nearly a quarter of all NBA teams had black head coaches, the highest percentage in the history of pro sports. The New York Knicks, Washington Bullets and Cleveland Cavaliers have their second black coaches in Stu Jackson, Wes Unseld and Lenny Wilkins; the Charlotte Hornets are coached by Gene Littles and the Houston Rockets are led by Don Chaney.

Other teams have had black coaches during the history of their franchises. The Boston Celtics, long thought of as a team led by whites, have had three black head coaches (Bill Russell, Tom Sanders, and K. C. Jones). Both Russell and Jones led the Celtics to two NBA championships each. K. C. Jones, one of two black NBA coaches in the 1983–84 season, is now with Seattle. Seattle is a fascinating franchise. In a city where the population is only 4.5 percent black, the Supersonics have now had six black head coaches and have been led by a black coach in all but one season. The Los Angeles Clippers have been coached by Paul Silas and Don Chaney. Sacramento's franchise started with Bill Russell as its coach. Detroit had Earl Lloyd and Ray Scott in the early 1970s. Lenny Wilkins was at Portland in 1974–76. Al Attles coached Golden State in 1970–83, the NBA's longest consecutive tenure by a black coach. Willis Reed, who also coached the Knicks, was with the Nets. In fact, sixteen of the twenty-seven NBA teams have had black head coaches; the NBA teams that have not had black coaches are Atlanta (they unsuccessfully tried to get Willis Reed for the 1990–91 season), Chicago, Dallas, Denver, Indiana (Mel Daniels coached for 2 games in 1988–89), Los Angeles (Lakers), Miami, Milwaukee, Philadelphia, Phoenix and San Antonio.

Until the mid-1980s, black NBA coaches rarely got a second chance after a losing season. In fact, up to that point, Lenny Wilkens was the only black coach to lose with one team and be hired elsewhere. Yet many whites like Larry Brown, Gene Shue, Dick Motta, Connie Fitzsimmons, Tom Nissalke, and Kevin Loughery were instantly rehired after failures. Now blacks are getting that chance. Willis Reed, who lost with the Nets, was offered the Atlanta job. Don Chaney was hired by Houston after coaching the hapless Clippers. Gene Littles lost at Cleveland and was hired by Charlotte. This certainly represents a significant turnaround.

In 1982–83, only four of the thirty-six assistant coaches were black. In the 1989–90 season, there were twelve blacks out of forty-two, almost triple the percentage of a few years earlier. The NBA was leading the way—no one was even a close second.

The NFL

Art Shell became the NFL's first black head coach in 1989, twenty-three years after the NBA and fifteen years after baseball had hired their first blacks in the equivalent position. There was an air of history on that October afternoon when it was announced that the Oakland Raiders had hired Shell, a Hall of Fame member from the Raiders' own family. Shell told a packed house that "It's a historic event, and I understand the significance of it. The main thing is, I know who I am and I'm proud of it. I'm proud to be a Raider." Just a few months earlier, when he had been inducted into the Hall of Fame, Shell had been asked if the NFL was ready to hire a black head coach. His answer: "It should be, but I'm not sure it is."

There had been some progress over the course of the decade as the number of black assistants rose from 10 out of 225 (4 percent) in 1980 to 50 out of 294 (17 percent) in 1990. Yet important questions remain unanswered as of the writing of this book. Was Shell hired because of a change in the NFL or because the Raider organization was run in a different fashion? At the time I wrote *Broken Promises* in 1983, many were saying that the hiring of two black head college football coaches at Wichita State and Northwestern was a good beginning. However, ten years later, there are still only two black football coaches at any Division IA program. For those in a self-congratulatory mood in the NFL after the hiring of Art Shell, a look at college sport would strike a sobering note of caution.

The chart on page 308 shows the coaching breakdown in the three major professional sports.

Clearly we had advanced since 1983. But will the pressures continue to sustain the progress?

The Front Office: A Long Road Ahead

The executives and members of the front offices in charge of professional sports in America are almost exclusively white. The

Coaches by Race in Professional Sport*

| | 1983 | | | | | |
| | Head Coaches | | | Assistant Coaches | | |
	No. Black	No. White	% White	No. Black	No. White	% White
Baseball	1	25	96	13†	123	90
Basketball	2	21	91	4	32	89
Football	0	28	100	27	242	90
Totals	3	74	96	44	397	90

| | 1990 | | | | | |
| | Head Coaches | | | Assistant Coaches | | |
	No. Black	No. White	% White	No. Black	No. White	% White
Baseball	2	24	92	N/A	—	—
Basketball	6	21	78	14	51	78
Football	1	27	96	50	247	83
Totals	9	72	89	64	298	82

*Charts include figures from the close of the 1983 and 1990 baseball seasons, the start of the 1983 and 1989 football seasons, and the 1982–83 and the 1990–91 basketball seasons.
†Includes Latins.

information that follows was derived from the 1989–90 publications of the individual teams in all three sports and information provided by the leagues themselves; it shows that this is the area where the most progress still needs to be made.

The National Basketball Association's Front Office

There was a time when it looked like Simon P. Gourdine, a black man, and former NBA deputy commissioner, might be chosen as commissioner. No one doubted his talents. Gourdine himself said, "If sports ever has a black commissioner, it will be in the NBA." Note that he did not say "when," he said "if." Some had hoped that Gourdine would be chosen, but David Stern got the job. However, in 1991, no one doubted that David Stern was a brilliant choice as his new $3 million contract indicated.

Under Stern's leadership, there has been considerable progress in the front offices in the NBA. Consider the state of the league in 1982: the NBA had blacks in only two of the thirteen positions in the league office. Wayne Embry was vice president of the Milwaukee Bucks. Arnold Pinkney was an executive in Cleveland. Al Attles was not only the coach of Golden State but was also sport's first black general manager. These were the only black executives in the NBA. There were one hundred twenty-one whites listed as executives (presidents, vice presidents, board chairmen, general managers, etc.). Embry, Attles, and Pinkney were the only blacks. There were three hundred people listed as administration and staff for NBA teams in that season. Larry Doby, unable to manage in Major League Baseball, was the director of community relations for the Nets. Will Robinson held the same post in Detroit. Wayne Scales was Portland's director of promotions. There were only nine other blacks in similar positions in the rest of the league.

1989–90 marked a significant year for minority opportunity and advancement in the front office. Prior to that year, there had never been a black owner in any major pro sport. However, in 1989 the Denver Nuggets were purchased by two black businessmen—Bertram Lee and Peter Bynoe. Lee, a financier and former president of the CBS-TV affiliate in Boston, led a group that included Bynoe, the executive director of the Illinois Sports Facilities Authority. Lee commented to *Sports Illustrated,* "As Afro-Americans, we're cognizant that we are participating in an event that is a milestone in sports history. If, along the way, we're viewed as role models or positive symbols, so much the better." He added that he hoped that within a year "at least two more sports franchises will be owned by Afro-Americans. That's one of the ways I'll measure my sense of success." This was a milestone only talked about in other sports; it had become a reality in the NBA. NBA Commissioner David Stern said at the time, "We are pleased that the NBA will be enhanced by a team whose management control is in the hands of black businessmen."

NBA Personnel by Percentage
1990–91

	White	Black
Front Office	88%	12%
Support Staff	83%	17%
Total	87%	13%

Neither Major League Baseball nor professional football has ever had a black general manager. Elgin Baylor (Clippers), Wayne Embry (Cavaliers), Bernie Bickerstaff (Nuggets), Bill McKinney (Timberwolves) and Willis Reed (Nets) headed the operations of their franchises at the start of the 1990–91 season.

The hiring of Susan O'Malley by the Washington Bullets as executive assistant and the addition of Glenn Sugiyama to the board of directors of the Chicago Bulls were important events that demonstrated that women and Asians are also breaking barriers in the NBA. The table above represents a breakdown of the NBA personnel for the 1990–91 season.

Minority advancement continues to take place in the NBA. Blacks held 12 percent (versus 6 percent in 1988–89) of front office management positions in 1990–91. Women occupied 16 percent of those management positions, a significant increase from the 11 percent they held in 1988–89. There was also a 5 percent increase in blacks holding support staff positions. Thus, blacks held 13 percent of all NBA front office jobs in 1990–91 versus only 9.7 percent in 1988–89. It was more than double the number seen in 1983 (5.3 percent). In conclusion, the 1990–91 data shows that the NBA offers opportunities for blacks far beyond any other professional sport.

The National Football League's Front Office

The NFL had a terrible record in 1983. Buddy Young was director of player relations for the NFL office until his tragic death in late 1983. Paul "Tank" Younger (San Diego) and Bobby Mitchell (Washington) were assistant general managers for their respective teams. They were the only two black executives out of one hundred seventeen working for the NFL teams. That was 1.6 percent in the NFL, whose players were 54 percent black in 1983.

There were four hundred fifty-two people listed as administration and staff for NFL teams, including assistants, receptionists, and secretaries. Only thirty-two were by blacks, including former stars like Rosey Brown (Giants), Lawrence McCutcheon (Rams), Otis Taylor (Kansas City), and Milt Davis and Elbert Dubenion (Miami), who were all scouts. Paul Warfield was director of player relations for Cleveland. The thirty-two blacks in the front office represent only 6.6 percent of all NFL front office positions, barely one-tenth of the total percentage number of black players in the league.

Combining all categories of executives, head and assistant coaches, administration and staff (as listed in the 1983 team media guides) there were 879 posts, 61 (6.9 percent) of which were held by blacks. An overview of the 1989 NFL personnel shows a very small increase in the front office (7% in 1989 vs. 6.9% in 1983). However, there were no black general managers and only one black in the ninety-three most senior management positions.

There was, however, some improvement below this level. Blacks occupied 11 percent of other management positions—an increase of 1 percent from the 1988 season. Men who moved near the top in 1989 included Rod Graves, assistant director of player personnel–Chicago Bears; John Wooten, pro personnel director–Dallas Cowboys; Patric Forte, assistant to the president–Philadelphia Eagles; Larry Wansley, vice president and general manager, Texas Stadium–Dallas Cowboys; Dick Daniels, assistant general manager–San Diego Chargers. Blacks also held 7 percent of support staff positions, up from 4 percent in 1988. The table below shows NFL personnel as it changed from 1988 to 1989.

An NFL official told me that minority employment had reaped modest positive results. Still there is much disparity for a league in which 60 percent of the players are black. The percentage of blacks who are employed in front office positions is small compared to blacks playing the game. However, the same NFL official maintained that not many players, minorities or non-

NFL Personnel
1988–1989

	No. People	No. Black	No. White	% Black	% White
Front office					
1989	369	25	344	7%	93%
1988	287	15	272	6%	94%
Support					
1989	610	40	570	7%	93%
1988	343	15	328	4%	96%
Total					
1989	979	65	914	7%	93%
1988	630	30	600	5%	95%

minorities, attain or even seek employment in an administrative capacity after they retire.

There seems to be a new level of awareness of race under Commissioner Paul Tagliabue. He has stated a commitment to hiring more blacks in the front office. While he can't dictate who the individual teams do hire, he sent a powerful signal to the sports community when he maintained that there would be no Super Bowl in Phoenix unless the state of Arizona recognized Martin Luther King's birthday as a holiday. Time will tell if his commitment will have the desired effect.

The Front Office in Major League Baseball

Most major league baseball media guides did not include photos in 1983 and still don't today. Therefore, it took some investigation to dig up the data for baseball's front office picture. That only was possible after Al Campanis's performance on *Nightline*. It was quickly discovered that only seventeen of the eight hundred seventy-nine management and administrative positions in baseball were held by black Americans in 1987. Another thirteen were held by Hispanics and Asians. Fifteen of the twenty-six teams had no minorities in management positions. Clifford Alexander, who was hired as a consultant by the league in the post-Campanis era to bring more blacks and minorities into the sport, provided me with updated information in 1990. It shows that opportunity for blacks and other minorities has improved in baseball.

According to Alexander, 273 (15 percent of 1,854 club front office positions) were held by minority group members in 1989—163 (9 percent) by blacks, 88 (5 percent) by Hispanics and 22 (1 percent) by Asians. There were 24 black and 11 Hispanic executive and department heads on the club level (7 percent of 485 total positions at that level). Data for on-the-field support staff revealed that 313 (20 percent) of 1,588 positions were filled by minority group members—207 (13 percent) by Hispanics, 102 (6 percent) by blacks and 4 (.3 percent) by Asians.

Those who are cynical about real progress in baseball point out that this information did not provide a breakdown of the positions held by minorities. How many of these are secretarial jobs and how many are managerial jobs is not known. The league needs to provide this breakdown to provide real clarity on its progress.

Nonetheless, the 1989 season, which started under the stewardship of the late A. Bartlett Giamatti seemed to send a signal of hope. Bill White, the president of the National League and the highest ranking black executive in pro sports, made several significant hires himself in the National League office, including Larry Doby and Joe Black. Faye Vincent, Giamatti's successor, was forthright at the 1990 league meetings and said more needed to be done.

Black professional athletes now do have a better chance of getting a front office job, but the opportunities are slim. What are the "retired" black athletes going to do? Surveys done by the Center for the Study of Sport in Society and by the respective players associations estimate that only 20 percent of the basketball players, 33 percent of football players and 16 percent of baseball players have college degrees. The employment records of former athletes isn't always encouraging.

Everything is compounded for the retiring black athlete. Drew Pearson played for ten years with the Dallas Cowboys in their prime (1973–83). He caught more passes than any receiver in the history of the Cowboys while leading them to three Super Bowls. Pearson told the *Dallas Morning News,* "There was nothing I could do wrong as No. 88 on the Cowboys, but it was a lot different in the business world because of the stereotype of the black athlete. . . . You've got to live down the stereotype that people think you want something for nothing." Trying to raise capital for his new company, Pearson felt the chill after he visited every bank in Dallas and many others throughout Texas. He felt betrayed.

It doesn't matter whether you are Bill Russell, Jackie Robinson, Bob Gibson, Hank Aaron, Ron Leflore, Tony Oliva, Frank Robinson, or Dave Winfield, all of whom wrote books. A black player out of uniform looks like any other black to most whites. A cop might back off once he sees the driver's license, but until then any athlete is just another black face. In 1984, when three members of the Harlem Globetrotters were held spread-eagled on the ground at gunpoint as suspects in a jewelry store robbery during the Christmas season in Santa Barbara, California, Police Lt. Charles Davis said, "They just looked like somebody we were looking for." The players were riding in a cab after shopping, were stopped by police, and ordered to the ground. Globetrotter Louis "Sweet Lou" Dunbar said, "If somebody points a revolver at your head, you don't just shake that off." Dunbar was arrested along with Ovie Dotson and Jimmy Blacklock. The trio sued the city for $3 million, eventually settling for $75,000. Testimony at the trial showed that they had been held even after they were identified as Globetrotters.

I recently received a letter from Philip Lawson, a learning skills counselor for the University of California, Santa Barbara. He related many moving stories about black athletes he has known, but none more poignant than that of his classmate and close friend, a state high-jump champion and top wide receiver who played pro ball in Canada. Lawson wrote, "In a case of mistaken identity, he was killed by a roadside store manager who thought that the only reason two black men would enter his store late at night would be to rob the store. They were merely en route from California to Canada to their training camp."

Dee Brown was the number one draft choice of the Celtics in

1990 out of Jacksonville University. He was in Wellesley, Massachusetts, a wealthy, overwhelmingly white suburb, contemplating buying a home. He and his fiancée, who is white, left a post office and were forced to the ground at gunpoint for ten minutes by Wellesley police, who allegedly thought Brown was the man who had robbed a local bank. The entire community was embarrassed when his identity was made clear. The incident reminded many sports fans in Boston of Bill Russell's complaints about frequent racial harassment by police when he moved into the all-white town of Reading, Massachusetts, three decades earlier. As in Russell's case, once Brown had been recognized everyone said they were sorry.

There are, of course, extreme examples of what happens to former pro athletes who suddenly find themselves facing the loss of their triple-figure incomes. No less than three current or former stars took their own life in 1988 and 1989. A small but growing number have turned to crime. They were among the one in nearly 7,325 who made it to the pros. Many of the others who "made it" soon will join the 7,324 who didn't. Back on the streets, they will have to decide what they will do. For most, the options are slim. The athlete has devoted most of his life developing the skills necessary to become a pro player. Because of that, he is not likely to become a surgeon, a lawyer, or an intellectual leader. When his career is over, his standard of living is likely to decline.

If sports are ever to live up to their promise as harbingers of racial change, then the press must tell us about the fates of all the Fred Buttlers as well as the Magic Johnsons. And we must learn about the deeds, not just the statistics, of multifaceted men like Paul Robeson, Bill Russell, and Kareem Abdul-Jabbar, if young blacks are to avoid the trap of devoting their youth to playing sports only to be trapped in unfulfilling jobs forever after. Everyone needs a role model to help draw out and build his natural talents. When poverty makes success seem a far-distant goal, children need so much more than a helmet, a glove, a bat, or a ball. Creatively used, sports can help the process of total education.

But only a thoroughly reformed sports system can help our young people, black and white, to value themselves not only for their bodies but also for their minds; to obtain an education to give them a full range of options in life; and to teach all who play the importance of embracing the diversity of our society before we consume ourselves with racial hatred.

We have really come much further in sport than I thought was possible when I wrote *Broken Promises* in 1983. When compared to society at large, sport *is* way ahead racially. But society is now dangerously close to the other side of midnight. We cannot afford to break any more promises.

Conclusion

As I have said several times throughout this book, I started my life in sportsworld as a starry-eyed player and fan; I then became a serious cynic about the value of sport. Now, after working in sportsworld, I have gained a new perspective.

That new perspective began in 1982 when I spent two weeks in Angola with an American basketball team, experiencing some of the best that sport has to offer. With no diplomatic relations between the two countries and five years of virulent rhetoric spewed from both Washington and Luanda, it was hoped that this basketball tour would soften the rhetoric and make way for better relations.

The American team, coached by Lou Carnesecca, was chosen from the Big East Conference. The players—eight blacks and three whites—did not know what kind of reception they would get from the Angolans in light of the prevailing hostility toward America in Angola. Their concerns melted away as they walked onto the big court of the Citadella arena in Luanda. Fifteen thousand Angolans cheered wildly for the team, which marched out behind the American flag. The flag had never been flown in Angola before. It was a stirring moment for everyone. A total of 75,000 came out to see the games, as much for their political as for their sports importance. Our players learned about Africa and Angola and the Angolan players learned about life in America.

Both teams transmitted their messages to their own people through the tremendous press coverage the tour received. This experience tempered my cynical feelings about sport and began to remind me what a positive force it can be.

There is little doubt that sport has the potential to deliver significant outcomes for individuals, teams, and nations. I now believe that a new, more humanistic sports system is possible with the reinvigorated NCAA Presidents Commission, the work of the Knight Commission, Dick Schultz's leadership at the NCAA, the work of the conference commissioners group, and the leadership of David Stern and Paul Tagliabue at the NBA and NFL.

While things may be getting better in sport, it definitely seems like they are getting worse in society. America's youth seem to be coming unglued as new phenomena like AIDS, crack, and gang violence have entered their world. All of these have made the already difficult teenage years even harder to bear as the economy sours and times grow worse.

Times like these usually signal a rise in racism, and 1990 seemed to be no exception as the Center for the Study of Sport in Society and the Reebok Foundation's survey of youth attitudes toward racism showed. The results were frightening. A majority (57 percent) of high school students have seen or heard racial confrontations with overtones of violence, significantly more than had been previously believed. These incidents were not isolated to any particular area and were commonplace in the nation's high schools.

One in four students reported that they have been the target of an incident of racial or religious bias. Almost half (46 percent) of the blacks surveyed said they had been targets. When confronted with a racial incident, 47 percent of students would either join in (30 percent) or feel that the group being attacked deserved what it was getting (17 percent). Only one in four would tell a school authority. More hopefully, a core of 30 percent of high school students were prepared to intervene to stop or condemn the incident.

Four in ten students report that when they see someone from another race or religion doing something they do not like, they are tempted to ask, "What else can you expect from those types of people." Patterns of human history show that teenagers, like their parents, are ready to blame the victim for his problems.

The foremost condition for meaningful change is to recognize the need for change. As will be seen later, teenagers are aware that discrimination and racism are serious problems in society. As has been seen throughout the last three chapters of this book, we are starting to face up to these problems in sports. This book is particularly concerned with race, so my proposals focus on the plight of black athletes; many of these proposals, however, apply across the board to all athletes.

Unfortunately, no one is in the position to propose changes that would totally eliminate racism in sport. Since sport free of racism can only exist in a society free of racism, it is more realistic to suggest changes that would ease the problem of racism in sport by giving the athlete a better understanding of, and thus more control over, his own destiny. For me, education is the key to this process.

Summary of Progress Thus Far

As has been shown, some but certainly not enough has changed for today's black athlete since sports integration began with Jackie Robinson. In college sport, we are finally aware of the academic problems not only of black athletes but of all athletes. Being aware of them is, however, only the first step, and much more needs to be done in this regard. There has been progress over the 1980s. There are more black head coaches in college; positional segregation is all but a thing of the past; there does not seem to be any remaining widespread quota system dictating that a certain number of whites need to be on the team; black athletes have occasionally spoken out on political issues without facing repercussions on campus; and the black athlete seems to face less overt discrimination on campus (unlike regular black students).

In pro sports, progress includes increasing numbers of blacks playing basketball and football; increased endorsement possibilities for black stars; near parity in salaries between blacks and whites; an apparent end to racial quotas for teams; a diminishing of positional segregation in football at quarterback and center and in baseball at shortstop and second and third bases; dramatically increasing numbers of black coaches and general managers in the NBA; small but significant breakthroughs for black managers in baseball; the first modern-day head coach in the NFL; black ownership in the NBA; and better representation of blacks in the respective halls of fame.

All of this progress, it must be noted, is relative. Black athletes still graduate at a significantly lower rate than whites, are overrepresented in basketball and football, are academically and sometimes physically separated from black students, have few black mentors on campus, have absolutely unrealistic expectations of making the pros, and still have a long fall back to the streets if they neither make the pros nor get a degree. In pro sports, the front offices of the NFL and Major League Baseball are still predominantly white outposts.

Changes have always emanated from current conditions. In the late 1960s, campus-wide protests provoked athletic protests under the inspiration of the likes of Harry Edwards and Jack Scott. There is now no such protest on the horizon. However, the media, especially in its more recent role of watchdog and informer on the inner turmoil of sportsworld, may prove to be a catalyst for necessary change.

Education: The Key to Keeping the Cheers Coming After the Last Game

Changes must come about at all levels to have the desired effects. At each level, the role of education is the key. Everything that happens to the athlete after his career ends depends on what knowledge and skills he has obtained while playing on the field or court. We can't realistically expect that individual and institutional racism will change quickly. Therefore, the emphasis must first be on exposing it and second on teaching young athletes to deal with it. Preparing them for the non-athletic job market is most crucial.

While it remains controversial, the NCAA's Proposition 48 has helped focus attention on the education of high school athletes. As we've seen, academic standards for high school athletes are probably the least rigorous of all levels. With 44 percent of black high school athletes believing they can play pro ball, the academic future of these athletes is in serious jeopardy unless they are required to devote themselves more fully to a balance between academics and athletics.

Increased Academic Standards in High School

Prior to the passage of Proposition 48 by the NCAA in 1983, less than 100 of 16,000 high school districts had a "C" average requirement for participation in extracurricular events. What does not having a "C" mean? In my state of Massachusetts, it means that a high school basketball player can be eligible for all four years and not only never get a "C" average, but never get a single "C" in any course. My question is: What have we prepared that young person to do in life?

Coaches were the largest opposition group during discussions about such "no-pass, no-play" legislation. They said that ineligibility would lead to dropping out and turning to a life of crime and drugs. Now there are six states and hundreds of localities with such higher standards. Coaches are running 7:00 A.M. study halls and their players see them involved in the educational process for the first time. Best of all, the student-athletes themselves have met the challenge and raised their grades.

Without higher academic standards, the lack of a mental challenge feeds on and fuels lenient admissions standards in self-fulfilling prophecies of academic failure. Without higher moral standards, we will see our youth seek the streets more than the classroom, join gangs instead of teams, and emulate drug dealers instead of teachers or coaches.

With athletes who love the game we have a captive audience. We can make a "C" average a condition for playing. We can also raise moral standards by demanding social responsibility on the part of our student-athletes. We need to create a Sports Ethics Corps of college student-athletes who will enter our high schools and challenge their younger brothers and sisters to stay in school, to stay off drugs and alcohol, and to treat each other with respect no matter what the color of their skin or their ethnic origin.

Later in this chapter I will discuss the more than two thousand athletes returning to finish their college degrees through institutions of higher education in the National Consortium for Academics in Sport. Those athletes work in school outreach programs counseling young people about academic balance, drug and alcohol abuse and teenage pregnancy, and now race relations. I am proud to say that by 1990 they had seen more than 533,000 high school and middle school students in the outreach program.

We must take up the charge of having our institutions of higher education work with the high school in our communities to raise the levels of academic expectations. If increased standards force high school athletes to take their studies more seriously, they will not only help those who actually continue to play in college but also those who aspire to do so but never make it beyond high school. As stated earlier, an average of 1 out of every 7,325 high school athletes make it to the pros. For most, their athletic career ends in high school. If they don't have some skills by their senior year, they almost certainly face a menial job or, worse, a place among the youth who are unemployed.

The Student-Athlete and College

As I said in an earlier chapter, I now believe that Proposition 48 has had a positive effect. However, it attacks the problem only at the high school level and does not address the student-athlete after he or she gains admission to college. By the time they are there, most scholarship athletes, including 44 percent of black athletes, are sure that the pros are in sight and academics are even less important than in high school. It is the ethical obligation of the university to ensure that they obtain a real education.

Increased minimum academic standards in high school and Proposition 48 will help prepare the student-athlete in high school. But selecting a college is very difficult. How can the athlete recognize the type of coach who might want him to help his team so badly that he would bend the truth about the school?

Publishing Graduation Rates

The Student-Athlete Right to Know Act was introduced in Congress by Congressmen Tom McMillen and William Townds and Senator Bill Bradley. The proposed legislation requires that prospective student-athletes be presented with a school's graduation rates, and that the rates be sport, race and sex specific. I had the opportunity to testify in both the House and Senate in favor of this legislation and noted that while graduation rates of all athletes would be helpful, figures had to be broken down by race, sex and sport as required by this legislation. The prospect of federal legislation in this area forced the NCAA to adopt its own legislation similar to the Student-Athlete Right to Know Act at its 1990 convention. These records should prove invaluable to high school athletes and their parents as they try to decide on the right school to attend. In spite of the NCAA legislation, Congress passed one Student Right to Know and Campus Security Act in 1990. It required publication of graduation rates for all students.

Concern with academic achievements starts with who is admitted to the university. The coach must consult with the admissions office to see if the athlete can make it academically. The coach needs a real evaluation of the academic potential of the recruit; if the recruit is borderline, the coach must be able to assure that sufficient academic assistance be available; if the recruit is beyond borderline, the recruiting process should stop.

Support Issues on the Campus

The 1991 NCAA Convention in Nashville proved to be a bench mark for college sport with more than two hundred thirty presidents taking control but also working cooperatively with athletic department and conference officials. While many of the reform proposals focused on cost-cutting (reduction of athletic scholarships, the number of coaches, etc), others will help the student-athlete stay on track academically. The new legislation effects the Division I schools the most.

Athletic dorms and training tables for athletes will be phased out, thus integrating the athlete into the regular student population. Significantly, the length of seasons and the number of games in all sports will be reduced. Athletes now can spend no more than twenty hours a week on their sport. Legislation passed requiring the provision of academic counseling and tutoring services for all student-athletes. A sampling of athletes must be given exit interviews when leaving the institution to help keep the institution knowledgeable about the needs of student-athletes. It will now be required that student-athletes fulfill more than half of their degree requirements prior to the commencement of their fourth year to remain eligible.

Two other academic proposals were voted down. One would have required a 50 percent graduation rate to participate in Division I. The other would have required minimum grade point averages for the student-athletes to remain eligible to play.

The 1992 convention has been designated as the "Academics Convention." If it is as effective in reform in this area as the 1991 convention was in cost-cutting, then the future of college sport will indeed be bright. However, as of this writing, many changes still need to be made to assure the quality of education for student-athletes that everyone now seems to want.

I agree with those who say the athletes deserve special treatment. Part of their being enrolled is an obligation to give the school literally thousands of hours of their time during their four years of eligibility. Their time brings the school entertainment, prestige, and frequently, handsome revenues. To argue against special treatment for athletes is naïve and irresponsible. However, what I mean by special treatment is the assurance of academic preparedness and not exemption from such preparedness.

The overall message to the players has to be that the school will provide special attention to its student-athletes to assure their academic preparation; however, in exchange for this, student-athletes will be expected to fulfill the same academic requirements as all students. Philosophically, the school must emphasize the *student* in student-athlete—not only their class attendance and graduation rates, but also the quality of their educational experience. Student-athletes must be encouraged to value education, not simply eligibility.

I divide the special on-campus responsibilities of the school into two areas: creating the best possible academic environment and the best possible social environment.

Several issues fall under both categories; I discuss these first.

Freshmen Eligibility

The transition for any ordinary student from high school to college is difficult. It is more difficult for an athlete, due to the time demands imposed on him; it is even more difficult for the black athlete who quite possibly has arrived in a culturally different atmosphere, with less developed academic skills as a result of the star syndrome and institutional academic neglect in high school.

One way to reduce the controversy surrounding Proposition 48 would be to eliminate freshman eligibility altogether so that all athletes can make a better transition. Given the proper advice and adequate time to grow into their new environments, athletes would begin the second year on a more equal footing with other students. This proposal is not meant to suggest a return to freshman basketball, football, and baseball teams. The freshman would have no athletic obligations in his first year although he would receive full financial support. This would increase costs to universities since they would be forced to carry more scholarship athletes on the varsity. However, athletes could be given an additional year of eligibility if they would be able to graduate in that year. This would reduce the financial burden.

The elimination of freshman eligibility would also end the practice of redshirting. The goal of all athletes and athletic administrations should be identical: every student should try to graduate in four years and no one should be deliberately delayed because of sports. Making freshmen ineligible would take care of this.

University Hiring Practices

More black coaches, assistant coaches, sports administrators, and academic advisors should be hired. As demonstrated, too little has been done to increase these numbers beyond a handful of head coaches and a few more assistants.

For that to happen, more blacks must become college presidents and athletic directors at schools that have major programs. Head coaches need to be hired in *all* sports, not just "black" sports.

Second, athletic departments should begin each academic year with an in-depth seminar for all athletes and coaches. Experts should be brought in along with former athletes to discuss the range of problems faced by today's student-athletes, including academics, drugs, and future careers either as pro athletes or ordinary citizens. In terms of race, such sessions should face all the issues honestly and directly. Black former athletes should meet with players and coaches. These discussions should deal with all the racial issues, both related and unrelated to sports.

The Transfer Rule

The transfer rule should be eliminated. As it stands today, very few athletes consider transferring to another school because they would have to sit out a year from sports competition. This rule is particularly unfair to the black athlete, who frequently finds himself in an uncomfortable social environment or faced with a coaching staff he can't deal with adequately and wants to transfer to another college. Under the present system, the athlete who leaves pays a high price in terms of competition. While the average college student can and does transfer easily, the athlete is trapped. To be at all fair to the athlete and his future, the transfer rule should go.

The Academic Environment

Certainly not all athletes need help. However, athletic scholarship recipients who are defined as being "at risk" academically should be required to attend an orientation program at the school prior to their freshman year which would include academic counseling, evaluation of the student-athlete's educational needs, and intensive workshops dealing with study skills, reading and writing skills, use of the library and basic computer skills. A year-round freshman adjustment program should be available for all freshman student-athletes.

Academic support services must be available, including academic advising, tutors and counseling. These services should work toward integrating student-athletes into the academic life of the university rather than furthering their isolation as a subculture that lies outside the mainstream of the university. Such an integrated system of services should encompass both the resources available to all students and a set of services based in the athletic department which are designed to supplement those resources. Better career counseling must be offered so that student-athletes take legitimate majors which will help them in the job market.

The coach should be part of the student-athlete's academic life. If problems develop with issues like class attendance, the coach is in the most powerful position to help by suspending game participation. The coach should be in regular contact with the school's academic advisors in monitoring the scholarship athlete's academic progress. Reasonable progress should be maintained—beyond NCAA requirements—so that the student-athlete will be as close as possible to graduation after eligibility has expired.

The question of financial support of athletes in general and black athletes in particular is a major one. Any serious reforms for athletes must include the guarantee of the chance to complete their education within a reasonable period. It should include a minimum five-year guarantee, with extensions if academic problems developed directly as a consequence of sports participation. Thus, the athlete would be certain that if he was sufficiently motivated, additional tuition and fees would never stand in the way of obtaining a degree.

Additionally, athletes who came to a school on a scholarship but failed to obtain their degree within their eligibility period may need help. This is especially true in the revenue sports where problems are magnified. Athletes should be able to return to complete their education at the expense of the university in exchange for community service. Such a policy should only apply to athletes who have already left school, so as not to be a disincentive for current student-athletes to complete their education as soon as possible.

This, of course, raises the question of whether or not athletes are motivated academically or are simply using college as a training ground for the pros. The results of the programs of the National Consortium for Academics and Sport, initiated by the Center for the Study of Sport in Society in 1985, go a long way toward proving that athletes do want an education. The seventy institutions in the Consortium have established important individual programs. Between 1985 and 1990, more than 1,244 college athletes who didn't make the pros and whose eligibility had run out either came back to school or continued on aid; almost half (617) of these returnees graduated. Another 702 current pros and 70 Olympians came back, either by paying their own way or having tuition paid by teams or by the United States Olympic Foundation.

These athletes were on campus without the glory of their sports careers and under much more difficult circumstances. They obviously did want an education and were looking for the support and self-confidence to obtain it. The fact that seventy colleges paid the tuition and fees of the 1,244 athletes who returned, at an estimated cost of $12 million and without the students performing in the arena, showed the institutional commitment to assuring an education to their former student-athletes.

The Social Environment

The student-athlete needs better representation on campus. A regular cast of individuals meets on campuses around the country to discuss the plight of the student-athlete in general or the black student-athlete in particular. Of the one hundred or so programs I have attended since the Center opened in 1984, less than ten had student-athlete participation.

One of the most poignant moments I have ever experienced took place on the campus of Loyola Marymount University in February 1990. I was the keynote speaker on the issue of "Ethics in College Sport." Members of Loyola's highly regarded basketball team shared the platform. After I gave a presentation about the problems in college sport, a student asked, "Who is to blame?" It is a question I always get. I usually sense the questioner is looking for a quick answer like "the coach" or "the athletic director." I try to explain the root and development of the problem, going all the way back to the home when parents go to games but not to parent-teacher conferences, or talk about their son's jump shot but not about his grades.

Mark Armstrong was sharing the platform with me. Mark is a graduate and former Loyola player who was then working for the university. He stood up, gently looked at the student, and said, "You're to blame. The only thing you ever asked me about was how I played the last game or what I thought about the next game. You never asked me about the economy or events in Eastern Europe or South Africa. To you, I was just a basketball player." Mark stunned the students in the audience with what struck them as a profound thought. It was profound, but I know from speaking to athletes in our degree completion program that what Mark said should have been obvious—and would have been if student-athletes were given a more direct voice on campus. They should be heard as valued advisors to presidents and the athletic directors in the creation and administration of programs and in evaluating programs. Any kind of collective voice of the student-athlete should be racially and sexually diverse.

In addition to student-athlete representation, coaches should be models to both the community and to players in hiring and social relations. If black players see the coach hiring and socializing only with whites, they will feel further isolated. All associations with exclusive social clubs should be terminated.

Athletic dormitories and separate athletic eating facilities will be phased out by 1996, as voted on at the 1991 NCAA convention. Athletic dorms can be especially harmful to black athletes, as they not only separate them from the entire campus but can also alienate them from black students who are not athletes. Team housing, road trips and meals should be integrated.

At the same time, minority student-athletes should be encouraged to be involved in university-wide social and academic student activities and be given the opportunity to take responsibility for their own affairs, both academic and social.

In the community, student-athletes should be encouraged to participate in summer corporate internship programs to gain real world experience. This would be especially valuable to the black student-athlete, who may have less opportunities for meaningful work experience.

Finally, an ombudsman in the president's office should be appointed to objectively hear the grievances of all athletes toward their coaches or athletic administrators. Hopefully, this person would operate preventively and diminish tensions rather than increase them. The ombudsman would need the respect of key athletic department people without being so close to them as to lose objectively.

Accreditation

These are all basic proposals designed to give the student-athlete a fighting chance to succeed academically and are realistically adoptable by universities.

However, being realistically adoptable doesn't mean they will be adopted. The NCAA has not had great leverage in enforcing academic standards. The recent interest shown by college presidents in changing this gives hope. But there must be a better way to induce universities to act.

The best suggestion I have heard came from Jack Scott more than a decade ago. He proposed that the academic progress of athletes should be part of the basis for the acquisition and maintenance of a university's accreditation. With the institution's overall academic integrity on the line, the university or college would have no choice but to establish the necessary programs that would ultimately lead to giving all athletes, black and white alike, the chance to obtain a useful education beyond the sports field. When their sports careers end, the athletes would be more prepared to control their own fates in the job market. In turn, this would help diminish the effects of racism.

The fact that the Knight Commission cites accreditation as one of its main pillars for reform should give this proposal additional credibility. The NCAA's Certification Program, which will require institutional standards for NCAA certification, is not far from accreditation.

One final and very important point: athletic departments should require their student-athletes to give something back to young people by participating in educational and drug outreach programs in area schools. This will help prepare future generations of student-athletes and reinforce educational values in the athletes who do the outreach. It will also put them in touch with racially diverse groups of people.

Project Teamwork

In 1978, I saw the other side of midnight as a victim of racial violence. It was a time when police and others said "these things don't happen anymore." I discovered that "these things" never stopped. Other victims taught me not to use anger as a flash point but to try to heal things. Backed by a $750,000, three-year grant from the Reebok Foundation, the Center for the Study of Sport in Society created Project Teamwork as a healing process. It is the Center's most ambitious undertaking. I see in it our greatest hope to use a multiracial group of athletes to reach our children, black and white, boy and girl, athlete and non-athlete.

I know athletes can reach children because they have been the basis of the Center's Schools Outreach Program. In 1984 we had no money, no athletes and nothing but hopes. But Scott Black, a local business leader and head of Delphi Management, stepped forward out of concern for the future of our children, especially minority children. Since 1984, Scott allowed us to grow by donating $300,000 to build the outreach program; by 1990, we had visited more than 220,000 Boston-area young people with messages about academic balance, drug abuse and teenage pregnancy. All our survey instruments and the responses from students, teachers and parents convince us that athletes do make a difference with young people. That is why we decided to launch a frontal assault on the pernicious problems of race with a similar model.

The Northeastern University/Reebok Foundation survey referred to earlier shows that our children have learned to hate and that racial and religious violence and harassment among our youth are now the rule rather than the exception. The wounds in our society are very deep indeed.

Yet the survey shows that youth have an underlying goodness and sensitivity. They are aware of discrimination; while nearly half might join in attacks or be silent partners, half would work to stop them. They have a knowledge of human rights around the world and an even higher standard of what human rights people are entitled to than exists in our system of government.

Young people need role models, and the survey shows that athletes are clearly the chosen ones. Project Teamwork is designed to enable our team of athletes to help young people convert what they feel into what they can do, to contemplate contribution and not destruction, to shed a sense of helplessness for empowerment. The team is made up of two blacks, two whites and a Hispanic and includes Luis Tiant, a star in the majors for nineteen years; Norm Van Lier, four-time NBA All-Star during his ten year NBA career; Robert Weathers, whose runs helped the Patriots make it to the 1986 Super Bowl; Holly Metcalf, world champion and gold medal winner in rowing in the 1984 Olympics; and Bob McCabe, who played center at Harvard and pro ball in Europe.

Integration was no more welcome in pro sports than it was in neighborhoods in Boston. But by being on teams together, athletes learned the principles of Teamwork. By becoming interdependent instead of exclusionary, athletes of different racial groups learned to respect each other, learned that they shared the same values and hopes for their families, and actually enjoyed living and working together.

That is the message that the Center's team of athletes brings into our schools. Young people must understand the principles of

Teamwork and incorporate them into their daily lives if we are to see an improvement in racial and ethnic sensitivity.

When my father was coach of the Knicks, he brought up Nat "Sweetwater" Clifton to the Knicks to help break the color barrier in the NBA. Clifton, like Chuck Cooper with the Celtics, became a master teacher of race relations for his teammates. Bob Douglas was my father's master teacher. Now our Team will be master teachers for our children.

Teamwork is a national program. Northeastern University's president, Jack Curry, called upon his fellow presidents in the National Consortium for Academics and Sport to join us in issuing the Teamwork message in their regions. They responded overwhelmingly in a positive way. We then sought cosponsors from the world of education, sports, and civil rights. The list goes from the NAACP to the NCAA.

The Team will work intensively in the Boston-area schools but will also travel to twenty-four Consortium cities, spending a week in the schools of each city. At the end of the week, they will train the Consortium school's athletes to carry on in the schools with Teamwork. Thus, by 1992 there will be twenty-five Teams around the country.

In Boston, the Team will create a living legacy in several schools called the Human Rights Squads. Modeled on the highly successful chapters of Students Against Drunk Driving (SADD), the Squads will meet monthly with several purposes: to learn more about civil and human rights issues, to build group respect, to work toward improved racial and ethnic relations in the schools and, most importantly, to create a core of activists in the schools and in their surrounding communities. The Northeastern University/Reebok Foundation survey showed that students wanted to be involved in adult literacy programs, work with the homeless, work in programs to help disadvantaged young people and their families, and participate in voter registration campaigns. These are the activities that the Human Rights Squads will address.

The hope I have for Teamwork grows from several sources. First, from lessons from my father, especially how competing with the Rens in cities where segregation was the law showed that some people accepted integrated sports before other forms of integration. This inspired me to understand the positive powers of sports and teamwork. Later my own limited playing career reinforced this, as many of my earliest black friends were athletes.

Another source of hope resulted from having worked in Norfolk, Virginia, in the 1970s. Norfolk was a major navy port; I became familiar with a series of controversial race relations seminars that navy personnel had to attend in the 1970s under the direction of Admiral Elmo "Bud" Zumwalt. In discussions with the participants I saw three different reactions. The hostility of racist whites remained unchanged. Those whites who had little contact with or knowledge of minorities but did not bear hostility were the most affected. They began to understand the origin of racial stereotypes and to grapple with them positively. Blacks saw clearly what they were up against with the racists but also saw hope with the other whites. Most importantly, they clearly comprehended where they stood in a primarily white institution and thus gained knowledge about what they had to do to successfully cope with the obstacles they would face. I believe the same type of program can help with students in high schools, where so much hate has been built up.

Whether in sport or in society, no rational people wants to admit it is racist. My own experience with the police and their accusations is a modest example. I have tried to show in earlier chapters how irrational the arguments of the police and medical examiner were. But the local press ran with them and I believe that the vast majority of white people from the area still believed the press when I left. Isn't that more comfortable than to think that violence can be directed at a college professor, even an outspoken one? Or that South Africa was involved in so small a matter? Clearly it is.

We must recognize that in some substantive ways blacks are actually worse off in society today than they were thirty years ago. In the 1960s it took blood and death to make us wake up to and effectively challenge racism. It took the courage of Tommie Smith and John Carlos in the Mexico City Olympics in 1968 to force us to examine racism in sport. Without such acts of resistance and rebellion, it is all too easy for us to become apathetic as a people.

Now racial violence has shown signs of reemerging. Race-hate acts have increased 149 percent between 1987 and 1989. Anti-Semitic acts are up 171 percent since 1988.

All of this is exacerbated by the fact that black Americans had their expectations raised by civil rights victories in the 1960s only to have them dashed in the 1980s. The frustration, disappointment, and anger of young blacks are reaching a new peak. This is also true of the black athlete carried by educational institutions for his or her athletic prowess until eligibility expires. It is equally true of the many black students socially promoted through American public schools. The result is the same—a lack of learned skills forces some blacks to become part of the vast sea of unemployed youth or to take up unskilled and low-paying jobs in the secondary labor market. The athlete at least has memories to go with the resentment. But those memories ultimately aren't very useful on the street.

Seventy years ago, my father was thought of as a "nigger–lover" when he and his teammates played against black teams. Forty years ago he was considered even more of a "nigger–lover" when he brought Nat Clifton up to the Knicks. Thirty years ago I was called a "nigger–lover" when I brought my black friends into our almost all-white neighborhood. For most of my adult life I have been a "nigger–lover" to some because of my work in the civil rights and anti-apartheid movements. Now my son Joey is a "nigger–lover" to others who hate his father or hate him because he has so many black friends in school. Where will it end? Will it end?

I am frequently asked how a family man can stay in the struggle and take such risks as I have been subjected to. It is precisely because I am a family man that I continue. In my forty-five years, I have never once felt totally free. No matter how good my personal and professional life might have been, no matter what short-term accomplishments I might have achieved, I have never been and can never feel totally free myself as long as others aren't. I want Joe, Chamy and Emily to know freedom, so I continue to join the thousands of others working for freedom.

When I joined the civil rights movement in the 1960s I was somewhat of an oddity as a white. When I joined the anti-apartheid movement in the late 1960s, I was an oddity as a white American working on an international racial issue. I worked for two and a half years for the World Conference of the United Nations Decade for Women on the issue of Southern African women. When I was hired for that position, I was informed that except for my race, sex, and nationality, I was perfect for the job.

But that is precisely the point. Problems of race relations aren't only the problems of blacks and other minorities, women's issues aren't only the problems of women, and restrictions on Africans affect people other than Africans. All such issues are ultimately human rights issues to be solved collectively by blacks and whites, men and women, Africans and non-Africans. Is there hope?

What greater sign of hope, of the forgiveness of the black community for all the wrongs that have victimized them for decades and centuries, than the attitude of Darryl Williams, the black Boston football player gunned down by a sniper in 1979 whose story I recounted earlier.

After the attack which nearly killed him and left him without the use of his arms and legs, after all the betrayed promises of medical and financial support offered to him immediately after the shooting, Darryl had this to say to the *Boston Globe*: "A lot of people perceive me as a white-person hater, because my injury was at the hands of a white person. I can't fault the whole race for that because there are bad people in the white race; there are bad people in the black race as well. You don't hate a whole race of people for one other person."

I have chosen sports as the vehicle through which I can best contribute to challenging racism. This vicious form of hatred has poisoned our people and artificially divided the human family for far too long. White America can no longer call the problem of race "the Negro problem" nor treat it with benign neglect. No form of neglect of racism is benign. White America needs to take a profound look at itself, understand what it has allowed itself to become, and work collectively as well as individually to initiate the transformation.

A close examination of sport can help us to confront the broader societal problems. If, however, we choose to continue ignoring the signs around us, we may be forever doomed to our current self-consuming fears of each other. Society doesn't get many second chances. This may well be our last chance. This time, promises must be kept.